Emerging Technologies for Library Management and Services

EMERGING TECHNOLOGIES for LIBRARY MANAGEMENT AND SERVICES

by

Neeraj Chaurasia

Deputy Librarian

Indian Institute of Technology Delhi

Ess Ess Publications

New Delhi

Emerging Technologies for Library Management and Services

ISBN: 978-81-7000-728-9

₹ 1295/-

First Published 2014

Published by:
Ess Ess Publications
4831/24, Ansari Road,
Darya Ganj,
New Delhi-110 002.
INDIA
Phones: 23260807, 41563444
Fax: 41563334
E-mail: info@essessreference.com
www.essessreference.com

Cover Design by *Patch Creative Unit*

Printed and bound in India at Salasar Imaging Systems.

Contents

Foreword

Information explosion, literature flood, publication deluge, mushroom growth of computer and communication technologies and networks worldwide has not only made the task of bibliographical control difficult, but also forced the contemporary librarians to make a paradigm shift from the age old traditional library operation to automation with the latest state-of-art. Such a change being imminent play a key role in increasing the aspirations, unlimited expectations and sky-high desire of the library clientele to a considerable magnitude. The contemporary librarians are quite aware of this current situation and psychologically prepared to adopt changes knowing fully well that, without such a change, the interest of the library and its clientele will not only be in a state of jeopardy, but also their very existence without computerization will cease to operate.

To the existing huge mass of knowledge and information is added a vast amount of information is generated by the community. The problem today is how to cope with this huge and different-to-control mass of information. To combat the impact of information explosion, the library professionals have developed new tools and techniques. In the process of managing and communication of information, the present day technological advances are playing a vital role. Information Technology is one of the most current tools, which has brought revolutionary changes in management of documents and information.

Computer and telecommunication technologies have joined hands in locating, organizing, storing, retrieving and dissemination of information to meet needs of the users. Networking which has made sharing and exchange of information among libraries and information centres possible is also the gift given by these technologies. Libraries today are getting shaped on the Internet and other networks around the world, and the possibility of a 'library without walls' is taking a concrete shape. Under changed environments and in their own interest the library professionals, shall have to move with the changing times and are to manage and disseminate information by using IT and through the Internet and other electronic sources. Today, time and distance stand collapsed and each library has global obligation. What is more important now is to access information rather than to acquire and collect the sources which contain it.

In the context of severe competition, the new dimensions are added to the services. They are quality consciousness, customer satisfaction, optimum use of resources etc. To enhance availability to wider information resources in the context of limited financial resources, the Library Information Centres are opting for consortia approach. Even the document delivery and resource sharing had gained the prominence in the agenda of Library Information Centres.

The emerging trends in the library and information services are compelling to agree that the Library Science is diminishing the challenges that are ahead and being faced by the librarians compel them to conclude that the entire concept of library science needs rethinking.

The present work of Dr. Chaurasia deals with new

innovations and emerging technologies which are influencing and dominating the LIS scenario and facilitating accessing information. Some of the topics dealt with are LIS Education in India, Accreditation of LIS education, Change Management, E-education,,Core Competencies for Librarians,, Cloud Computing,, Digitization, RFID, Web 3.0, Electronic Books, Federated Search Technology and Discovery Tools, Networking and Resource Sharing, Industry-Institution Relationship, Marketing of Library Products and Services, Physical Stock Verification, Weeding-out Library Collections; and Innovative Technologies for University Libraries.

Dr. Chaurasia deserves our congratulations for bringing out a useful publication, dealing with the application of information technology to library work and services so as to improve accessing information and serve the seekers better. This book without doubt remains a significant addition to LIS literature, particularly in the present context.

Sambalpur, Odisha

Prof. K.C. Sahoo
Formarly Professor & Head, DLIS
Dean, School of Arts & Information Science (AIS)
Dr. H. S. Gour Vishwavidyalaya, Sagar (M.P.)

Preface

The world today is witnessing a new kind of revolution - the *Information Revolution* - ushered in by technology. This revolution is far more sweeping than any other revolution in history in its reach and influence, bringing fundamental changes in all aspects of human life. Information and Communication Technologies (ICT) has a profound impact on all spheres of activities in the libraries. Its impact has been noticed on the way the libraries are to build its collection, its technical activities, its outreach activities, its budgetary strategies, its manpower development, its infrastructural requirement and the most important its library services.

With the invention of Information and communication Technology, libraries are now using various types of technologies to aid the services they render. Everyday new technological advances affect the way information is handled in library information centres. The impacts of new technologies are felt by libraries in every aspect.

Selected papers written by the author on various topics have been included in this volume. Some of the articles are primarily published in the seminar proceedings and the learned journals. Present work by the author is a compilation of papers on various aspects on technologies which are influencing and dominating the LIS scenario and facilitating accessing information.

This book reviews innovative emerging technologies and their impacts on library management, library information resources, services and in-house operations. Some of the topics focuses on the recent emerging technologies which might impact on library administrations, resources, services, and teaching programs. The book contains discussions about a variety of topics dealt with LIS Education in India: Emerging Paradigm and Challenges, Accreditation of LIS education in India, UK and USA, Change Management in Library and Information Centres in Modern Era, The Phenomenon of Knowledge Management (KM) and Human Resource Development (HRD), E-education,, Core Competencies for Librarians,, Cloud Computing and Libraries,, Digitization of Library material,, RFID Technology, Web 3.0 : Emerging Technology, E-Books : Latest Trends and Future Directions, Federated Search Technology and Discovery Tools, Use of Information Technology in Public Libraries, Networking and Resource Sharing in Library and Information Services, Industry-Institution Relationship, Marketing of Library Products and Services, Physical Stock Verification of Library Collection, Weeding-out Library Collections, Quality Improving Quality of LIS Education; and Emerging and Innovative Technologies for University Libraries.

In the process of managing and communication of information, the present day technological advances are playing a vital role. Telecommunication networks are there to handle digital machine readable data and to use micro-waves and communication satellites to transfer such data. ICT advances have made it possible to provide library services and access to information even outside the library. A *library without walls or a virtual* library is now becoming a reality.

The LIS scene is changing fast in the face of new challenges and in response to new demands. The advent of new technologies and their applications to library services is further accelerating the pace of this change. Library professions are experiencing a transition from stand alone libraries to library and information network; from printed publications to digital documents; from ownership of graphic to access to information. Development of internet technology, emergence of web 2.0/3.0 concepts, new and upcoming technologies, equipments and services are some of the major influence in the transformation of the libraries and information centres. Library professionals and users have taken cognizance of this transition and are redefining their roles.

The emerging technologies have gripped the entire society under its impact domain. The industrial and service sectors are witnessing multiple changes in operation management. The Knowledge Resource Centres are also being affected by these technologies. The storage, retrieval and library management technologies have solved century old problems. In this publication I have made an effort to touch all possible areas of emerging trends and technologies in libraries and information services.

June, 2014
New Delhi

Neeraj Chaurasia

1

LIS Education in India: Emerging Paradigm and Challenges

1. INTRODUCTION

Advancement in telecommunication has made the dream of networked environment and resource sharing a reality. Internet has made it possible to access information from anywhere in the world. Advancement in storage technology has also made a significant effect on information handling. Use of electronic storage devices has greatly reduced the problem of space and finance. It also allows quick retrieval. Due to these advancements, today we face not the problem of dearth of information but the problem of excessive information. The traditional libraries with their system cannot meet the onslaught of information explosion and the only alternative before them is to brace up and undergo technological changes. The information-based society of today calls for a vast range of information provision, which in turn, requires a new breed of library and information professionals to provide it effectively.

The management today is not only looking for a candidate with high academic qualification, but also a person with good computer and communication skills who can develop and manage IT-based information delivery systems. Library and Information Science (LIS) education has a significant role for the growth of information society in developing countries like India, because, through LIS education a skilled, knowledgeable and tactful library professional is born. The diversity in the information environment now demands multi-modal role of LIS professionals who can respond to the dynamic nature of information sector.

Hence, the challenge before the contemporary LIS education is to train future information managers in traditional principles as well as in information and communication technologies (ICTs). In this context, the emerging challenges in LIS education have been discussed and some suggestions are made for the improvement of LIS education in India in future.

2. LIS EDUCATION IN INDIA

LIS education in India is nearing centenary celebrations. Sarkhel (2006) highlighted that W. A. Borden, Librarian of Young Man's Institute, New Haven, Connecticut, USA started the first training program for library workers at Central Library in Baroda in 1911. In 1915, Asa Don Dickinson, another American Librarian, established a training course in erstwhile Punjab University (now in Pakistan), which was considered to be the second library school in the world, the first being the Columbia School. Both Borden and Dickinson who paved the way for LIS education in India were the students of Melvil Dewey. The birth of full time P.G. Courses dates back to 1931 in Madras University, mainly through the efforts of Dr. S. R. Ranganathan. Since then this profession is progressing steadily. The outstanding contributions of Dr. S. R. Ranganathan gave a new impetus to the spread of LIS education at the university level in India. LIS education in India has expanded since independence in the form of increase in number of LIS departments in the universities and institutions offering specialized courses in LIS, and in the increase in number of students as well as courses. Research has also been initiated and accelerated in different facets of the subject with the support of the universities and different funding agencies (Satija, 1993).

UGC, from its inception, has attached due importance to the university and college libraries, together with LIS education. UGC set up the "Ranganathan Committee on University and College Libraries" as early as in the year 1957. "Ranganathan Committee on Library Science Education" was set up in 1960 and its report has been serving as Bible in matters relating to teaching of Library Science in Indian universities (Report of CDC, 2001).

Another attempt in this direction was initiated by the UGC in early 1990s when the UGC constituted CDC (Curriculum Development Committee) on Lib. & Inf.Sc. under the Chairmanship of Prof. P.N. Kaula. The committee recommended a new curriculum strengthening the information science components. The UGC set up a Subject Panel in year 1997 with Prof. C.R. Karisiddappa as Convener. The panel discussed the earlier CDC report on Lib.& Inf.Sc. and expressed their concern for immediate restructuring of CDC Report in the wake of rising impact of IT on libraries. Regional meetings at Kurukshetra University, Kurukshetra, Utkal University, Bhubaneswar, Osmania University, Hyderabad and NEHU, Shillong followed this.

National Knowledge Commission has also recommended promoting Information Communication Technology (ICT) applications in all libraries. To achieve this it recommends revamping library and information science education, training and research facilities. It has recommended that the proposed Mission/Commission on Libraries must assess as soon as possible the manpower requirements of the country in the area of LIS management, and take necessary steps to meet the country's requirements through library and information science education and training. To keep the LIS sector abreast of latest developments, necessary encouragement should be given to research after evaluating the research status in the field. Establishing a well equipped institute for advanced training and research in LIS and services would provide the necessary impetus to this task (NKC Report, 2006, p.28-29).

Now after almost hundred years, library science profession is at a crossroad of diversified factors involving management of several different tasks hitherto not handled.

3. MODES OF LIS EDUCATION

Teaching-learning process basically remains theory oriented. Teaching fraternity acts as a channel for transfer of information rather than channel. The concepts, tools and techniques that are taught in the classrooms hardly find environment to practice, experiment and relate to society. The mainstream LIS education in India provides courses in two modes, like :

a. Conventional classroom teaching and

b. Open and distance education.

There may be variations of either of these modes of instruction like personal tuitions and self-education. Murthy (1997) stated that after the advent of IT, educational instruction has taken new modes like television (TV), audio, video programs, etc. The use of IT in LIS education can be broadly classified into the following modes:

- Audio and video taped lectures or instruction,
- Online access to course materials,
- Video-conference-based instruction or teaching, and
- Hypertext and artificial intelligence (Al) based teaching and instruction.

An offshoot of IT which has entered the LIS education is that of virtual-reality (VR) which would provide virtual classrooms, virtual libraries and similar situations. These developments are going to have a strong bearing in the LIS education in several developing countries also. However, generally three forms of e-learning are available and used namely; web-based training, supported online training and informal e-learning (Mason, 2002).

4. LIS COURSES OFFERED BY THE UNIVERSITIES AT VARIOUS LEVELS

Library and Information Science is not a mere academic discipline. It is a professional course, which involves practical, observational and experimental study. At present, education in LIS is provided at seven levels, viz., Certificate (CLIS), Diploma (DLIS), Bachelor degree (BLIS), Master's degree (MLIS), Associateship, M.Phil. and Ph.D. Following LIS courses are offered by various universities and educational institutions under regular and/or open and distance mode in India:

4.1. Certificate Course in Library and Information Science (CLIS)

The certificate course of six months duration leading to the award of CLIS is open to candidates who have passed the 10+2 examination. Usually the professional associations of librarians offer this course.

4.2. Diploma in Library and Information Science (DLIS)

DLIS course of one-year duration is available mostly through distance learning mode. Entry requirement for this course is also 10+2. Some polytechnics also offer diploma courses.

4.3. Bachelor Degree in Library and Information Science (B.Lib.I.Sc./BLIS)

For the degree courses of one-year duration, graduates in any discipline are eligible.

4.4. Master Degree in Library and Information Science (M.Lib.Sc./MLIS)

Those who obtain the BLIS degree can pursue the Master's degree course, also of one year duration. On the recommendation of UGC curriculum model 2001, several universities have now started two-year integrated course leading to Master's degree after graduation.

4.5. Associateship in Information Science offered by NISCAIR, New Delhi and DRTC Bangalore

AIS form NISCAIR, New Delhi/DRTC Bangalore is a two-year programme equivalent to Master's degree in Library & Information Science recognized by Govt. of India and many Indian Universities. The students of this course are selected through a written test and interview. Persons having a minimum of 50% aggregate marks in (i) Master's degree or (ii) four-year *plus* degree like B.E./M.B.B.S. or (iii) Bachelor's degree *plus* B.Lib.Sc. *plus* one year of relevant experience after B.Lib.Sc. are eligible to apply.

4.6. Master of Philosophy in Library and Information Science (M.Phil.)

The duration of the courses is one year and the eligibility is MLIS degree.

4.7. Doctor of Philosophy in Library and Information Science (Ph.D.)

Besides the above courses, various advanced level short-term training programmes like Certificate in ICT application in library (CICTAL), P.G. Diploma in library Automation and Networking (PGDLAN), etc., are being offered as part of continuing education programmes by the NISCAIR, New Delhi; NASSDOC, New Delhi; DELNET New Delhi; INFLIBNET, Ahmedabad; IIM, Lucknow; and various library and information science associations like ILA, IASLIC, etc.

There is a well-known list of Indian universities available online namely 'Library and Information Science Education in Asia' which provides information of different courses available in LIS and their respective address for correspondence (*http://dis.sci.ntu.edu.sg/cisap/schools/india.htm*).

According to a compilation by Rawtani (2002),there are 105 Library Science schools in India offering BLIS, 85 schools offering M.L.I.S. or its equivalent degree, 14 schools offering M.Phil. and 51 schools offering Ph.D. programmes. While detailed content analysis of LIS syllabi is not the objective of this paper, it has been observed that LIS Education in Indian universities including the open universities gives an impression of diversity in the course curricula of LIS Education.

5. RESTRUCTURING LIS CURRICULUM

The syllabus of any course has to be structured within a fixed framework. Professional training has a life cycle and a transitory period. The quality of future professionals' habit depends much on having up-to-date curriculum. It needs to be so oriented that it is able to cope up with the rapidly changing needs. The syllabus of LIS courses taught at University level is varying.

In the recent past, advanced topics like computer application and networking technologies have been included in the courses. The increasing use in the number of electronic information materials such as CD-ROMs, especially in the area of science and technology and R & D information systems necessitated for their inclusion at the postgraduate level. Since curriculum development is a process rather than purely a product, it is expected to take into consideration the trends in the socio-economic front and link it with the needs of the profession. The important changes taking place in higher and tertiary level education are the changes in learning process. There is an increasing trend of adopting a combination of teaching methods and a skill from 'Chalk and talk' method. The traditional teaching methods are supplemented by project work, seminar, group discussions, fieldwork, tutorials, in-service training, internal assessment, etc. The Library Science profession is demanding specialized skills from the LIS professionals in addition to simply disseminating information. These skills have to be acquired through learning process. For example, when students are expected to give seminars based on their project work, they are disseminating the information that they have understood. It needs skill to present what they have grasped, justify what they have to say and understand human interactions. Learning and grasping abilities of students are generally checked by three means(Ganesh Kumar and Chaurasia, 2004):

Writing Skill : Generally revolves around memory and retention power.

Doing skill : One learns best by 'doing' something.

Thinking skill : Involves interpreting the facts learned by 'doing', through trial and error and seeking solutions.

One of the most important activities in higher educational institutions, more precisely in universities (where Library and Information Science is taught), is learning through research, which may be in the form of project work, dissertation, investigation work and so on. Today, library is a part of worldwide network and the requirements of the users cannot be predicted with absolute certainty. Therefore, LIS Education needs to be structured in such a way that the professionals develop necessary abilities and skills to withstand the pressures, while they are in learning process.

Satija (2009) opines that though temporal curriculum is vital to education in every sense. It is important for training of the minds and to instill employable skills in the learner. School time has to be judiciously divided between class room teaching and extra co-curricular activities. Academic programmes should be restructured not less often to ensure their relevance to immediate market needs and the basic academic and social needs. He suggests establishing a consultative committee constituting of past students and prospective employers.

6. QUANTITY VS QUALITY EDUCATION

The gradual improvement in LIS education in the country has manifested more in quantity rather than in quality. Although, the number of departments and professional associations and other institutes along with the students' enrollment has steadily increased, the quality of outgoing students leaves much to be desired. The current course content of LIS programmes shows no relevance to our present day informational demands. Keeping in view the veracity of the curricula, few years back, UGC has constituted a committee, Curricular Development Committee in LIS Education, which has partially focused on the steps to be taken to bring out necessary improvements in curriculum standards so that the quality can be maintained in LIS education.

7. TRAINING FOR QUALITY SERVICES

Quality in education is an evaluation of the process of educating, which enhances the need to achieve and develop the talents of the customers of the process, and at the same time meets the accountability standards set by the clients who pay for the process or the outputs from the process of learning. The six sigma approach developed by Motorola is a statistical unit for measuring quality. Although it is aimed at upgradation of business, there should not be any difficulty in applying the quality concept involved in it for giving quality services in the libraries. It may be achieved partially by adopting the following means(Mahapatra, 2006):

- Making conscious efforts for improving communication skill - verbal, written or even body language.
- Teaching critical thinking and problem solving.
- Making a plan for computer assisted instructions.
- Developing "Intelligence Learning Technology" by having self teaching guides.
- Organizing library's collection with new zero effect, which is absolutely essential for speedy information retrieval.
- Managing library budget with no duplication with every conscious effort to avoid overhead expenditure.

8. SKILLS REQUIRED FOR THE LIS PROFESSIONALS

Libraries are undergoing transformation and so also users' expectations due to rapid technology changes. Skills and competitions acquired during early career stages are not likely to suffice beyond 10-15 years. The status of libraries in the market place is partly determined by their ability to disseminate the knowledge. Libraries deal with the information in content. In addition to access the information, they are expected to add value to it, and repackage information. They will have to be in dialogue with specialists in computing, networking, finance, marketing and so on. The services would be more customer based. This will require that LIS professionals should acquire skills such as (Gokhale, 1999):

- Excellent communication skill – both oral and written with polite aggressiveness.

- Professional attitude to critical thinking for problem solving.
- Broad knowledge of networked information and deep knowledge of specific subject field.
- Knowledge of setting up web sites for libraries.
- Developing attitude towards marketing of information.
- Knowledge of writing on-line publications using SGML code.
- Skill for developing multimedia packages.

Like other professionals, LIS students as well as professionals need to acquire skills to cope with challenges of changing paradigm. Most required skills are pinpointed here(Ganesh Kumar and Chaurasia, 2004):

- Effective communication
- Project management
- Problem-solving
- Critical, reflective, and creative thinking
- Team work
- Self management
- Life-long learning and professional updating
- Information and communications technology (ICT) application
- Information literacy

Education providers also need to consider the career-long learning needs of the profession.

9. LIS EDUCATION: CHANGING PARADIGMS

Change is a characteristic of life - whether it is that of an individual, institution or even that of a discipline. Starting with 'Librarianship', it became 'Library Economy' then 'Library Science' and then came the concepts 'Documentation' and 'Library and Information Science'. And today, it is 'Information and Library Studies',

'Information Studies', etc.

With the approach of this new millennium, it is presumed (Missingham, 1999) that "all signs indicate that it will be the age of 'wired' citizens and workers." E-learning provides increasing access to learning resources, interactive teaching and learning environment, increasing student convenience, reducing educational delivery cost, developing a scholarship of web based pedagogy and providing 21st century learning environment. Advancement in Information and Communication Technology (ICT) and multimedia application has facilitated Web Based Learning/E-Learning beyond the conventional learning.

Prof. C.R. Karisiddappa (2001) being the Chairman of Curriculum Development Committee (CDC) recommended that, "in view of the emerging network environment, in view of the fundamental shift in the goals of the library, and in view of the changes in information storage and delivery mechanisms, the educational programmes should cater to the needs of these changed settings by including in their course contents, the knowledge and skills required to function effectively in such an environment".

Varaprasad (2006) stated that "Knowledge management will become an integral part of LIS education beyond the understanding of technology-centric solutions. Library curriculum would need to embrace both tacit and explicit knowledge management skills." Teaching/learning strategies like independent learning, field trips, problem-based learning, case studies, independent group work, etc., could make students active.

Due to emergence of Library 2.0/Web 2.0, the current trend is changing drastically and LIS professionals need the capability, insight and knowledge to influence this dynamic work environment.

10. RECENT TRENDS AND DEVELOPMENTS IN LIS EDUCATION AND RESEARCH

Application of ICT as a tool of information handling has revolutionized the entire concept of libraries, the system of information storage and retrieval and ways to access the information. Traditional concepts are changing with high speed, i.e. collection development to content development, conventional education to web-based education, information society to knowledge society and Library Professional to Information professional. New forms of library like Digital Library, Virtual Library, etc. have developed. Library cooperation is made through resource sharing networks or consortia. The growth and development of library as well as LIS profession in digital era has proved Dr. S. R. Ranganathan's Fifth Law of Library and Information Science, "Library is a growing organism".

Therefore, the objectives of LIS education have been revolutionized with the E-concept. To incorporate a considerable number of IT components in LIS curricula, CDC (2001) has made maximum efforts. At the same time the report has recommend that the "revision of syllabus is required to be undertaken very cautiously with break – even manner, not entirely overawed either by the invasion of IT or by sentimental attachment to various philosophical and historical components". Another trend is the broadening of the curriculum, the introduction of new areas of specialisation and flexible options for higher education. Establishment of The Knowledge Commission has also elevated the entire field of LIS.

Though each program tries hard to balance LIS education with an IT emphasis in response to market demands, many of them are facing problems in expanding LIS education to meet the requirements for information professionals in an IT-based society. At the same time, it becomes more and more difficult to attract new students into traditional library oriented programs, as graduates tend to have difficulty securing employment. This situation calls for a radical reform of the curricula and systems of LIS education, by taking into consideration the market needs of the entire information service industry.

According to a study by Miwa (2006), following are some of the implications for the future reform of LIS education in Asia, including:

- the need for new job markets for LIS graduates,
- the need to connect research and practice,
- the need to redefine the identity of LIS,
- the need to enhance information professionals' social standing, and
- the need to match qualification systems with employment procedures).

Library schools could help by teaching students how to develop a strategy for continuing their education once they are out of library school, how to develop skills for learning new technologies and how to develop a strategy for troubleshooting technologies. No library school student should be allowed to graduate without basic Internet skills and search skills (Markey, 2004).

We have identified the following common trends of LIS education in Asia:

- changes in core subject areas from an emphasis on manual-based collection development to ICT-based information/knowledge management,
- shift in the educational level from undergraduate to graduate,
- increase in the number of faculty with doctoral degrees, who prefer to teach cutting-edge courses rather than traditional library oriented courses.
- elimination of the word "library" from the names of LIS programs in order to attract students,

- decreasing opportunities for new employment in library markets because of over production of LIS graduates and economic recession,
- depreciation of LIS education for school librarians,
- lack of understanding among employers to accept LIS graduates as capable knowledge workers, and
- low interest among well-educated graduates in the public library market, which is characterized as offering relatively low social status and wage levels compared to national and academic libraries,

11. ISSUES AND CHALLENGES BEFORE INFORMATION PROFESSIONALS/EDUCATORS

To cope up with issues and challenges of today's Information Society, LIS educators have to balancing tradition and technology. Proliferation of information in digital era has elevated application of ICT and web technology to organize information. Due to growth of information in digital form LIS professionals need to acquire ability or capacity to use and exploit e-resources and its management. Also, balancing of education and practice or research is highly demanded. So, LIS educators, researchers and practitioners need to identify thrust areas of education and research, which may provide future direction, keeping in view the potential market demand.

The emergence of the networked information society has changed the landscape and roles of information professionals dramatically. **Six challenges** have been identified by Johnson (1998) facing these professionals:

i. assisting users to deal with information overload through higher selectivity and screening;

ii. high level of technical skills to manage new ICTs;

iii. competition with other professionals for positions in increasingly converged library, information and computing services;

iv. need for new skills drawn from those traditionally seen as separate sectors of the information industry such as publishing;

v. higher level of skills for teaching and facilitating information literacy; and

vi. the ability to work with other people.

Against this backdrop, we have seen library and information schools rise to the challenge to train such a new breed of information professionals by reinventing themselves and engaging in the revision of their LIS curricula, rightly recognising the lack of expertise in traditional LIS departments and thereby fostering and creating collaboration and cooperation opportunities with other departments to offer new specialisations within the framework of a generalist programme of education.(Foo et al., 2006).

Inspite of the intent, LIS departments of developing nations fail to achieve their goal of producing information managers of future because of the many constraints faced by them. A study of LIS Departments of universities of M.P. (Thapa and Sahoo, 2002) shows that there is lack of faculty; lack of latest books and periodicals on LIS in the university libraries; lack of funds for purchase of books for the departmental libraries; lack of availability of literature in regional language; lack of supporting staff; lack of space to accommodate departmental library, workshops and even classrooms; lack of latest information technology products and services and also lack of co-ordination among faculty members. They recognize the need to revamp LIS curriculum to produce skilled and capable future information mangers but also emphasize that this is possible only through a planned and sustained effort both on the part of State Government, UGC, University authorities and also LIS community.

Because of the rapid shift toward an information and knowledge-oriented society, librarians and information professionals need to develop the required knowledge and skills to take advantage of ICT. These needs have driven the shift of LIS education from traditional librarianship toward ICT-oriented informatics. Many colleges and universities have modified their curricula to emphasize ICT and have changed the names of their LIS programs from Library Scienceto Information Science. These days, some countries avoid the word "Library" in the names of these programs. This is because it is difficult to interest students in traditional LIS programs and the name change helps to attract more applicants. However, many employers do not yet recognize that graduates from ICT-oriented LIS programs are capable of taking on information and knowledge management jobs. Such research findings suggest that we need to cultivate new employment opportunities for these graduates when we restructure LIS programs into ICT-oriented one.

12. SUGGESTIONS

LIS curriculum and syllabus needs radical change keeping in view the requirement for information workforce in the national/global market. IT has to be made an integral part of LIS education. Thapa and Sahoo (2009) have suggested some measures which can help LIS departments to gear up for the IT onslaught:

i. Practical training through internship programme should be introduced.

ii. Regular training, orientation programmes, workshops, refresher courses, seminars and conferences need to be made mandatory at different levels of staff and student.

iii. Awareness needs to be developed especially among senior staff towards use of IT.

iv. Demonstration of latest IT tools should be conducted at the departments.

v. Infrastructure for sharing of knowledge, among departments through video conferencing, should be developed.

vi. Change in existing course content, like IT based classification and cataloguing and introduction of new subjects like multimedia application, preservation of print and electronic media, industrial library information system, agricultural information system and rural library information system.

Motivation is the fuel that feeds progressive thinking. Positive motivating impacts the teaching-learning process which ultimately determines the overall academic development of the students. The University Grants Commission, universities and colleges have since long stressed upon a change in the teacher's role from that of a mere transmitter of information to that of a facilitator of learning. Therefore, there is a need for proper planning and the implementation of a well-thought out plan for the welfare of the student community. This would invariably lead to the development of independent thinking, originality, productivity, critical thinking, scientific temper and proper social approach, etc.

To support the students in their endeavor to perform well it will be a good practice to share the teaching material with the students. All material so collected, collated and planned to be delivered should be digitized with proper references.

There is a need for National Accreditation Agency for quality assurance and to achieve standards of excellence. Highly demanded issue is to have a LIS degree that is at par with international standards. LIS education should be internationalized so that LIS professionals from India can compete in the national as well as global market. Finally there is a big demand for a National Council in LIS education.

13. CONCLUSION

The changing paradigm of LIS has compelled Library professionals to become Information Professionals through "Education for Information". International initiatives and developments have forced the developing countries to keep pace with such developments. The crisis in library education is a crisis of understanding. Distanced from LIS programs by their roles in the field, many practitioners have assumed an adversarial role against library education and have been unsympathetic when institutional demands coupled with insufficient funding result in library school programs to be different from those they envision. Instead of assuming the worst, practitioners should thoughtfully consider how schools are evaluated and what it takes to educate a librarian while seeking cooperative means through which they can help LIS programs to more effectively accomplish their goals. Special efforts may be made to identify such professionals who have strong leadership qualities and have the potential of being visionaries to take the profession ahead successfully.

"Library schools don't function in a vacuum. . . . LIS education needs a healthy infrastructure involving faculty, students, alumni, and practitioners," observes Ling Hwey Jeng. LIS Schools and Educators must be committed to act as qualitative problem solvers and effective information managers, possessing broad range of capabilities to meet the highest demand in the information sectors (academic, corporate, government), to meet the challenges in new millennium. The curricula in Library Science should provide sufficient scope for continuous learning, as well as it may be designed in such a way that every professional feels confident and comfortable over handling technology.

Quality assurance is not the destination but a journey to continuously improve. We need to develop strategies with consensus at national level, which will help recombine points of strength in a synthetic framework and work to overcome the weaknesses and the flaws.

REFERENCES

1. Foo, Schubert et. al. (2006).Working together in developing library andinformation science education in the asia pacific. InSugimoto, S. et. al. (Eds.): ICADL 2006, LNCS, pp. 4-11.
2. Ganesh Kumar and Chaurasia, Neeraj Kumar (2004). Quality management of libraries through LIS education. 20th IATLIS Seminar on Globlization of Library and Information Science Education, held on 21-23 November, 2003 at University of Madras, Chennai, pp. 194-198.
3. Gokhale, Pratibha (1999). Quality Management Through Library & Information Science Education. Workshop on Information Management,held on6 - 8 Jan 1999 atDRTC Bangalore.
4. Karisiddappa, C. R. (2001). Model curriculum: Library and information science. New Delhi: UGC.
5. Mahapatra, G. (2006). LIS education in India: Emerging paradigms, challenges and propositions in the digital era. In, Asia-Pacific Conference on Library & Information Education & Practice 2006 (A-LIEP 2006), April 3-6, Singapore.
6. Markey, Karen (2004). Current Educational Trends in the Information and Library Science Curriculum. *Journal of Education for Library and Information Science,* 45 (Fall), pp.317–339.
7. Mason, R. (2002). Review of e-learning for education and training. In networked learning 2002: Proceedings of the third International Conference on Networked Learning 2002, Sheffield, UK. 26-28 March, pp.9-26.
8. Missingham, R. (1999). Science and technology: A web of information; impact of electronic present and future on scientists and libraries. In Proceedings, Information on-line & on-disc 99, 9th Australian conference & exhibition, 19-21 January 1999.
9. Miwa, M. (2006). Trends and issues of LIS education in Asia. In, Khoo, C., Singh D. & Chaudhry, A. S. (Eds.), Proceedings of the Asia-Pacific Conference on Library & Information

Education & Practice 2006 (A-LIEP 2006), Singapore, 3-6 April. Singapore : School of Communication &Information, Nan yang Technological University, pp.18-26.

10. Murthy, S. S. (1997). Use of information technology in library & information science education. *DESIDOC Bulletin of Information Technology*, V.17(3), pp.3-7.
11. National Knowledge Commission (NKC). *NKC Report 2006*. (New Delhi: NKC, Govt. of India, 2006) 28-29.
12. Rawtani, M. R. and Others (2002). A regional study of Library and Information Science education in India : some observations. *ILA Bulletin*, V.38(4), pp.108-117.
13. Report of Curriculum Dcvclopment Committee in Library and Information Science. 2001. University Grants Commission. New Delhi.
14. Sarkhel, J. K. (2006). Quality assurance and accreditation of LIS education in Indian universities: Issues and perspectives. In, Khoo, C., Singh D. & Chaudhry A. S. (eds.). Proceedings of the Asia-Pacific Conference on Library & Information Education & Practice, Singapore, 3-6 April, pp.427-431.
15. Satija, M. P. (1993). Research in librarianship before and after Ranganathan. In, Navalani K. & Satija, M. P. (eds.), Pettits petals: A tribute to S. R. Ranganathan New Delhi: ABC Publishing, pp.27-45.
16. Satija, M.P. (2009). Need for revamping the LIS education in India. Iaslic Bulletin, V.55(1), pp.3-11.
17. Thapa, Neelam and Sahoo, K.C.(2009). Education and training of Future Information managers: Role of UGC and Universities in M.P. *JLIS*, V.27(2), pp. 122-134.
18. Thapa, Neelam and Sahoo, K.C. LIS Departments of Madhya Pradesh: Geraing up for the Information Technology Onslaught. *JLIS*, V.34(1), pp. 17-32.
19. Varaprasad, N. (2006). Keynote address on Singapore's vision of the 21st century library service. In Proceedings of the Asia Pacific Conference on Library and Information Education and Practice, Singapore: Nanyang Technological University.

2

Accreditation of LIS Education in India, UK and USA

1. ACCREDITATION

To lay down standards of education in consultation with the institution imparting such education and to recognize the organizations whose degree in the subject concerned is considered to be the qualification for certain professional positions is called accreditation. The purpose of accreditation by professional associations is to see that courses met the professional standards of the associations, thus, saving the society from poorly prepared professionals. Accreditation serves as a mechanism for quality assessment and quality enhancement with quality defined as the effective utilization of resources to achieve appropriate educational objectives.Technology may be making the LIS global in its reach, but certain things about education remain stubbornly local. One of those things is accreditation.

2. DEFINITIONS

Accreditation may broadly be defined as a process whereby an outside reputed independent agency evaluates and examines the courses of instruction framed and offered by an educational, institution under its jurisdiction according to a set of predetermined norms and standards.

a. A Voluntary, non-government system of evaluation used to protect the public, interest and to verify the quality of service provided by member institutions'.

b. According to *Bicentennial Commission on Education*, Washington, DC - "A Profession is organized into one or more professional associations which within broad limits of social accountability are granted autonomy in control of actual work of the profession and conditions which surround it admissions, educational standards, examinations & licensing, career, ethical, performance standards and professional discipline."

c. Accreditation is "the means employed for all professions for evaluating the quality of the professional program of a given college or university"

d. According to *Kent & Cancour* - "Accreditation refers to approval or recognition of one party by another on the basis of some standards".

3. NEED FOR ACCREDITATION

Absence of accreditation leads to inconsistency in the course contents, infrastructure, intake capacity, examination, apprenticeship requirements, nomenclature, etc. It may lead to substandard education, malpractices and unethical activities in the profession.

Accreditation is a degree of excellence or a uniform pattern of practice or process specified by a standing body. In order to achieve academic excellence, it is very essential to lay down norms of education and ensure their adherence consistently and regularly. Proper quality control and guarantee by some recognized body of the professionals is necessary to achieve this goal. Accreditation presupposes the maintenance of a good quality and ensures the identification of best one so that the bad one which does not follow prescribed standards get eliminated. Accreditation helps in maintaining uniformity, quality and level of performance.

Accreditation requires in achieving uniformity in respect of procedures, processes and products, etc. and may prove to be useful in LIS education in many ways. Since the traditional educational programmes in LIS lack proper objectives and to accommodate changes, the LIS syllabi of different schools need to be restructured and redesigned keeping in mind the local requirements and introduction of modern techniques and to establish an accrediting agency, which will formulate standards for LIS education in India.

In the light of the above, there is a dire need for accreditation of professional courses to maintain academic standards. Accreditation in the field of LIS education is found to be useful for achieving and maintaining desired objectives, targets and goals.

4. AREAS OF ACCREDITATION

a. Curriculum

- The existing course-module be restructured and remodeled by supplementing the newly emerging topics like information systems, information and data processing, information technology.
- The new aspects in information organization and management have revolutionized and brought about rapid and dynamic changes in LIS education.
- It may be admitted that a well-designed curricula will ensure quality product both in library profession and teaching. Therefore, a definite policy should be planned for a new curriculum which should be based on the manpower requirements of the present day needs of the professions.
- The model syllabi recommended by the UGC Review

Committee (1965) and UGC Panel on LIS (1982) may be accepted as an ideal.

- The curriculum of library and information studies encompasses information and knowledge creation, communication, identification, selection, acquisition, organization and description, storage and retrieval, preservation, analysis, interpretation, evaluation, synthesis, dissemination and management.

b. Teaching Faculty

- Full time faculty members are qualified for appointment to the graduate faculty within the parent institution.
- A quality teaching standard presupposes that there are faculty members having good academic background and sound knowledge and experience on the subject. But in practice it is found that as compared to other disciplines the strength of faculty is very small in many schools.
- Part-time faculty, when appointed, balance and complement the teaching competencies of the full-time faculty to enrich the quality and diversity of a program.
- The number of faculty members should be made available according to the UGC recommendation of teacher-student ratio.

c. Admission Procedure and Intake

- Different schools have their various admission criteria. No library school follows standard admission criteria while granting admission to the students in the department. The admission criteria should be based on some principles in relation to manpower requirements in future. However, admission may be granted to a student either on the basis of merit or admission test and interview or combination of the two. Both the methods have their advantages and limitations.

- The intake in both the levels be restricted to a certain number in order to ensure individual attention, management of practicals and quality among the products. However, there should be a balance between the demand and supply of manpower.

d. Students

- The school formulates recruitment, admission, financial aid, placement and other academic and administrative policies for student.
- The school has policies to recruit and retain a multicultural, multiethnic and multilingual student body from a variety of backgrounds.

e. Physical Resources and Facilities:

- Physical facilities provide a functional learning environment for students and faculty; enhance the opportunities for research, teaching, service, consultation and communication and promote efficient and effective administration of the schools program, regardless of the forms or locations of deliverys to the physical facilities available for the library schools, the condition of the library school is still worse. In many schools there are no separate rooms for faculty members, no workshop and even no classroom. Many schools are to share with some other departments or house in a small part of a university library. However, the building must have adequate space for the library, lecture rooms, staff rooms and common room for students.
- The building should be modular, so that future extension can be made according to the requirements. A program has access to physical resources and facilities that are sufficient to the accomplishment of its objectives.

5. ACCREDITATION OF LIS EDUCATION

5.1. India

There is no accreditation agency in India like the ALA Committee on Accreditation (USA) to ensure reasonable standards and quality of output. The Report of the Committee on National Policy on Library and Information System has stressed the need for such a body. So far departments of LIS in the universities have broadly adopted the scheme of papers recommended by the UGC Review Committee on Library Science in Indian Universities (1965). In order to overcome the problems of diversity in LIS education in India and maintain their academic standards, it is very essential to establish some professional agency at national level which can undertake the work of accreditation of the LIS education, as is being done in certain other professionals within the country and abroad. The agency will also be responsible for constant revision and evaluation of the existing LIS course offered by different universities. This agency will set and recommend minimum standard in terms of faculty member, curriculum development, finance and physical apparatus, etc.

The immediate task is to establish a mechanism for accreditation of LIS courses followed in different library schools in India. The value of accreditation has been discussed and emphasized repeatedly at national seminars and conferences. But no concrete effort has yet been made in this direction. However, there are number of professional organizations like ILA, IATLIS and IASLIC on national level and government body like UGC, which can act as a body for accreditation.

In view of the fast growing number of schools imparting training in librarianship, emerging diversity of standard and the recent trend of training through correspondence, the need for a regular control and enforcement of minimum standards in training and education for librarianship can hardly be overemphasized.

5.2. UK

In the UK, two professional bodies – the Library Association (LA) and the Institute of Information Scientists (IIS) – separately equipped themselves with accreditation instruments designed to assist in the recruitment of quality-assured graduates into their registers of members. These instruments provided a conceptual map of the subject discipline against which the content of each submitted course could be compared. They also offered a framework for assessing aspects of course delivery and management. University teaching departments in LIS have generally been keen to submit themselves to such external scrutiny, because accredited status contributes to the marketability of a course and its graduates.

The criteria for assessment of courses incorporate the IIS Criteria for Information Scientists and the LA Body of Professional Knowledge and have five main areas:

a. Information Generation, Communication & Utilisation

The processes and techniques whereby information resources are created, analysed, evaluated, moderated and manipulated in order to meet the requirements of defined user populations

b. Information Management and Organisational Context

The application of techniques for planning, implementing, evaluating, analysing and developing library and information products and services within the context of the organisation's culture, aims and objectives. The impact of information systems on the structures and procedures of organisations.

c. Information Systems & Information & Communication Technologies

The availability and functionality of manual and electronic information systems and information and communications technologies insofar as they apply to the principles and practices of information management. The application of techniques to identify, analyse, specify, implement and evaluate appropriate systems.

d. Information Environment & Policy

The dynamics of information flow in society, in (and between) nations, governments and the information and media industries.

e. Management and Transferable Skills

Principles and techniques associated with business and institutional management, together with transferable skills of literacy and numeracy urements and graduate employment data. Panel members also seek evidence of institutional support, and expect to meet senior representatives of the university from whom assurances are sought regarding a continuing commitment to the subject discipline, and to the allocation of human and physical resources sufficient to deliver the course in future.

5.3. USA

The American Library Association established a Board of Education for Librarianship, which developed standard for library schools in 1924 and evaluate them (Rochester). The Committee on Accreditation (COA) is now the section of the American Library Association responsible for accrediting library school. Twelve members are appointed by the Executive Board for two year terms. The current standard in the USA is that of 1992. There were previous ALA Standards in 1925, 1933, 1951, and 1972.

The Standards for Accreditation of Master's Programs in Library and Information Studies 1992 the following address six areas:

i. Mission, Goals and Objectives
ii. Curriculum
iii. Faculty
iv. Students
v. Administration and Financial Support
vi. Physical Resources and Facilities

6. CONCLUSION

Accreditation has served a worthwhile purpose. However, accreditation cannot raise the program quality by itself, because it speaks only about the minimum requirements for accreditation. In view of the wide range of skills and expertise needed for the efficient provision of information and the effective management of library and information services, the accrediting bodies should not seek to stipulate precise requirements for course contents. The accreditation should be based on the objectives of the course, its structure, syllabi, teaching/ learning methods, and assessment methods and criteria. The value of accreditation has been discussed and emphasized repeatedly at national seminars and conferences. But no concrete effort has yet been made in this direction. However, there are number of professional organization in India like ILA, IASLIC & IATLIS on national level and government body like UGC, which can act as a body for accreditation.

REFERENCE

1. Agarwal, S P (1997). "Library and Information Studies in India." In, Library and Information Science: Parameters and Perspectives. Vol.1. Ed by R G Prasher. New Delhi, Concept. P.88-104.
2. Bansal, G C (1997). "Accreditation of LIS Schools in India

and US: A Proposal for Collaboration." In, Library and Information Science: Parameters and Perspectives. Vol.1. Ed by R G Prasher. New Delhi, Concept. P.245-251.

3. Barua, B. (1997). "LIS education in India : Need for standardization". In, Proceedings of XV IATLIS National Seminar, Dept. of Studies in Lib. & Inf. Sc., University of Mysore, Mysore, P. 171-181.

4. Hurt, C D (1992). "The Future of Library Science in Higher Education." In, Advances in Librarianship, 16, 153-181.

5. Isaac, K A (1996). "Future Prospects for Education for Librarianship in India." In, Library Science with a Slant to Documentation and Information Studies, 33 (2), 57-64.

6. Jebaraj, V. Franklin David (2004). "ALA accredited schools Vs Indian LIS schools". In, Proceedings of XX IATLIS National Conference, Dept. of Lib. & Inf. Sc., University of Madras, Chennai, P. 258-265.

7. Konnur, M B (1997). "Education for Librarianship: Some Pertinent Issues." In, Library and Information Science: Parameters and Perspectives. Vol.1. Ed by R G Prasher. New Delhi, Concept. P.186-192.

8. Ward, Patricia Layzell (2000). "Professional Education in Australia, the United Kingdom, and the United States in 20th Century." In, Advances in Librarianship, 24, 103-137.

3

Change Management in Library and Information Centers in Modern Era

1. INTRODUCTION

In Ancient days libraries used to be treated as the storehouse of books and the librarian merely a custodian of stored books. But now the situation has totally changed due to the various developments in library techniques, Accordingly library treated as the center for the creation and recreation of information products of academic pursuits. The dawn of 21st century has brought in a phenomenal change in every organization. The change management is a major theme of management studies. It tries to answer the question of why some organizations change with times and go from strength to strength, whilst others either stick rigidly to the old ways and die, or attempt to change but goes horribly wrong. Library and information centers are no exception to this universal phenomenon of change. There are the dynamic changes in the approaches of the process, services and products, which led to the changes in its collection, technology, staff and users. It is necessary for the library to evolve continuously for its successful growth and development.

If the changes are not managed properly, and the needs of the users are not met, they will be in a week position to effectively deliver the library and information services. It is only through planned change and its efficient management; the organization can cope with changing environment and may discover more profitable use of resources.

2. AREAS OF CHANGE IN THE LIBRARY AND INFORMATION CENTERS

According to*H.J. Leavitt (1965)* there are four areas of an organization, which are subject to change. They are:

- **Task :** Task refers to the product or service that is produced, and the processes that are undertaken;
- **Technology :** The equipment that is used to deliver the services;
- **People :** It is fairly obvious, but includes the beliefs and ways of doing things that the staff follows; Library users and staff;
- **Structure :** It means the structure of the library & information center.

So these changes in management are necessary for smooth flow of work in library and information center.

2.1. Task: Products and services

21st century librarian must be an information manager who is a custodian of millions of documents and does all the transactions for his customer satisfactorily with the help of desktop or laptop computer. Thus the modern libraries are becoming bigger in respect of information storage and retrieval. In recent years, information technologies have advanced to such an extent that, their impact on libraries is significant. Development of digital libraries, Internet, CD-ROMs, electronic publishing, etc., are forcing the libraries to change the way they used to function in the past. The developments that emerged during the present century have provided many opportunities and challenges for the libraries. Developments in information and communication technologies have changed the type of coilections in the libraries.

It is a well-known fact that, library collection is the sum total of library material that make up the holding of a particular library. Collection development is an operation that involves regular addition to the collection of information sources in print and in other modern forms, and weeding out on regular basis, of such materials from the collection that turn obsolete or deteriorate physically over time. Collection development is not any single activities; it is planning and decision making process.

2.2. Change management: Technology

Modern libraries equipped with modern forms of technologies like computer networking, optical fiber, networking support, Internet and intranets make the sources of the library and information centers globally available. The technological developments are going to change the very complexion of library and information services of all categories. The roles of the library personnel are more dynamic and ever changing. The duties of librarian are different from that of the conventional librarian. He has to look after more valuable databases and retrieve information more speedily. Hence the librarian of today should be willing to tune with the changes of time and technology. Otherwise technology will change him and information manager of other sectors will capture his positions.

The new technologies audio technology, audio-visual technology, cnline search, CD-ROM technology, e-mail, Tele-conference, networking technology are more used in the libraries today. The Internet is one of the main technologies, which changes the whole activities of the information centers. Another important technology, which has more impact on libraries, is multimedia information system. It integrates several media such as text, audio, graphics and image. All the technologies are useful in modern libraries to cope with challenges of new information scenario. So the staff training is most important, to adjust changing work environment. And the installation of new technologies consumes more budgets. So wise expending of money on these technologies and train the staff and users to use technologies in a right way should be planned systematically.

Emergence of Internet is another development in the field of information technology. It is being used worldwide for personal and group communication, file transfer and accessing database on remote computers. Through Internet some publishers allow free access to their e-publications, so it is an opportunity to the libraries to provide services to the users without subscribing the printed version of journals and magazines. Internet can be used in the libraries right from the selection of documents to delivery of information or service to the end user.Many resources can be accessed on Internet e.g. Online dictionaries, Internet yellow pages, digital encyclopaedias, manuals and handbooks, patents, standards, textbooks, almanacs, bibliographical sources, digital maps, etc. All these are greatly influencing the collection development in the libraries.

2.3. Change management: Peoples (Library Staff and Library users)

a. Library staff

Keeping the changes in the mind there is a need for developing new skills demanding by the introduction of new technologies in the libraries.

"The demand for professionals qualified for handling

digital resources and products has increased significantly in recent years and today there is a lack of staff with competencies corresponding to the demands of the information society in most of the libraries. However, new competencies are needed if new and interesting products are to be developed in order to make library services prosperous. This is also an important issue for the library, which needs to be requalifying staff in order to compete with other libraries on the provision of information. This implies that information profession and knowledge workers must be educated and further trained. New qualifications are needed within the traditional cultural industries and institutions."

The skills required for library professionals in changing environment are as follows:

i. Acquire and process information, mediate and market information products;

ii. Be aware of the various needs and requirements of different user groups and professionals;

iii. Be aware of the various needs and requirements of different user groups and professionals;

iv. Have the ability to transfer cultural and social developments to the process of producing and disseminating information;

v. Have market and service-oriented attitudes;

vi. Evaluate appropriate media, information services and products in view of the different types of information, user requirements and markets.

In addition to the above requirements, the information professionals also need to possess certain basic skills attitudes. They are:

a. Language skills(knowledge of English);

b. Professional education in the field of electronic documentation and archives;

c. Knowledge of information and communication

technologies;

d. Knowledge of database suppliers, database language and search systems;

e. Analytical capacity;

f. Ability to summarize complex information;

g. Flexibility and adaptability;

h. Communication skills;

i. Creativity;

j. Team ability;

k. Readiness for life-long learning.

The application of IT helps the library professionals in creating database of their collection and making them available for easy access to the users both within the library and as well as outside the library through library networks.The technology is developing rapidly, which requires different knowledge and skills. Traditionally the staffs have expertise in work but not with technologies. Therefore improvement of skill for new era is an important task. For knowledge of emerging technologies and skills, the library manager must arrange training programmes for library staff. Training and awareness programmes to staffs help to improve and develop their skills and also identify the needs of users.

2.4. Library users

As a result of the introduction of emerging technologies, change in-house activities calls for change in the entire work environment. Now a days the users are more enthusiastic and active for making use of all the library services. However, at the same time, the increasing number of users will also burden the library staff, as for retrieval of information is concern. The problems being faced by the library staff are generally that many users are not computer literate and as such may not know how to send and read the mail.

To cope with all these problems it is necessary to instruct the users, and enable them to be efficient in the use of new technologies like OPACs, e-journals, etc. Therefore some sort of training is necessary in order to access information, and also for efficient use of new technologies like e-mail, OPAC and Web-browsing, etc. For this, users are to be given some training; it will save the time of the staff in the long run when the users find their information independently.

It is assumed that users of 21st century will be more aware of information needs and also more enthusiastic while coming to the information centre. Therefore keeping in view the interest and need users it becomes necessary to instruct them in such a way that they do not feel handicapped while using the new system. In this way one can manage the change and educated the users. So this is the way, where we manage the users in the changing environment.

2.5. Change Management: Withering Traditional Structures

Change is a departure from the status quo of from the conventional trends. Structural change for libraries could signify adoption of computer and communication technologies, starting new services for their clients, redefining the purpose and mission of the library, restructuring the library to create a new positions, etc.

The change that is introduced in one element is bound to influence the other elements in the system, because the library is not a system of disjointed parts. The change in the process, the users and their expectations, the change in technology in the overall policies of the parent organization and its objectives and mission is bound to have effect on the library structure also. "At the operational level restructuring is intended to distribute administrative authority and responsibility more widely throughout the organization in order to develop more efficient operations." The traditionally hierarchical structures are withering and are giving way for more accountable, transparent, and decentralized structures. The decisions are to be taken at different levels in conformity with the holistic vision and mission of the organization. The new structures demand for new skills, new responsibilities at different level of leadership. By creating flexibility in structure, it is hoped that the library will be able to manage resources better, define processes better, and eliminate boundaries and the cold wars that have historically existed in libraries.

3. STRATEGIES FOR LIBRARY MANAGERS

The modern libraries attached to any organization have to basically understand the vision and the mission of the parent organization and modify themselves to cope with the changing times.

Heery and Morgan (1996) have identified five fundamental characteristic features of an adaptable library. they are:

i. Integration into institutional life

ii. Strategic planning

iii. Participative management

iv. Service-orientation

v. Consultation

The effective management of change comprises or encompasses all these aspects. "Whether these issues are addressed the library is more likely to develop, to innovate and realize the new role that is appropriate to the changing times."

Every library whether it is public, academic or research library needs to be watchful to the changes that are taking place in its environment, carefully analyze the factors and forces responsible for the change. To do so the library mangers must not be alienated from the institutional life, then only are positioned in a right place to watch and respond, or to visualize the future course of developments and prepare to face the challenges ahead. But in reality the position of library managers (librarians) in majority of the institution with exception of some special libraries is precarious.

4. CONCLUSION

The library manager is facing new challenges because of unprecedented explosion of information unleashed by globalization, privatization and liberalization of every aspect of human life on one hand and the emergence of knowledge economics on the other hand. The modern librarianship is in search of solutions to the problems created by the chaotic world of information environment. However, the right solutions to the problems can be found only by making the whole system responsive and sensitive to the overall environment, because after all library is only a part of a system. Library and information center's responsibilities in the process of information generation, communication and access to the information published anywhere in the world-pin-pointedly exhaustively and expeditiously for the benefit of its users has acquired new dimensions in the fast changing world of information and communication technologies. Libraries no doubt are required to change but they should not push aside their traditional ethos on which the super structure of modern librarianship is built.

REFERENCES

1. Ashok Babu, T. (1999). Modern Information Technologies: Their Impact on Library Services. Library Information Technology in Modern Era. New Delhi : Common wealth Publishers, p.68-69.
2. Boughey, Alan (2000). Implementing the 'New Library : The People's Network' and the Management of Change. *Aslib Proceedings, v. 52 (4),* p 143-149.

3. Bryson, Jo (2002). Change Management: Effective Library and Information Centre Management. New Delhi : Gower Publishing Limited, p. 250.

4. Gupta, D. K. and Jain, S.L. (1996). Managing change in libraries. *ILA Bulletin, v.32(1-2)*, p.29.

5. Lekhi, Renuka and Arora, R.L.(1998). Collection Development in an IT-based environment. *Journal of Information Sciences,v.9(1)*, p.9-13.

6. Nandwana, H.B.(2000).Changing Roles of Libraries in the Management of Library and Information Services in the 21st Century. *In*, Bavakutty, M. and Parameswaran, M., *ed.* Management of Libraries in the 21st Century. New Delhi : Ess Ess Publications, p.22.

7. Nirmal Singh (2002). Management change: Principles of Management: Theory, Practices, and Techniques. New Delhi: Deep and Deep Publications, p.568-570.

8. Prakash, Jaya A. (2001). Management of change for quality improvement in library and information centres. *University News, v.39 (46)*, p.11.

9. Rama Reddy, E. (2003).Manpower Development for Information Management in Competitive Environment. *In*, Laxman Rao, N. and Others, *ed.* Manpower Development for Information Management in Competitive Environment. Hyderabad : IATLIS, p. 22.

10. Sangam, S.L. and Vatnal, R.M. (2003). Managing Electronic Resources : Skills Required for LIS Professionals. *In*, Laxman Rao and others, *ed.* Manpower Development for Information Management in Competitive Environment. Hyderabad : IATLIS, p.120.

4

The Phenomenon of Knowledge Management (KM) and Human Resource Development (HRD)

1. INTRODUCTION

Knowledge management is the key factor in the development of human society. It enhances the organizations ability and capacity in four dimensions viz. mission, competition, performance and change. Knowledge Management is the process of transforming information and intellectual assets into enduring value. It connects people with the knowledge that the need to take action when they need it. According to *Ran Yong*, Knowledge Management is a radical and fundamentally new way to create new technology, to share knowledge much faster than ever before. This has a significant impact on the organizational development. It should be remembered that we are in the area of people, process and technology fusion at all levels within the organization. The outstanding growth of the Internet, intranet and other electronic and digital media generally transformed our work and personal lives. To manage knowledge effectively and efficiently the library and information professionals have to play a vital role. They have to develop professional and personal types of competencies and skills to show their efficiency over others in the digital environment:

2. KNOWLEDGE AND ITS BASIC KINDS

Knowledge is the totality of all existing information that is known; every piece of information that is recorded in logical and systematic manner creates knowledge. Knowledge is all that has been perceived or grasped by the mind; learning, enlightment. Knowledge applies to anybody of facts gathered by study, observation etc, and to the ideas inferred from these facts, and connotes an understanding of what is known (man's knowledge of the universe).

According to *Denham Gray* "Knowledge is the full utilization of information and data, coupled with the potential of people's skills, competencies, ideas, intuition, commitments and motivations."

Beckman, T. defines "Knowledge is reasoning about information and data to actively enable performance, problem solving, decision-making, learning and teaching".

According to *New Webster's World Dictionary & Thesaurus* "Knowledge is defined as acquaintance with facts, range of information, awareness or understanding.

There are basically two kinds of knowledge that are recognized Knowledge:

(i) Explicit Knowledge : Explicit Knowledge is that which is written down or expressed in some tangible form. This is verbal, theoretical, objective and easily codified and is found in memos, manuals, annual report and the like.

(ii) Tacit Knowledge : Tacit Knowledge is communicable through mechanism like observations, conservation on- the-job learning and so on. Its very intangibility makes its management a challenge. It is informal, hidden, highly complex and personal, and is the type that forms the basic of intuition, hunches and insights.

(iii) Knowledge Management : *Meaning and definitions* : Knowledge management is the ability to manage "Knowledge". It refers to the basic elements include accessing, evaluation, managing, organizing, filtering and distributing information in a manner that is useful to end users. It includes the identification and analysis of available and required knowledge, its planning and control to fulfill organizational objectives.

Knowledge management may be defined as the set of processes that create and share knowledge across an organization to optimize the use of judgment in the attainment of mission and goals. It is an audit of intellectual assets that highlights unique sources, critical functions and potential bottlenecks, which hinder knowledge, flow to the point of use.

Hibbard writes "Knowledge Management is the process of capturing a company's collective expertise wherever it resides-in data bases, on paper or in people's heads, and distributing in to wherever it can help produce the biggest pay off".

According to *Peter Drucker and James Quinn* "knowledge Management is a process of a question of proper vision, organization networks, educated decision and the best use of lessons learned as the key of organization learning".

According to *Nonaka* " Knowledge Management is a form of application of sound management practices to human resources as whole which are the carrying vectors of knowledge. Knowledge management in a sense, is the management of the organization towards the continuous renewal of the organizational structures, facilitation of organizational members putting informational technology instruments with emphasis on teamwork and diffusion of knowledge into place.

According to *O'Dell* "Knowledge Management applies systematic approaches to find, understand and use knowledge to create value".

Knowledge Management is a discipline that promotes the integrated approach to identifying, managing and sharing of all of an expertise's information assets. These information assets may includes databases, documents, policies and procedures as well as previously unarticulated expertise and experiences resident in the individual workers.(As defined by Gardner Group, 1996)

Unfortunately, there's no universal definition of KM, just as there's no agreement as to what constitutes knowledge in the first place. For this reason, it's best to think of KM in the broadest context. Succinctly put, KM is the process through which organizations generate value from their intellectual and knowledge-based assets. Most often, generating value from such assets involves sharing them among employees, departments and even with other companies in an effort to devise best practices. It's important to note that the definition says nothing about technology; while KM is often facilitated by Information technology, technology by itself is not Knowledge management.

4. STEPS IN KNOWLEDGE MANAGEMENT

KM has three fundamental steps, which are as follows:

i. Knowledge Acquisition/Creation : Knowledge acquisition is the process of development and creation of insights, skills and relationships. Creation of documents and moving documents onto computer system.

ii. Knowledge sharing : Implies dissemination of knowledge, and making available what is already known.

iii. Knowledge utilization : Educating employees on the use of knowledge.

5. PRINCIPLES OF KNOWLEDGE MANAGEMENT

Thomas H. Davenport, one of the well-known

experts in Knowledge management concepts, framed the following ten principles of knowledge management:

i. Knowledge management is expensive.

ii. Effective management of knowledge requires hybrid solutions of people and technology.

iii. Knowledge management is highly political – Knowledge managers have to acknowledge and cultivate politics. They will act as brokers between those who have knowledge and those who may use it.

iv. Knowledge management requires knowledge managers.

v. Knowledge management benefits more from maps than models, more from markets than from hierarchies.

vi. Sharing and using knowledge are often unnatural acts.

vii. Knowledge management means improving knowledge work processes.

viii. Knowledge management access is only the beginning.

ix. Knowledge management never ends.

x. Knowledge management requires a knowledge contract.

6. TOOLS AND TECHNOLOGIES FOR KNOWLEDGE MANAGEMENT

There are very few tools and technologies providing a truly integrated set of functions to support the tasks integrated set of functions to support the tasks associated with KM. Some of the tools and technologies that support KM include knowledge repositories, Internet/Extranet, expertise access tools, e-learning applications, help desk technology multimedia and intelligent tutorial systems, content management, record management, workflow management, groupware, metadata tagging, discussion, NetMeeting and chat technologies, synchronous interaction tools, and search and data mining tools.

7. CORE PROCESS OF KNOWLEDGE MANAGEMENT

There are different views of different persons; according to *Probst* Knowledge management process consists of identifications, acquisition, developing, sharing and distributing, using and presentation of knowledge. Whereas *Devenport* explains the KM processis about acquisition, creation, packaging and application or reuse of knowledge. *Heising* has outlined the following four key processes involved in KM are, Create new knowledge, store, and distribution and apply knowledge.

8. HUMAN RESOURCE DEVELOPMENT AND LIBRARY

Human Resource Development (HRD) is a continuous process to ensure the development of employee's dynamism, motivation, effectiveness and competencies in a systematic manner. The growth and development of any library depends upon the human and material resources. The proper training of manpower will help to utilize the available material resources in a proper way. Training should we given to the professionals, how to use current technologies and how to identify and implement the latest methods of service delivery to the users of information.

9. CONCLUSION

It is a fact that Knowledge management will play a critical role in near future due to rich Knowledge based marketing. Since Knowledge is the key strategic elements played an important role in any organizations for improving internal productivity and efficiency. The arrival of Information technology challenged the established roles of libraries, publishers, producers and consumers. It helps the organization, improve the effectiveness of its knowledge process.Knowledge management requires a holistic and multidisciplinary approach to management processes and an understanding of the dimensions of knowledge work. It should be the evolution of good management practices sensibly and purposively applied. As we are living in a global village, need global knowledge available on the web. To acquire this knowledge we need new HRD skills, competencies. There are a greater variety of competencies necessary to accomplish the role of the professional librarian, while the responsibilities of librarians in the collection, organization and dissemination of information does remain the same. The ability to use the most current technology and to identify and implement the latest methods of service delivery is essential.

REFERENCES

1. Neelameghan, A. Knowledge resources management. Information Studies, V. 6, 2000, p. 203-204.
2. Satyanarayana, M. and Ravichandra Rao. L. Knowledge management. Vs. Academic libraries. *In,* Proceedings of the National Conference on the Recent Advances in Information Technology (REDIT-2001), Sept. 18-19, 2001, p.276-279.
3. Competencies for Special Librarian of 21st Century, Report : Chair : Bill Fisher, Lynda Moulton and Roberta Piccoli, May 1996.
4. Abels, Eileen and others. Competencies for Special Librarian of 21st Century, (http://www.sla.ng/conf/pcp/prodev.html)
5. Mitra, Subrata Kumar. Udog Pragati. 25(3). July-Sept. 2001. p.33.
6. Santosus, Megan and Surmacz, Jon. The ABC's of Knowledge management (http://www.cio.com/research/knowledge/edit/kmabcs.html)
7. Keeble, John and others. The Rise and role of the knowledge manager (http://www.kmmagazine.com)
8. Davenport, Thomas H. Principles of knowledge managements (http://www.itmweb.com/essays538.htm)

9. Sivasubramanian, V. Knowledge management: Task ahead for Library professionals. In, Proceedings of the National Conference on the Recent Advances in Information Technology (REDIT-2001), Sept. 18-19, 2001, p.269-275.

5
E-Education : An Online Perspective

1. INTRODUCTION

During the last few years it has been seen, an almost exponential development and growth of the digitalization, automation and the Internet, with little sign of a slow down. No longer is Internet access restricted to a few select educational establishments; it is now available to anyone in their place of work, local libraries, the Internet cafes and even in the home. It is the information that has become the key to the success in different walks of life. The information technology has two aspects of retrieving correct information and able to disseminate to the right person and this is the information age paradigm shift that has attached the concept of Library and Information Science. It too has seen a fundamental shift in the concept, manner and method by which the information managers deliver their services, and this is the practice of education, which has the purpose of teaching, training and learning. Today when the people talk about education, the conversations unknowingly turns to a new type of education called 'E-education'.

2. WHAT IS E-EDUCATION?

The term E-education means electronic education and it is basically the online delivery of information, communication, training and learning. E-education seems to have a multiplicity of definitions to each of its users and the term seems to mean something different. A very comprehensive definition has been given by the Cisco System, which defines 'E-education is Internet-enabled learning. Components can include content delivery in multiple formats, management of the learning experience, and a networked community of learners, content developers and experts. E-education provides faster learning at reduced costs, increased access to learning, and clear accountability for all participants in the learning process. In today's fast-paced culture, organizations that implement E-education provide their work force with the ability to turn change into an advantage'.

3. NEED FOR E-EDUCATION

Due to the social technological and economical transformation, E-education has become an important aspect of learning as globalization encompasses local economies like never before, the development of a skilled work forced becomes an international concern. The W.R. Hambrecht report lists some general E-education benefits as seen from the corporate side of E-education are given-

The new global economy poses more complex challenges to workers, requiring higher levels of education, computer literacy, critical thinking, information analysis, and synthesizing skills. However, educational deficiencies have brought the organization of curriculum and teaching methods as they relate to labour market preparation is needed. Academic and corporate environments must be redesigned to adequately prepare people to function in an information society.

At the beginning of the new millennium,

corporations view learning increasingly as a competitive weapon rather than an annoying cost factor. Business success depends more and more on high-quality employee performance, which is turn requires high-quality training. Corporate executives are beginning to understand that enhancing employee skills is key to create a sustainable competitive advantage. In the quest to remain competitive in today's labor market, companies are exploiting advances in technology to train employees more rapidly, more effectively, and at less expense than in the past.

Organizations and training providers need to evaluate whom they train and how. Today, traditional students in higher education make up less than 20% of all students. The fastest growing group attending higher education institutions are working professionals. This new group of "learning adults" is seeking education principally to advance their careers and increase their salaries. For universities and business-to-consumer (B2C) training provides, these individuals are excellent candidates for education delivered to their homes or offices.

The emergence of online education is not only a matter of economic and social change, but also of access. One estimate states that, by 2003, the number of Internet users worldwide will grow to about 502 million, up from 87 million in 1997. Through its increasing reach and simplicity of use., the Internet has opened the door to a global market where language and geographic barriers for many training products have been erased.

4. SCOPE OF E-EDUCATION

This new mode of education promises to transform the experience of the classroom in a number of fundamental ways: by augmenting traditional textbook materials with online resources; lectures through the use of rich multimedia and interactive content; and by extending student discussions beyond the walls of the classroom via a wide range of new communications platforms supporting inter classroom collaboration. As human capital becomes the chief source of economic value, education and training become lifelong endeavors for the majority of workers. E-education offers us potentially less expensive, more convenient, and richer ways of becoming educated, and of coming into contact with more diverse groups of fellow learners than ever before.

5. TOOLS OF E-EDUCATION

To take the better opportunities of E-education we have to know the tools associated with E-education. Some of them are:

5.1. E-mail

E-mail is the foundation for all forms of online learning and teaching. Although we are taking email in a casual way but still it is very highly appreciable tools of E-education. http://www.ncsi.iisc.ernet.in/ncsi/services/lisforum.html is a good example of this, where library and information professionals share their knowledge with other people through e- mail.

5.2. Real-Time Conferencing

Real-Time Conferencingcovers any form of online synchronous interaction. One of the simplest forms of real- time conference is online chatting. Here participant's exchange typed messages with everyone having common interface. Others can see what a person is typing on the other side, all in real time. Each message is preceded by the name of the sender to identify who said what. For example: Different messengers for instant messaging, such as Yahoo messenger, MSN messenger. The instant messaging software provides interesting features for communication or sharing of knowledge.

5.3. Desktop Video

The most advanced form of real-time conferencing is desktop video system. A desktop video system is basically a chat system that uses video images instead of text messages. The video images (including audio) are captured by a small digital camera that is connected to the Personal Computer. These cameras are relatively inexpensive and can be connected to any computer (including laptops). Using software, that comes with the camera or is obtained separately, it is possible to connect to a server running a video conferencing program — or make a direct link with another person using their IP address for a two person video session (called a point-to-point connection).

6. WHAT THE 'E' IS ABOUT?

E-education is electronic education, but the 'e' in E-education has a number of other implications as mentioned below :

Exploration : e-Learners use the Web as an exploratory tool to access a plethora of information and resources.

Experience : The Web offers e-Learners a total learning experience, from synchronous learning to threaded discussions to self-paced study.

Engagement : The Web captivates learners by enabling creative approaches to learning that foster collaboration and a sense of community.

Ease of use : Not only is the Web easy to use for learners who are already familiar with the navigation capabilities of the medium, but to learning providers as well, as they can easily make content immediately available to learners across all technical platforms (Windows, N4AC, Unix, etc.).

Empowerment : The Web puts learners in the driver's seat with a set of tools that enables personalization of content and allows learners to choose the way in which they best learn.

7. IMPLEMENTING E-EDUCATION

Des Casey, (1998) has illustrated four learning models for web based tuition. In the first, he suggested the web as an information source. Here traditional paper based course material is reproduced as a web document. This is much as was originally used by academics and still represents much of its importance today.

In the second model, the web becomes an electronic book. The course material is presented in a more structured format. Using hyperlinks it is possible to provide an optimal path through the material, multimedia clips can illustrate and further explain issues and finally on-line tests allow the level of comprehension to be assessed. However, the interaction is only between the student and the web page.

In the third model the web becomes more like the tutor. There is some simple interaction between the student and tutor through e-mail or chat rooms. Clearly, there is less of an interaction than would be provided by a face-to-face meeting, as the link may not necessarily be real-time.

The final model proposed by Casey is where the web actually becomes the medium of communication between the tutor and the student. Rather than publishing the course material on the web and the student learning from it, the tutor is involved in a direct interaction with the student. The difference here is that the student is not learning from the web but learning through the web.

7.1. Students perspective

For the student it would seem that the advent of on-line education has many potential advantages that would allow them to fit their education in with their way of life, that is other commitments. The need to be physically present for a range of lectures and tutorials is alleviated however there will need to be a greater self-motivation.

7.2. Tutors perspective

For the tutor there are new requirements that e-education needs addressing. In order for the course to be interactive there much more planning and preparation are required. Similarly as there could be a larger number of users and with that, a wider range of skills and usage of the material these will also have to be pre-empted.

7.3. University perspective

Many of the commercial services that have moved their services to Internet have done so because they offer customers a better or a faster service. In reality, the driving force will most often be cost savings for the company. When we look towards education these may still hold but the primary advantages that are gained are the conquering of time and distance. The geographical location of the students and tutors is not an issue.

8. REQUIREMENTS FOR IMPLEMENTING E-EDUCATION

Taking on board many of the points raised above here are some requirements for a successful implementation of E-education. Clearly most of these need addressing before attempting to implement any electronically based education system.

- Provision of free or low cost access
- Collaboration to be encouraged between various organisations
- Mixture of different teaching models
- Closer monitoring of individual student progress
- Provision of greater support to motivate students

where needed

- Standards require monitoring
- Readily scalable service with high bandwidth an availability

9. E-EDUCATION IN LIS EDUCATION

In the present scenario the information needed the users have been changed. Thus, many library schools all around the globe have already introduced E-education as a tool for continuous learning in Library and Information Science. In United States, there has been a fast adoption of E-education techniques in the LIS schools, as such; this has immensely benefited the students and practitioners. Usnews.com and World Report carried out a survey on the best online LIS schools accredited by American Library Association. The survey reveals that the first on line LIS education was started in the year 1993 by Syracuse University, New York. 12 LIS schools accredited to ALA organizing online programmes in different courses, such as, Master in Library and Information Science, (MLIS), Master in Library Science (MLS), Master of School Library and Information Technologies (MSLIT), etc. These schools have been using varieties of learning technologies, such as Chat rooms, threaded discussions, audio & video, simulations, laboratory exercises, etc., In most of the schools (66.66%), the programme participants need not visit the school campus. All the schools, ranging from 4-24 hours daily provide online technical help. It is evident from the results of the survey that E-education/online learning has been playing a strategic role for the developments of quality education and professional practice in library and information science.

In India, the E-education initiatives have already begun. The following messages mentioned in a mailing list depict the development of E-education in Indian education sector. Satyam in E-education partnership with Canadian firm. Toronto, Dec.6-ISOPIA Inc. an E-education infrastructure software provider here, and Satyam, Infoway, a premier Indian information technology (IT) company, have announced a partnership to launch on online learning site in India. Through its newly formed subsidiary, Satyam Education Services Limited (SESL), Satyam Infoway will promote online learning courseware and offer India's burgeoning web population the opportunity to expand its education to meet growing skills requirements.

10. CONCLUSION

The effective use of information technology in the learning process can best be achieved by taking an integrated approach to change involving the examination of pedagogy, curriculum and organizational structures within the community. Library and information science schools and other educational and professional bodies should take up the challenge of electronic education and integrate the appropriate learning platform. The cooperation of teachers, professionals and students would make the centre a great success and thereby making provision for a continuous quality in the field of LIS education.

REFERENCES

1. Casey, D. (1998). Learning from or through the Web: models of Web based education. *Proceedings of the 6th annual conference on the teaching of computing 3rd annual conference on integrating technology into computer science education on Changing the delivery of computer science education,* 1998, pp. 51–54. *http://www.acm.org/pubs/citations/proceedings/cse/282991/p51-casey/*
2. Neumann, P G. (1998) Risks of e-education. Communications of the ACM, 40(10) October 1998, p.136.
3. United States Distance learning Association's Preamble : National Policy Recommendations. (http:/www.usdla.org)

4. Hambrecht, W.R. (2002). The corporate E-learning : Exploring New Frontier (report).
5. Salz, Edith(1998).E-education for Libraries : How to keep track of the latest developments.
6. Sahu, S.R. and others (2002). E-learning : A myth or reality. In, Workshop on Information Resource management, held on 13th –15th 2002, DRTC Bangalore.
7. *WWW.CiscoE-education .Com*
8. Salmon, Gill (2002) E-moderating : the key to teaching and learning online. Epping Forest, Feb.2002.
9. Duggan, E (2002). E-education, its virtually here. *http://bizjournal.com*

6

Core Competencies for Librarians

1. INTRODUCTION

Competencies are the skills, technical knowledge and personal attributes that enable individuals to contribute positively to their organizations and the library profession. These core competencies apply to librarians and library staff, although some aspects of each of the competencies may not apply to every staff person.

There are greater variety of competencies necessary to accomplish the role of the professional librarian, while the responsibility of librarians in the collection, organization and dissemination of information does remains the same. The ability to use the most current technology and to identify and implement the latest methods of service delivery is essential.

In the past librarians' role was limited to acquiring, classifying,and cataloguing books. After doing this, they worked as acustodian of their collection. They were mere 'storekeepers.'Today information technology has ushered in a revolution to theeffect how knowledge is developed, stored and accessed to.Librarians are, therefore, faced with the tremendous challenge of maintaining their relevance, responding to the imperatives oftheir changing role in a constantly evolving academic scenario.By successfully meeting these challenges, librarians cantransform themselves into effective information professionals andcan tread along the fast track course by seizing the innumerableopportunities thrown by new breakthroughs in information technology.

2. PROFESSIONAL COMPETENCIES

2.1. User services

- Understands user needs and preferences for information, which builds and drives thc selection of resources and services.
- Improves user services in response to changing needs.
- Presents welcoming behaviors and practices effective interviewing skills to best determine the user's actual needs;
- Understands information-seeking behaviors and facilitates the user's successful information retrieval.
- Instructs in information gathering, research and technical skills, including how to use and evaluate information sources.
- Acts as a user advocate during the development of information products and systems.
- Tailors services and information products to support the user's needs.
- Acts as a consultant to the parent organization and community on information issues.

2.2. Assessment

- Continually analyzes and investigates the information and service needs of the targeted user base
- Continually analyses and investigates the use, quality and effectiveness of current services.

- Continually scans the local and global environment for societal changes and service opportunities.
- Evaluates and selects resources to assure their quality, accuracy and pertinence and delivers them in a form appropriate to the situation.
- Focuses on the outcomes of library use and conducts related research towards solving identified information management problems

2.3. Knowledge of Information Sources and IT

- Coordinate the development and application of library technology. This includes selecting, designing, implementing, evaluating, and monitoring computer equipment and software.
- Continuing education is essential to update skills, keep current broaden knowledge and integrate new techniques and methodology into everyday practice.
- Design and implement automated systems for resource collection, management, and access that are responsive to the organization's goals.
- Regularly evaluate and adjust automation requirements for the library.
- Evaluate, select, implement, and monitor computer equipment and software for the library.
- Develop, oversee, and evaluate Internet and organizational Intranet applications.
- Attend conferences, workshops, seminars, and classes to maintain knowledge of changing technologies.
- Can identify materials appropriate to user's requirements and their abilities.
- Can identify, interpret, and access varied information resources.
- Designs and locally produces resources in a wide variety of formats to anticipates and meet user needs.

2.4. Resource management

- Prepare and maintain library resources. This responsibility includes all technical service activities such as acquiring, processing, cataloging, maintaining, and circulating resources.
- Establish guidelines for collection development that reflect the library's goals and objectives.
- Develop policies and procedures to evaluate, acquire, discard, process, organize, maintain, and circulate or loan information resources.
- Perform evaluation studies to ensure information resources are responsive to client needs and library goals.
- Process and prepare print or electronic resource additions and maintain the condition and order of resources to ensure their availability to library users.
- Catalog or index resources in accordance with national and international standards.
- Select or design classification schemes to make resources accessible to users.
- Administer copyright compliance and contractual commitments.

2.5. Expertise and Technical Knowledge

- Demonstrates broad, in-depth, and up-to-date knowledge of pertinent fields and awareness of current Technology understands
- Understands and uses the latest relevant technology to manage and deliver services.
- Scans the environment for emerging technologies that are relevant to library services.
- Looks for opportunities to use and expand knowledge, skills, and experience.

- Keeps up-to-date with new practices, trends, and standards in the field by reading journals, attending professional meetings and conferences, holding discussions with experts, etc.
- Asks for and is willing to take on more challenging work acts as a resource to others; freely and willingly shares new technology with others.

2.6. Administration

- Manage and direct library operations and facilities. This responsibility includes establishing goals, monitoring statistics, developing work plans, managing facilities, and supervising on a day-to-day basis.
- Assesses strength, weaknesses, opportunities, and challenges to the organization and develops strategies for dealing with them effectively without compromising vision and values.
- Creates a culture which promotes change.
- Identifies, develops, administers and evaluates both internal and external resources to support the library's mission.
- Develops and implements policies and procedures for the efficient and effective operation of library functions.
- Continually adjusts programs and services to respond to social changes and service opportunities.

2.7. Advocacy

- Communicates the value of library and information services to decision makers.
- Promotes literacy.
- Promotes intellectual freedom and equal access to information.

- Can identify and enlist the support of strategic partners to complements strengths and weaknesses of the organization and to obtain key resources and assistance to support the achievement of mutual goal?

2.8. Collaboration

- Understands and works to realize the mission, values and vision of the library organization.
- Uses effective team process skills to develop and achieve organizational objectives.
- Collaborates to achieve common goals in a spirit of collegiality and mutual respect.

3. PERSONAL COMPETENCIES

3.1. Education

- Continuing education is essential to update skills, keep current broaden knowledge and integrate new techniques and methodology into everyday practice.

3.2. Service commitment

- Understands and meets the needs of users and addresses their interests and the concerns of those affected.
- Is interested in the goals of users, co-workers and suppliers and strives to provide effective support in helping them achieve these goals.
- Demonstrates and understanding of and a respect for diversity.
- Demonstrates a sincere commitment to user service.
- Remains knowledgeable with current events, popular and local culture.

3.3. Flexibility/Adaptability

- Performs a wide range of tasks, responds to changes

in direction and priorities, and accepts new challenges, responsibilities, and assignments

- Anticipates and manages change effectively and participates in change.
- Consistently maintains a positive attitude in responding to unpredictable situations.
- Adapts personal styles and preferences to the demands of the situation.
- Takes risks, experiments and makes mistakes and supports this behavior in others.

3.4. Leadership

- Sets and models high performance standards characterized by integrity; earns trust and respect of others by coaching, inspiring, and empowering teams of people to achieve strategic objectives
- Sees the long view, articulates the direction clearly and enlists others to jointly work to achieve it.
- From any position within the organization, sets a positive examples for others to follow.
- Sets and models high performance standards characterized by integrity; earns trust and respect of others by coaching, inspiring, and empowering teams of people to achieve strategic objectives.
- Helps others to achieve their full potential.
- Values the contributions of others.

3.5. Communication skills

- Listens effectively, transmits information accurately and understandably, and actively seeks constructive feedback.
- Provides timely, accurate, and candid information on critical issues (planning/progress/results) to the users.
- Identifies the critical issues to be communicated in

complex situations.

- Presents information or data in a format that is efficient and understandable.
- Effectively shares what is learned with others.
- Communicates openly and directly.
- Practices effective learning skills.
- Demonstrates effective and informal presentations skill.
- Writes clearly, logically, and concisely.

3.6. Ethics

- Treats others with honesty, respect and fairness.
- Protects and values user confidentially and organizational security.

3.7. Self-motivation

- Takes responsibility for managing the development of one's own carrier within the organization and beyond, including a commitment to lifelong learning and periodic retooling of personal skill set.
- Keeps current with professional literature and discussion groups.
- Takes initiative and demonstrates innovation.
- Seeks opportunities to serve one's personal goal and those of the organization.

4. CONCLUSION

Today, Information and communication technology has fundamentally transformed the learner and the learningenvironment. Librarians must be prepared to serve as champions of this transformation. They must be prepared to move with the challenges of digital technology, globalized information access and networked resources. Acquiring such skills will create very tempting new opportunities and new roles for librarians.The core competencies necessary for Librarian and other library staff to function in the future are changing as fast as the changes in higher education that drive them. Flexible, adaptable staff will allow libraries to move forward to meet the needs of their users. Through core competencies, libraries can recruit, hire, train, and retain valuable library staff responsive to the new and continuously changing library environment. Core competencies are an integral part of the move toward a learning organization and will help to the Libraries to move forward and to meet changing users needs and expectations.

REFERENCES

1. Andersen, A. (1998). Knowledge navigators: Changing practice of librarians. Information Outlook, 2(9), 17-26.
2. Klobas, J.E. (1999). Networked information resources: Electronics opportunities for users and libraries. OCLC Systems and Services, 15(2), 10-11.
3. McCleskey, Sarah E. (2003)."Staffing Standards and Core Competencies in Academic Art and Architecture Departmental Libraries: A Preliminary Study." Journal of Library Administration 39(1): 1-21.
4. Oketunji, I. (2003). Professional challenges in the digital age. Lagos Journal of Libraries and Information Science, 1(2), 12-17.
5. Omekwu, C.O. (2002). Challenges of information systems in the modern library. In E.C. Madu & M.B. Dirisu(Eds.), Information Science and Technology for Library Schools in Africa (100-114). Ibadan: Evi-Coleman Publications.
6. Richard, B. (1998). The digital information revolution. In G.I. mihalas et al. (Eds), Medire Aread: Vasile Goldis University Press, 7-10.
7. Syracuse University (2002). Third Annual 21st Century Librarian Award : Recoginging Librarians Work in shaping the New Information Environment, Syracuse : University of Syracuse school of Information studies, 3.

7

Cloud Computing and Libraries

1. INTRODUCTION

Cloud computing is a new technology model for IT services which many businesses and organizations are adopting. It allows them to avoid locally hosting multiple servers and equipment and constantly dealing with hardware failure, software installs, upgrades and compatibility issues. For many organizations, cloud computing can simplify processes and save time and money. Cloud computing is a technology that uses the web (Internet) and central remote servers to maintain data, software and application. Cloud computing allows users to use applications without installation in their local machine to access their personal and official files on any computer with internet access. This technology allows users to access much more efficient computing by centralizing storage, memory and processing. This is not a new technology; it's associated since inception of the web. In the libraries cloud computing is used to a digital library and to automate housekeeping operations using third party services, software and hardware. Cloud computing refers to both applications delivered as a service over the internet and the systems software in the data centers that services. In simple words the datacenters, hardware and systems software is what we can call a cloud. One does not need any software or server to store them. These services are free to all users till some limit, any extra storage capacity and advanced services are available at cost.

Cloud Computing, with its inception since 2006 has become a buzzword and a latest rage not among the corporate and big business houses, research institutes, libraries but the common masses also like using face book, twitter, smart phone applications, online bank transactions or using IRCTC services for booking online railway tickets etc. with the advent of cloud computing age-old and archaic server centric application integration technology has become a thing of the past. Archaic server centric technology required expensive services of domain experts and software developers and it lacked the ability of using the computing power of the client system and storage capacity to its maximum limit.

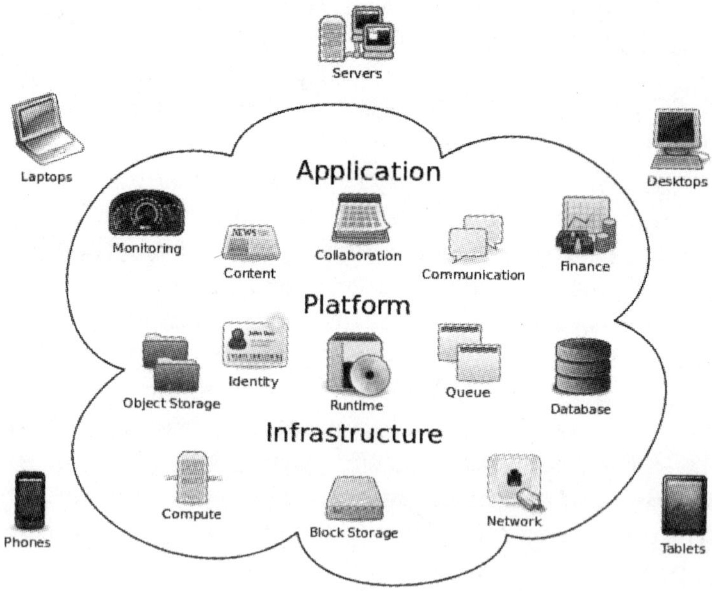

Fig. 1. Cloud Computing technology

Cloud computing offers information retrieval systems, particularly digital libraries and search engines, a wide variety of options for growth and reduction of maintenance needs and encourages efficient resource use. These features are particularly attractive for digital libraries, repositories, and search engines. The dynamic and elastic provisioning features of a cloud infrastructure allow rapid growth in collection size and support a larger user base, while reducing management issues. The pace of growth of information available on the Web and the challenge in finding relevant and authoritative sources of information make information retrieval systems very useful. Anyone connected to the Internet is probably using some type of cloud computing on a regular basis. Whether they are using Google's Gmail, organizing photos on Flicker or searching the Web with Bing they are engaged in cloud computing. As Geoffrey Moore points out, the interesting thing about cloud computing is it did not start as a technology for the business enterprise, but was driven by the public with services like Face book and Flicker. The Gartner Group defines cloud computing as "a style of computing in which massively scalable and elastic IT enabled capabilities are delivered as a service to external customers using Internet technologies.

In the new concept of the clouds, software's are doing the role of service providers, outsourcing and hosting providers, network and IT infrastructure providers while adding the name of software companies contributing in the process of commercial boom in the internet world.

Cloud computing is a computing paradigm, where a large pool of systems are connected in private or public networks, to provide dynamically scalable infrastructure for application, data and file storage. In this technology, information is permanently stored on the internet servers and it can be cached by the users temporarily. The cloud application is created using resources from more than one service and from more than one location. It is a subscription-based service where a person can obtain networked storage space and computer resources.

2. WHAT IS CLOUD COMPUTING?

What is "cloud computing"? To put it simply, cloud computing is a synonym for the internet. To say that a company or institution is engaged in cloud computing is to say that they are involved with projects that base applications and computing services on the internet in a widely distributed environment. There are many synonyms for cloud computing: "on-demand computing", "software as a service", "information utilities", "the internet as a platform", and others. In some ways, cloud computing is simply an extension of the client server model that was introduced in the 1980s. Cloud computing means cloud based networking environment. Cloud computing contains set of software and hardware resources which are available on the internet and its services are managed by third-party. These services provide access to advanced software applications and high configured servers. Service provider performs role of consultant. Cloud computing is a web based computing where shared resources, applications and information are provided to the set of computers and other devices on demand using web technology. Cloud computing is based on internet; generally the internet is commonly visualized as a cloud. Therefore, the process of cloud computing is being done through set of web enabled applications loaded on the server with proper access rights.

There are many reasons why this form of computing is attractive to organizations. It shifts the bulk of the responsibility for infrastructure support out to another vendor, and basically outsources all data center and software support to a company that specializes in web-based computing. There is no need to perform client-based software upgrades, which can be costly in both personnel costs and software licensing costs. The issue of storage, network security, operating system upgrades, hardware costs and all of the various and sundry activities associated with maintaining a local computing infrastructure are pushed out to the service provider. Also, the cost of purchasing Individual or bulk licenses for software products is mitigated because the application is centrally installed and utilized. There is no need for a per-host license to run the software. All of us are familiar with the pain of dealing with license issues for locally hosted software. There are many disadvantages as well.

Cloud computing is a new technology model for IT services which many organizations and individuals are adopting. It allows them to avoid locally hosting and operating multiple servers over an organization's network and constantly dealing with hardware failure, software installation, upgrades, backup and compatibility issues and also enables them to save cost. In other words, it refers to "the delivery of computing as a service rather than a product, whereby shared resources, software, and information are provided to computers and other devices as a metered service over a network, typically theinternet".2 In this model rather than investing on hardware and software, organizations buy and pay for the services as needed basis. Cloud computing also helps to increase the IT requirements quickly and easily to accommodate the changes in demand. In other words, it enables organizations to add or remove hardware/ software as per the needs just by requesting the service provider to do so.

Various definitions and interpretations of 'Cloud' and 'Cloud Computing' exist. "Internet based computing in which large group of remote servers are networked so as to allow sharing of data-processing tasks, centralized data storage and online access to computer services or resources."

"Cloud computing is Internet-based computing, whereby shared resources, software, and information are provided to computers and other devices on demand through the Internet".

The Christy & Carina of Gartner Group define cloud computing as 'a style of computing in which massively scalable and elastic IT-enabled capabilities are delivered as a service to external customers using Internet technologies'.

To simplify the concept, cloud computing can be defined as 'simply the sharing and use of applications and resources of a network environment to get work done without concern about ownership and management of the network's resources and applications'.

In other words, information and software do not need to be stored on your personal computer. This abstraction of hardware and software allows you to take different approaches in selecting and implementing library services.

3. FEATURES OF CLOUD COMPUTING

ICT is playing pivotal role in the development of libraries in the World. Characteristics of cloud computing technology are attracting library professionals to make use of it in routine library house-keeping operations. Changes in the services, digitization, up-gradation in existing or introduction of new hardware/software are the routine process carried out in the library. Cloud computing technology takes care of these changes and allows users (library management or organizations) to make request for these changes and also for additional bandwidth, storage space and speed. Such scalability is possible in this technology. On-demand self service is another characteristic of cloud computing, in which being a customer library can request and manage its own computing resources. Cloud services are available on Internet. End users of the library can avail the library services and access required information through Internet from their destinations. Moreover library staff may also work for his/her library on Internet. The characteristic i.e. Broad network access allows for enjoying this facility. The services obtained by the cloud service provider can be measured. Library can request for the additional band width for fast and smooth access of its information to the users, specific numbers of user license, space for storing the digitized information and so on as per the requirement. These requests of library can be measured easily to pay the service charges. Following are different features of cloud computing:

3.1. Elasticity and Scalability

Elasticity is one of the essential and core features of cloud systems. This is very important feature of this service that any modification and enhancement in the services are very easy and fast which make this service very scalable and resilient. One can easily add up required bandwidth, processing speed and data storage or number of license in very short time. One need not to plan any more for project costing, procurement, project implementation or project closer; but one need to place a purchase order to service provider to get the service in due time.

3.2. Energy consumption

Energy consumption is relevant to reduce additional costs of energy consumption. In case of traditional system one has to keep all the servers on as the data loaded on the server for round the clock access. Cloud is a based on network environment and therefore, principally allow reducing the energy consumption.

3.3. Reliability

It's an amazing characteristic of cloud computing. Reliability is one neededcharacteristic of cloud computing that will increase when redundant websites are accessed. Reliability is improved by having multiple sites for the same service, such that if one faces an outage, the other can take over the load.

3.4. Security

Security is obviously essential in all systems dealing with potentially sensitive data and code. The cloud is managed and administered by the team of IT expert. Therefore, the data will be secure in terms of data loss and system crash.

3.5. Consumption based billing

The capability to build up cost according to the actual consumption of resources is a relevant feature of cloud systems. Pay per use strongly relates to quality of service support, where specific requirements to be met by the system and hence to be paid for can be specified. One of the great features of cloud is, if you don't use the resource and you pay nothing.

3.6. Data Management

Data management is an essential aspect in sense of storage, where data is flexibly distributed across multiple resources. Implicitly, data consistency needs to be maintained over a wide distribution of replicated data sources. At the same time, the system always needs to be aware of the data location at the time of replicating data across the data centers. Therefore, data management is a tremendous feature of cloud environment.

3.7. Managing Cloud Activities

One of the most considerable features of the cloud is a management and monitoring of cloud application. As cloud manager works within a distributed wide area network infrastructure; one can monitor it from all over the world. One of the biggest shifts from the traditional data center is that all the data stored, managed and administered in a cloud.

3.8. Multi-tenancy

Multi tenancy is a highly essential issue in cloud systems, where the location of code and / or data is principally unknown and the saine resource may be assigned to multiple users (potentially at the same time). This affects infrastructure resources as well as data / applications / services that are hosted on shared resources but need to be made available in multiple isolated instances.

3.9. Self Service Model

The one of the reason behind popularity of cloud based environment is self service model. In some cases users have the ability to upload files, build programs, deploy, schedule, manage, and generate reports. This service is available to the users based on demand.

4. CLOUD SERVICES

4.1. Software as a Service (SaaS)

In SAAS users could have software as service delivery over network as per requirement. Service as a platform is admired in cloud computing world for its easy to use model. Redeeming feature of SAAS being its application ready for running directly without any installation or downloads. There is absolutely no need for installation and running it on personal computers. Maintenance and continuous support for applications users are immense.

In SaaS, instead of buying required software in the library and installed it on the server of the library, it can be acquired on rent basis from cloud service provider. In this case the software is available with the service provider. It is installed on the server of service provider. Library has to subscribe the services of software from service provider. So far as data is concerned, it may either available on the local server of the library or with the service provider.

The major benefit of the SaaS is that the library management need not to invest funds in buying the software. However, the software required for the specific local work of the library may not be available with cloud service provider. In such a situation library itself has to purchase it for its users.

4.2. Infrastructure as a Service (IaaS) :

In this model cloud service consumers uses the facility of virtual desktop while consuming resources like resources storage, network, virtualized servers etc.

Using these services is chargeable and it all depends upon the actual use of the IAAS service. In fact IAAS service provider permits the user to use its IT infrastructure to install a virtual server.

Characteristics and components of IAAS include:

i. Utility computing service and billing model.

ii. Automation of administrative tasks.

iii. Dynamic scaling.

iv. Desktop virtualization.

v. Policy-based services.

vi. Internet connectivity.

In modern library, ample memory space is required to preserve and organize the digitized documents. Large capacity with sufficient memory space and latest configured hardware are required for library. Purchasing, developing and then maintaining this infrastructure in the library is a tedious job. In Indian scenario, unavailability of well IT skilled manpower is the biggest problem before the library management. Further, continuous development and up-gradation of hardware is the another problem. To overcome these problems, infrastructure required by the library can be made available from cloud service provider by paying subscription. In this kind of services, library management can think to subscribe server space, storage space, network equipment etc. from service providers.

4.3. Platform as a Service (PaaS)

PAAS offers computational resources through a platform. It is basically tailored for system administrators, developers, and testers. PAAS users are not needed to buy hardware and software's and using this platform development and deployment of customized software takes place. In this model networking, storage, virtualization, servers, middlemen and runtime are handled by the service provider whereas data and application are managed by consumers themselves.

In computer system, platform is the essential thing to run the software or programs. In computerized/ automated libraries various software are required to perform different task.

Many a time different operating systems such as Window NT, Linux are required for these software. Investing funds in purchasing these operating systems may not be possible due to shrinking budget or on technical ground. In such situation, it is better to subscribe it for certain period. PaaS through cloud service provider allows this facility to its clients. Under this facility, service provider extents PaaS on monthly rental basis.

PaaS offers application development, design, testing and hosting, web service integration, database integration, security, storage facilities to the end users.

Collection of knowledge is the prime factor of library. The collected knowledge is to be managed in the library so as to disseminate it to the proper user at right time. Now a day digitization is the buzz word in the library. Organization and proper storage of this digitized knowledge is a challenge before the library management. Further, much attention is to be paid in providing the security to this huge data. Cloud solves this problem with great extent by extending

4.4. Data as a Service (DaaS)

Therefore, so far as library is concerned this kind of service can be demanded from cloud service provider.

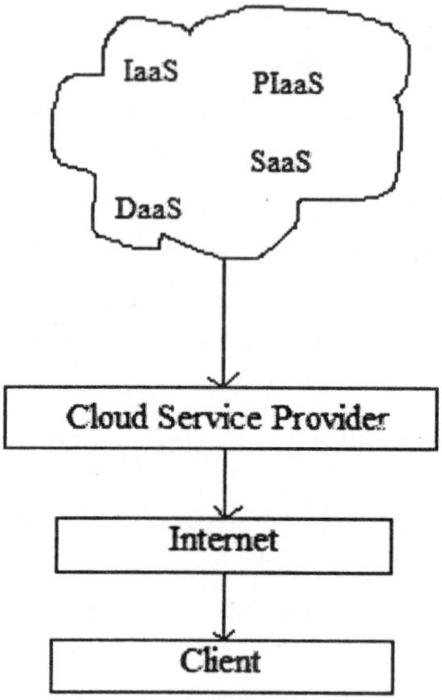

Fig. 2. Cloud Computing Services

5. CLOUD COMPUTING IN THE LIBRARIES

Libraries have been using some cloud computing services for over a decade. Online databases are accessed as cloud applications. Large union catalogs can also be defined as cloud applications. However, a look outside libraries is warranted to better understand the value proposition of cloud computing. Cloud computing has large prospective for libraries. Libraries may put more and more contents into the cloud. Using cloud computing user would be able to browse a physical shelf of books, CDs or DVDs or choose to take out an item or scan a bar code into his mobile device. All historical and rare documents would be scanned into a comprehensive, easily searchable database and would be accessible to any researcher. Many libraries already have online catalogues and share bibliographic data with OCLC. More frequent online catalogues are linked to consortium that share resources.

Libraries are moving towards cloud and trying to provide network based services. Moving to cloud based services means, the library housekeeping operations, digital libraries etc are hosted on cloud based network. In the recent era many libraries are using Google web technology knowingly or unknowingly to provide services. Earlier, if a person wanted to create document or spreadsheet he was using Microsoft's Office package, nowadays many Libraries are processing documents, using Google web technology (Google Docs) on day-to-day basis. Use of Google apps and other similar tools in the libraries shows a radical shift from traditional to advance technologies. Now libraries are providing good number of services to their users to access various resources and computer applications from a single platform. This is an advantage of the cloud computing. Libraries have been adopting cloud-based solutions for different services including

- Electronic journal access management,
- Statistics tracking,
- Digital library hosting,
- And even integrated library system (ILS) hosting.
- Cloud computing has allowed libraries to make strategic choices about the allocation of resources and to offer better service than would be possible if relying on in-house solutions.

The concept of cloud computing is not much accepted in Indian libraries. The reason behind that is the lack of good service provider in the field of library management using advanced technology. Many libraries are thinking to adopt cloud computing but they are facing some problems in relation to standardize software, administrative procedures, budget constraints, connectivity problem etc. Nowadays, some foreign companies are providing cloud based services.

In today's scenario libraries are adopting advanced technology in their day-to-day activity and the concept of cloud is one of them. In libraries Automation of Housekeeping operations and Digital Libraries are main two areas which can be moved on the cloud.

India is not as fast as US and Europe in the development and considering the timelines of research to reach market-readiness as opposed to the fast movements in the market itself. The time is a critical resource with respect to positioning India in the global cloud development market. Implementation of cloud in the libraries is not easy task as there are many administrative and financial matters involved. Adopting cloud services means we have to be depending on the service provider. Many Indian libraries does not have even internet connection to connect with the cloud, in this case, it is very difficult to implement cloud based services.

India is an emerging market for IT industry and, Indian government is also providing help to Indian university libraries to get high speed internet connection for research purpose, in view of these libraries/ institutions/universities can consider cloud based library services to serve their users. Using cloud computing libraries can offer modern information services in user friendly format. With the use of these advanced technology library staff can also get an opportunity to learn new technological changes occurred in the field. As the cloud is a third party service if, any problem occurs, then the experts will provide the quick solution without interrupting library services.

With a view to Indian libraries one need to examine

all the criteria before choosing any cloud service. Because, when it is planned to use third party services one need to have thorough idea about the whole system. If one thinks that our all day-to-day activities can be moved then, first of all searching the standard company who has set of various software and hardware and experience in handling such services. There are many companies in the market which provide this kind of services. (e.g.Ex Libris, Duracloud, Polaris Library System). Following are some of the service providers of Cloud computing for libraries:

- **Ex Libris :** Ex Libris is a well known cloud service provider based in USA. They are providing cloud solution in the field of library with all the software and hardware support needed to provide services to the users. Ex Libris is available for all type of libraries and also for consortia. Ex Libris is built on various standard and contains number of features like compatibility with Unicode font, flexibility, migration of data, customization etc.,
- **Polaris Library Systems :** Polaris is one of the cloud based library automation system available in the market. The company also provides standard acquisition and processing system. Also, with a Polaris ILS Client License, the library can integrate various PC and print management systems at no extra cost. The systems uses number of well know standards like MARC 21 for bibliographic data, XML, Z39.50 for information retrieval, Unicode etc.
- **Dura Cloud :** Dura space provides open source repository solutions by undertaking turnkey projects for organisations and libraries to enable them to share scholarly literature using DSpace and Fedora Commons. It is providing cloud solution for digital library services. Dura Cloud is a sister concern of the Duraspace which is a collaboration of the Dspace digital library software and Fedora

Commons. Fedora Commons is a frame work for digital repository. It offers complete solution for digital library with standard software and hardware solution. Dura cloud also provides open source code and the code needs to be installed on your machine.

- **OCLC's Web scale :** OCLC has set an example for making use of cloud computing for libraries. Years together OCLC has been functioning as a cloud computing vendor because they provide cataloguing tools over the internet and allow member institutions to draw on their centralized data store.
- **OSS Labs :** OSS labs from India is using Amazon's elastic cloud computing platform owing to the various capabilities of Amazon such as high durability of data, strong information security based on ISO standards, capability, and flexibility.

Cloud computing is nothing but a collection of servers, sharing data and resources on a shared platform. It is a recent technology and still it is not commonly used. So far as libraries are concerned very few libraries in the World are involved in this technology. OCLC, Library of Congress etc. could be the examples of cloud libraries.

In digital library the storage of huge digitized data for dissemination is the major task to be performed by the professionals. It requires strong configured machines having adequate storage capacity. And as we know due to continuous and fast developments in ICT, new hardware and software with changing platforms are introducing day by day. It is very difficult for library managers to cope up with these technological changes with shrinking budget. Therefore, in near future libraries will be thinking to apply cloud technology in data storage area. Moreover, library databases, OPAC, Institutional Repositories etc. could also be put on cloud. A well-stocked library is an asset to any academic and research institute. It has to play pivotal role in teaching-learning process. As library is the momentous ingredient of higher education in teaching and research, it should be sound in terms of academic resources as well as new technologies. It has to be acted as a 'Knowledge Resource Hub' to percolate the essential information up to end stakeholders. Moreover, these library stakeholders are expected from library that the adequate resources should made available at their work station/s. Further any single library can't fulfil the requirements of its stakeholders. With the help of other libraries (Member libraries) and cloud computing technology it can be done effectively.

6. SEGMENTS OF CLOUD COMPUTING

Following are different segments of cloud computing:

6.1. Application

The application segment is the part of internet technology which is proved already as the constructive and helpful model. When many individual applications are accessed through the central server of cloud, the library (Institute) will demand severe cost. On the other hand, the applications of on-demand are not similar in the price scheme and delivering process to the users. In short an application is the first segment without which a concept of cloud computing cannot be survived.

6.2. Storage

The backbone of the main concept of Cloud Computing is called infrastructure or storage. All the vendors will permit the users to create their own cloud applications within the limited space. The popular S3 of Amazon is considered as a storage segment.

6.3. Connectivity

Most important part of the cloud is connectivity. Without high speed internet connectivity there will be no use of application and storage. Therefore, the high speed leased line internet connectivity is necessary to connect with the cloud. All above three segments are inter-related with each other and out of three if, anyone is missing then a concept of cloud will remain unfulfilled.

7. TYPES OF CLOUD COMPUTING

Cloud computing technology makes feasible interconnectivity of immense resources through the gateway of public and private networks.Cloud computing is considered as a third revolution of Information Technology after the revolution of Personal Computer and web technology/Internet. These revolutions have brought the great changes in the sphere of knowledge. Library is a place where the knowledge is to be stored and preserve for further use for next generations. So the utmost care is to be taken in its preservation. After the invention of paper, the knowledge in the form of written information has been preserve on it. However, with the emergence of PC and web technology, library professionals are now interested to put this knowledge in digitized form. Of course, developing required IT infrastructure for it and maintaining of it is an expensive affair for individual library. Cloud computing system is an option with library management for solving this guanine problem of library. Instead of maintaining this huge and eternally increasing knowledge locally in the computer, it can be put on cloud. Many options in the form of models are available for uploading the knowledge on cloud. Library can choose the proper one as per its convenience amongst the following models discussed in forthcoming paragraphs.

7.1. Private Cloud

Dedicated cloud infrastructures relating to organizations are known as private clouds. Private clouds permit only specified users to host applications in the cloud in a secure cloud based environment. Private clouds, within a virtualized environment, using underlying physical computing resources makes available computing power as a service. When the individual organization develops the cloud for its different services purpose and sections, it istermed as Private Cloud. This kind of model is useful for large organizations such as Bank, Railway, etc. Generally in the individual organization for storing data and for other task, every section required hardware as well as software. Repetition in purchasing this infrastructure is observed in this process. In such a situation resource sharing in terms of hardware and software is possible through private cloud.

If organizations develop their own cloud, the sections of these respective organizations can put their data on it. Library can avail the facilities of cloud, in case the cloud is developed by its parent institution. Security of data is the biggest problem in cloud computing. However, in case of private cloud as data is stored and maintained by the cloud of parent institution the problem of data security is solved in large extent.

7.2. Public Cloud

Public cloud service providers hosting a cloud operate the infrastructure and offer access over the internet. Noteworthy feature of this model is sharing of same infrastructure kitty with finite configuration. Public cloud service provider provisions e.g. applications and storage to users over the internet. In this model cloud computing is publically accessible also. Public cloud computing service is offered by the service providers either free or pay-per-use model.

When the cloud service provider provides cloud services to the general public on Internet, then such a service provider is known as Public Cloud Service Provider and the model is called Public Cloud. Some of the typical examples of Public Cloud are given below.

- Amazon EC2 (http://aws.amazon.com/ec2/),
- Google App Engine (http://code.google.com/appengine/),

- Webfusion (http://www.webfusion.co.uk/cloud-hosting/),
- Rackspace Cloud (http://www.rackspacecloud.com/) etc.

Services offered by such a model may be free or pay as per usage. In certain cases cloud services can also be availed by paying periodical subscription. Libraries may also think to take the services of Public Cloud. The major benefit in this kind of model is that the library or its' parent organization need not to invest funds in purchasing hardware/software.

7.3. Hybrid Cloud

As public cloud allow any organization to outsource their part of infrastructure to service provider, at the same time organization would lose the control over resources and data management. In this type of cloud a part of cloud will be given to public for use. (e.g. Google Apps)

Combination of Private Cloud and Public Cloud forms a Hybrid Cloud model. In this combination at least one Private Cloud and at least one Public Cloud are required. In hybrid model the individual organization manage its data along with infrastructure for its sections as Private Cloud and also extend the services to other organizations on their demand either free of charge or on payment basis. Amazon's Virtual Private Cloud (VPC) is one of the leading examples of a hybrid cloud.

7.4. Community clouds

Community clouds are specifically organized clouds and are limited for specific group (e.g. Institutional Gmail of Google Apps)

7.5. Special cloud

Special clouds are extensions of normal cloud system to provide additional services. (e.g. Google App Engine)

7.6. Resource clouds

Infrastructure is referred as resource clouds. Resource (Infrastructure) is being provided by third party as service to the users to use them the way they want. (e.g.Amazon S3)

8. SHARING OF E-RESOURCES USING CLOUDS

Cloud computing offers information retrieval systems, particularly digital libraries and search engines, a wide variety of options for growth and reduction of maintenance needs and encourages efficient resource use. These features are particularly attractive for digital libraries, repositories, and search engines. The dynamic and elastic provisioning features of a cloud infrastructure allow rapid growth in collection size and support a larger user base, while reducing management issues.

The Digital Library has brought new opportunities for the advancement of digital library. Cloud computing can take the library facility at the most convenient state to its stakeholders than other technical approaches. Many people are getting more used to with the e-copies of books, journals, newspaper and other resources than paperback format. Cloud computing can provide the optimum library services to the people by centralizing the resources and disk spaces of any digital library. Cloud computing can provide an uninterrupted service to its stakeholders. The implementation of cloud computing in digital library can provide many scopes for people from different professions. Librarians, Computer experts, and people from other professions have different scopes while cloud computing has integrated as part of any digital library.

The three typical kinds of cloud computing services are processing clouds, storage clouds and application clouds. Processing Clouds that provide scalable and mostly affordable computing resources that run enterprise programs, which is also sometimes known as

Infrastructure as a service (IaaS), Storage Clouds that offer an alternative to local file systems also known as a Platform as a Service (PaaS), and Application Clouds also called Software as a Service (SaaS), that allow a thin client to interact with services that are completely hosted on an external infrastructure. The libraries can use cloud computing applications to create personalized portals for users, the Library could use cloud computing as their back up methodology. Libraries have already begun to adopt cloud services to alleviate their IT departments and increase efficiency.

9. ADVANTAGES AND DISADVANTAGES OF CLOUD COMPUTING

Like any other technology, cloud computing do also have its advantages and disadvantages, which need to be taken into consideration before implementing this new technology:

9.1. Advantages Cloud computing

Cloud computing seems to offer some incredible benefits for communicators: the availability of an incredible array of software applications, access to lightning-quick processing power, unlimited storage, and the ability to easily share and process information. All of this is available through your browser any time you can access the Internet. It means computing ability also can be a kind of commodity, as gas, water and electric, easy to use and cheap cost. "Could Computing" brings such a change – "computer storage computing center" are set up by professional network companies such as Google and IBM, through one cable and user can access easily with browser, make "Could" as the center of material storage and application services.

9.1.1. Cost effective

Cloud computing is cost effective whereas using the

proposition of traditional software development for the need of the organization by domain experts and developers and consultants took years and always remained a costly affair. Upfront costs of cloud computing are very reasonable and updates are never a problem.

9.1.2. Flexibility

By using cloud computing, concept of working from office is gone. Working from any location remains the user's choice. With the result, network dependency i.e. using internet is more in vogue.

9.1.3. Speedy in response to unexpected business events

After cloud deployment it remains the responsibility of vendor to take care of capacity and location planning and this results in quicker response from companies to unforeseen business changes.

9.1.4. Easily accessible latest updates of software's

It remains the onus of cloud vendor to provide latest update of the soft ware's being used by the organization from time to time and without incurring any burden on the pockets of the consumer. This results in most modern user interface to cope with emerging business demands.

9.1.5. Providing cloud solutios is time savvy

In providing cloud solution and roll it out takes couple of months whereas on-premise solutions requires years to be serviceable. Another plus point is reduced IT resources requirement for shaping a cloud solution and making it more profitable for the organizations.

9.1.6. Easy to adopt web based user interfaces

Cloud applications can be had by the user company anytime and from anyplace using standard web browsers. Web styled interfaces are more easy to adopt without any need of specialized training. EBay and Yahoo are an example to cite with.

9.1.7. Addressing security concerns

For all the companies data security is their prime concern and critics of cloud computing are always suspicious on this count. Placing data's outside internal firewall always remained a hot topic to discuss in companies opting for cloud computing. With the provision of strict ISO security protocol, cloud providers are bound to follow it, resulting in greater security of data's of cloud users.

9.1.8. Pay as you use and quitting easy

Using cloud computing services requires less expenditure initially compared to on premise solutions. Quitting is also easy in case satisfaction level is not good.

9.1.9. Virtualization

Increased utilization, sharing of servers and storage is one of the key features of cloud computing. Migration from one server to another is quite easy.

9.1.10. Agility

To make a provision of new computing resources took a considerable time. Cloud computing has enabled consumers t access computing resources using an on-demand self service interface as demanded by the user resulting in scaling up and down of the applications to give a response to external business forces than the need of IT procurement.

9.2. Disadvantages Cloud computing

Cloud computing system has many benefits. However, no system is full proof in the world and as cloud computing is in infancy stage, it has also certain drawbacks. As in other organizations the biggest hurdle in applying cloud computing in library is the data security.

In cloud computing system, the data is to be handed over to cloud service provider in case of opting DaaS i.e. Data as a Service option. Cloud backup option is available to reduce this problem. Besides, Crypto cloud computing is also for securing cloud computing architecture. It helps to provide protection to data at the system level.

Besides, strong Internet facility should be available on the part of library clients. In case of interruption in Internet service, the clients can not avail the library facility. Further, if any technical problem arises on the part of cloud service provider and stop the services, then all the job of the organization/library will stop.

i. Constant connectivity required
ii. Dependency
iii. Failure in compliance
iv. Quality problems with cloud service provider
v. Risk or data loss
vi. Since all the development and deployment have been done by Cloud service provider, it is very difficult to get good grip on overall system.
vii. Time and Budget Constraints

10. RISKS IN USING CLOUDS

10.1. Vulnerability testing reports

Cloud service providers are hesitant to furnish vulnerability testing reports and often refuse to allow scanning for the fear of compromising their infrastructure.

10.2. Third Party Audit report of Cloud service provider

Cloud providers usually don't welcome asking for the third party audit reports unless enshrined in the contract clause.

10.3. Excessive dependency on internet

Basic drawback of Cloud computing is its dependency on the internet for accessing cloud and because of this dependency service interruptions and outages at any time always remains there to count for.

10.4. Difficulty in developing Hybrid System

It's difficult to create Hybrid Systems of cloud computing. Big organizations holding sensitive information's normally have their inbuilt IT services and don't like to share it offsite despite the benefits of efficiency and performance.

10.5. Security and integrity of data's

Security and integrity of data's hosted in- house remains at risk when we put it off site to take the services of cloud computing.

10.6. Sustainability

The emerging problem with the use of cloud computing is phenomenal increase in the use of electricity and it is propelling us to the polluting energy sources instead of clean energy abundantly available today.

10.7. Over-concentration on a single service provider

"Cloud computing is undergoing a seismic shift and is fundamentally shifting the economics of IT, of businesses and of delivery of governance, however the biggest hindrance that is stopping us from adopting cloud is the fear of losing control," said Bhaskar Pramanik, chairman, National Committee on IT, ITeS & e-commerce, CII & chairman, Microsoft India Corp. Pvt. Ltd. Innumerable users relying on a single service provider and subsequent over concentration may cause failure in service resulting in catastrophe.

10.8. Infrastructural and Logistics concern

For a healthy and secure growth of cloud computing environment it is imperative for cloud service providers to follow all relevant organizational information technology policies and possess capabilities essential for implementation and managing it. To name with, demand management, relationship management, data security management, application life cycle management risk and compliance management are those capabilities. Mushrooming of cloud computing providers lacking these capabilities is making a mess of the foolproof cloud environment.

11. CONCLUSION

Cloud computing enables innovation by alleviating the need of innovators to find resources to develop, test, and make their innovations available to the user community. It is in the evolving stage, requires some amount of careful considerations before organizations think about hosting some of their services. However, this technology has certain advantages, which definitely help organizations such as libraries in managing their services, which will relieve library staff from managing the servers.

The cloud computing has its own merits and demerits. Moreover, newly coming up libraries which do not have sufficient budget to acquire high end technology with proper hardware and software can choose cloud. To cope up with the new technological innovation in the field one need to know and explore the cloud computing. From Indian perspective the concept of cloud is not much accepted in libraries as there are many issues involved. But, in future it may increase looking into the advantages of this technology, which relieves libraries and library professionals from maintaining the servers and software.

The cloud computing may help libraries to undertake modern ICT activities without worrying about technical side of it, except adding content of resources. Library professionals many a times find it difficult to manage the technologies owing to their skill levels, lack of support from IT departments or for not having IT facilities within the organizations. This kind of situation always hinders library professionals in undertaking automation of library activities, developing digital library services, etc. Here, cloud computing may help libraries to undertake modern ICT activities without worrying about technical side of it, except adding content of resources It is evident from the literature that some service providers have already pitched in to help libraries to automate and establish digital libraries on the cloud.

Indian IT industry can be an important commercial factor for the western countries to consider in their future cloud related development. Accordingly, an Indian library does not have the economic strength to impact on the western countries. The main strength and hence advantage of India, however, consists in its consolidated and synergetic efforts to address new technological innovations, trends and governmental issues. As India has strong IT industry now, up-coming Indian companies are offering cloud services for Indian libraries at affordable prices. Moreover in India many institutes are not in condition to purchase high end server and costly software for their library, in this situation the cloud computing will provide grate platform to host their data on cloud to serve their users.

The future of cloud computing in India as well as abroad is very promising irrespective of certain snags in the nascent technology of cloud computing. Security and integrity of data's , sustainability are the major concerns of cloud computing arena and is required to be addressed soon to win the confidence of user organizations. "It is imperative to make optimum use of IT infrastructure and reuse applications, since in a large country like India, we can't afford to have individual applications for all states.

We have to adopt rapid deployment methods that we can measure and monitor," said Dr S. Satyanarayana, a noted cloud computing technology expert. The way cloud computing is progressing the day is not far that cloud services would become part and parcel of daily lives.

Library is a service institution. It is successfully shouldering the responsibility of disseminating the information and knowledge to all kinds of users including teachers, administrators, researchers, students since its beginning. Library professionals are always thinking to improve their library services. They have successfully applied the Information and Communication Technology in library for improving library administration, house-keeping jobs and services. Cloud computing is a new emerging technology and library professionals have an opportunity to use this technology in improving the library operations and services.

REFERENCE

1. Buyya R, "Market-Oriented Cloud Computing: Vision, Hype, and Reality of Delivering Computing as the 5th Utility," 9th IEEE/ACM International Symposium on Cluster Computing and the Grid, pp. 1, 2009.
2. Dudin, E.B. and Smetanin, Yu.G. (2011). A Review of Cloud Computing. Scientific and Technical Information Processing, 38(4), 280-284
3. Ex Libris: The Bridge to Knowledge. Available at *http://www.exlibris.co.il* (Accessed on 02/06/2014)
4. Fox, R. Library in the clouds. OCLCSystems & Services, 2009, 25(3), 156-161.
5. Ghanam, Yaser, Ferreira, Jennifer and Maurer, Frank (2012). Emerging Issues & Challenges in Cloud Computing—A Hybrid Approach. Journal of Software Engineering and Applications, 5, 923-937
6. Golden, B. The Case Against Cloud Computing, Part Four. *http://www.cio.com/article/480595/The_Case_Against_Cloud_Computing_Part_Four* (Accessed on 02/06/2014)
7. Goldner, Matt (2010). Report on Winds of Change: Libraries

and Cloud Computing. OCLC Online Computer Library Center, Inc.

8. Gosavi, Nandakishor, Shinde, Seetal S. And Dhakulkar, Bhagyashree (2012). Use of cloud computing in Library and Information Science field, International Journal of Digital Library Services, 2(3), 51-60

9. Gurmeet Singh & Sachdeva, Vineet, Impact and Challenges of Cloud Computing in Current Scenario. International journal of Social Science & Inter disciplinary research. Issue10, Vol. I, Oct. 2012, pp 136-146.

10. *http://www.dictionary.reference.com/* (Accessed on 02/06/ 2014)

11. Liz Eversoll Available at *http://www.lizeversoll.com* swot-strengths-weaknesses-opportunities, threats/(Accessed on 02/06/2014)

12. Pandya, Miteshkumar (2012). Cloud Computing for Libraries: A SWOT Analysis. 8th Convention PLANNER-2012 INFLIBNET Centre, Ahmedabad, p387-393

13. Polaris Library Systems. *http://www.gisin\fosystems.com* (Accessed on 02/06/2014)

14. Sanchati, Rupesh and Kulkarni, Gaurav (2011). Cloud Computing in Digital and University Libraries, Global Journal of Computer Science and Technology 11(12), 36-41

15. Shiau, Wen-Lung, Chao, Han-Chieh and Chou, Chia-Pin (2012). An Innovation of an Academic Cloud Computing Service. Journal of Software Engineering and Applications, 5, 938-943

16. Terrence, William. Features of Cloud Computing Available at *http://www.eddyarticles.com/computers/features-of-cloud-computing/* (Accessed on 02/06/2014)

8

Digitization of Library Material

1. INTRODUCTION

The impact of current information revolution and information technology have changed library totally in to an important media of communication of knowledge. In the information age, demands will be focused on knowledge and knowledge of what to gather, how to gather and how to process communicated. Using modern information technology, the libraries of today have changed the methods of collection, storage, dissemination and retrieval of information. Today, digitization has become one of the important activities in the library and information centre which is an excellent way of providing open access to library resources. Through digitization, libraries are able to access, preserve, maintain the digital collections easily and provide effective services to the user requirements. The digital age create new delivery and access alternatives for libraries as well as new preservation challenges. The goal of a digital preservation system is that the information it contains remains accessible to users over a long period time.

Digital conversion of library materials has advanced rapidly in recent years, prompting some casual observers to believe that everything of importance can be found on the World Wide Web in digital form. But instant access to all the world's wisdom is still more than mouse click away. It is important to resist the urge to digitize everything in a library or archival collection and destroy the originals in a mad rush to save space or occupy a place on the cutting edge. Digitization is an excellent way of providing access to library materials, but the technology, in its current state of development, is not adequate for archival preservation. Digitization has proven to be possible for nearly every format and medium presently held by libraries, from maps to manuscripts, and moving images to musical recordings. The use of hardware and software for capturing an item and converting it into bits and bytes, matched by a quickly developing set of practices for describing and retrieving digital objects, is giving form to the talk of a "library without walls" But such a virtual library has a very real price, for policy matters related to digitization often find themselves struggling not only to understand the new technologies, but also, and more importantly, to grasp the implications of those technologies and to understand what digitization of their collections means for their institution, its patrons, and the public." This paper will provide an overview of the digitization of library collection.

Digitization of materials may occur in both library and archival environments. In the case of archives, candidate materials for conversion often include unpublished materials such as correspondence or corporate records, as well as items as diverse as photographs, film and videotape, advertising flyers, train tickets, and handwritten manuscripts. In the discussion that follows the term "library" and "archives" may occasionally be used interchangeably depending upon the source material to which reference is being made, but the primary focus of this paper is on library digitization.

2. WHAT IS DIGITIZATION?

In its most basic sense, the term "digitization" refers to the conversion of materials that were originally created in another format into an electronic from. Conversely, this definition excludes materials that were initially created digitally, such as email communication. Technically, the process of digitization involves converting an analog image into its corresponding numeric values. The word "image" is literally true because the digital scanner creates an image of the original analog item, whether that item is a photograph, a word-processed document, or a handwritten letter. The digital image created by the scanner is stored in numeric form.

For example. When a photograph is digitized for viewing on a computer screen, the original continuous tone image is divided into dots with assigned values that are mapped against a grid. The pattern of the dots is remembered and reassembled by the computer upon command. Following are some of the main objectives of digitization :

i. To provide accessibility to all or part of the content of manuscripts and books,

ii. To capture, store, manipulate and distribute information,

iii. To digitize the documents for preservation and for space saving,

iv. To improve the cost effectiveness of library operations.

v. To introduce and provide new services,

vi. To make available the reading specially rare and fragile materials;

vii. To provide facility for networking and resource sharing,

viii. To provide need-based and retrospective search services to the user,

ix. To search across the different title and to draw together materials relating to a wide range of research and learning topics;

x. To support library functions such as circulation, serial control, acquisition control, stock maintenance and other routine office works and developing in house database.

3. WHY DIGITIZATION?

In the digital world, all knowledge is divided into two parts. The binary strings of 0s and 1s that make up the genetic code of data allow information to be fruitful and multiply, and allow people to create, manipulate, and share data in ways that appear to be revolutionary. It is often said that digital information is transforming the way we learn, the way we communicate, even the way we think. It is also changing the way that libraries and archives not only work, but, more fundamentally, the very work that they do. It is easy to overstate- and underestimate-the transformative power of a new technology, especially when we do not yet understand the full implications of its may application. Nonetheless, people have embraced this technology enthusiastically, often as an answer to questions that had not, in many cases, yet been posed.

One of the most important qualities of information in digital form is that by its very nature it is not fixed in that way that texts printed on paper are. Digital texts are neither final nor finite, and are fixed neither in essence nor in form except when a hard copy is printed out, for they can be changed easily and without trace of erasures or emendations. Flexibility is one of the chief assets of digital information and is precisely what we like about text poured into a word processing program. It is easy to edit, to reformat, and to commit to print in a variety of iterations without the effort required to produce hard copy from a typewriter. That is why visual designers like computer-assisted design programs. It is easy to summon up quickly any number of variations of value, hue, shape, and placement to see, rather than to imagine, what different visual options look like. Furthermore, we can create an endless number of identical copies from a digital file, because the file does not decay by virtue of copying.

4. ADVANTAGES OF DIGITIZATION

Digital imaging projects offer unique advantages. Information and content may be delivered directly to end-users, and can be retrieved remotely. Image quality can be quite good, and is often enhanced, with capabilities continuously improving. There is added advantage with the possibility of full-text searching, cross-collection indexing and newly designed user content. Flexibility of the digital material is another advantage. Since the data is not "fixed" as with paper or printed text, it is easy to reformat, edit and print.

Moreover, the ability to provide a large number of user's access to unique or special collections material (normally viewed only on-site) may be the most attractive feature of digital conversion projects. Online resources serve local, national and international needs. Increasing access by any means, specifically remotely, makes historical or literary research much easier. Allowing for a wider audience to view digital surrogates of primary material provides a great service and increased utility to the collection (de Stefano, p. 13). There are no travel costs involved and this interaction may allow for the creation of new knowledge.

Providing access to primary material can help to "publicize" the material to other departments and peers, and to demonstrate the importance of the collections. The special collections departments may present the "jewels in the crown" from the research library.

Profound changes in professional attitudes, private and public funding, availability of images reproductions, and electronic communications technologies have resulted in museums and archival institutions reevaluating their target audience. The general education market is the new target audience, and the new method of providing information is through electronic media, most often through the World Wide Web. Digitization projects allow for extended data recovery, enabling scholarship that was previously not possible with analog material. Computer enhancements, such as enhanced optical character recognition (OCR), allow for more in-depth analysis.

But institutions need to realize that digital resources are institutional assets in their own right, resources are institutional assets in their own, right, and not merely surrogates of an analog object; they must be managed, preserved and migrated over time.

Participating in digitization projects, allow for professional development as staff gain new skills, knowledge and expertise while completing the project. An institution and its staff also become "assets" and may share expertise and lessons learned with other institutions. Not only does digitization provide "added value" to the resources; it may also breathe new life into older institutions.

Another advantage of creating digital surrogates is, use of the surrogate reduces handling of the old or fragile material, hopefully extending the life of the original.

5. DISADVANTAGE OF DIGITIZATION

Required staff expertise and additional resources are often the greatest costs in digitization projects. Not only are large budget allocations needed to fund research and intellectual selection, but also time must be spent for feasibility assessments, training, and methodical prioritization of items or collections to be digitized. These requirements pull staff away from their regular workloads. Cataloging the new material adds additional base costs to the budget. Digital conversion projects require added levels of work not needed in traditional reformatting project. Many institutions lack expertise and preparation must be well-planned.

Digital conversion is not a yet a form of preservation; which relies on long-term, stable media, which cannot be expected with today's technology. The only accepted long-term preservation media are durable acid-free paper of preservation microfilm.

Access to successful digital surrogates often encourages people to wish to consult the original. This impacts staff in other ways with more calls, letters, and requests for publication or reproduction of the materials, and added reference service is necessary. High-quality surrogates must be created in order to satisfy the user's needs, or they will need to go back and consult the original.

Financial costs are extremely high and cultural institutions usually operate with either flat or marginally increasing budgets. Operational environments must have fundraising and accountability, with such great costs of staff time and funding, the "risk of loss" is very high.

Another disadvantage of creating digital surrogates is that users are completely reliant on computers and stable internet connections to view and retrieve the digital information. Depending on user's hardware and software capabilities access may be frustrating because of the large variety of computer models, platforms, software and hardware around the world.

Ease of access to a digital collection leads to high expectations of end-users. There is a tendency to believe that everything is available online, that every piece of information is true and accurate, and that everything available online is free. Rarely do users understand or appreciate the scope of the collection and its relationship to other parts of the collection.

6. DETERMINATION OF LIBRARY MATERIALS TO BE DIGITIZED

Institutions select collections for digitization based on specific goals. Each decision should be weighed against a cost and benefit analysis for the end users and the institutions. Subject specialists (familiar with both the collection and how it is used) must be key decision-makers.

Selection for digital conversion continues to work under the premise of access and ease of use. Rather than physical deterioration. Digital conversion projects should be goal driven rather than technologically driven.

Institutions contemplating digitization projects should research what other institutions have done and review their successes, mistakes, and lessons learned. Selection of material may be based on a desire to educate and provide access to "hard-to find" items of great intrinsic value. Selection may also be based on the value of the original item. For some institutions it is most important to spend the time and money to create a perfect reproduction in order to protect the original item. The rare of fragile material often requires special handling. Material chosen for digital conversion often require preservation and conservation treatment prior to photography or scanning.

Some key issues that most institutions agree upon are: Does your institution have a legal right to digitize the items and make them available online? Does the material or collection have intrinsic value to make it highly used by the target audience? Is there added value by increasing extended access to the collection? Is the parent organization and technological infrastructure to make the project possible? If the answer are "yes" the project should be good to go forward.

Often microfilm is the only copy of an item after the original was destroyed and may also be scanned. However creating digital files after several generations may not provide the highest possible image quality.

Providing expanded access and exposure to collection material on the internet may also work as promotional device, by increasing donations, or both funding and "gifts" to the institution.

7. DETERMINATION OF LIBRARY MATERIALS NOT TO BE DIGITZED

Selecting collections or material to digitize should be based on a clear understanding of the users needs, and of what digital materials can do, that analog material.

It is often difficult for libraries and to determine if they have the legal right to scan and display material, even if they own the physical item. Institutions should determine if they have a legal right to digitize the material and make it available to the public. An institution may choose to digitize a collection that it does not have the copyright to, for "in house" use only. The material may be fragile, or it may u be used a great deal.

Collections that are rarely used or in low demand should not be selected for digital conversion, as the costs in time, resources, and money cannot be justified.

Digitization does not replace collection management. Digital surrogates should never replace the original analog item, even when trying to save shelf space. If an institution decides to deaccession brittle newspapers, it should first obtain microfilm copies to serve its patrons.

8. TECHNICAL REQUIREMENTS FOR DIGITAL PRESERVATION

Following are some of the requirements for digital preservation :

i. Proper preparation of the original in sequence

ii. High quality microfilming of the documents

iii. High quality Optical Character Recognition of the scanned images

iv. Quality assurance of the scanned images

v. Software to index individual articles and to enable search facility

vi. User-friendly software to provide a host for the data, and to permit users to access it viaInternet.

9. CONCLUSION

Books, manuscripts, are decaying. Some of them are still useful, but the damage is beyond restoration.To preserve their information contents it is urgently needed to digitize them. Digital preservation ofrecourses is finding ways to maintain our cultural heritage. Digital preservation will ensure the longterm maintenance of a byte stream sufficient to reproduce the document and provide continuedaccessibility of the contents over time and through evolving technology.

If the manuscripts are digitized and made available on web, then they are easily accessible fromevery nook and corner of the entire world; the manuscripts users will not come to those placeswhere the manuscripts are physically preserved. The importance of digital preservation cannot beignored.

Advances in technology create new challenges and workloads, for staff and institution, not present before. Part of the problem lies in the fact that currently there is no consensus regarding digital conversion or preservation of digital material.Professionals must work together to address the problems stemming from the fact that there are no set standards for preservation of digital material.Even after one has addressed the legal, ethical, technical, and professional issues surrounding digital conversion projects, what still needs to be addressed are the needs of the end-users. Providing access to digital collections in an unmediated environment creates continued challenges. Digitization is an excellent way to provide access to library materials, but it is not currently a viable preservation technology. More must be done than simply run materials through a scanner. With numerous issues to consider, selection criteria to develop and follow, and physical and intellectual preparation to accomplish, the undertaking of a major archival project, or even a minor one, can be very costly indeed. Such a project should not be rushed into without careful consideration and expert advice. Cultural institutions house rare and unique artifacts recording the history of humankind. Providing greater access to collections may bring together vast, disparate collections and may inspire new scholarly work. By prioritizing digital projects, allocating funds, and working together, cultural institutions provide added utility to collections.

REFERENCES

1. Beamsley, T. (1999). Securing digital image assets in museums and libraries: A risk management approach. Library Trends, 48(2). 358-78.
2. Conway, P. (2000). Overview: Rationale for digitization and preservation. *http://www.nedee.org/digital/dighome.htm*
3. Gertz, J. (2000). Selection for preservation in the digital age: An overview. Library Resources & Technical Services. 44(2). 97-104.
4. Ingram, G. (2000). Selection of special collections material for digitization. In Kenney, A & O. Reiger (Eds.). Moving theory into practice : Digital imaging for libraries and acvhives. pp. 18- 19.

5. Library of Congress (2000). Digitizing the collection: American Memory. Retrieved February 24, 2001 from the World Wide Web : *http://leweb2.loc.gov/ammem/daghtml/dagtech.html*

6. Ogden, S. (Ed.). (1994). Preservation of library & Archival materials : A manual, Andover, MA : Northeast Document Conservation Center.

7. Smith, A. (1999). Why Digitize? *http://www.clir.org/pubs/reports/pub80-smith/pub80/html*

8. Tennan, R (2000). Selecting collections to digitize. Library Journals. 125 (19). 26.

9

RFID : An Innovative Technology for Libraries

1. INTRODUCTION

In their quest for serving the patrons better, the libraries are continually adopting newer and most advanced technologies. RFID is an innovative automated library system for automatic identification and tracking of library material. It is combination of radio-Frequency-based technology and microchip technology and can be used to identify, track, sort or detect library holdings. This is an effective way of managing collections of the library and providing enhanced services to the users having benefits like: to control increasing theft, to find misplaced reading material, inventory accuracy, stock verification procedures, security control, etc. It is an automatic data capture technology that uses tiny microchips and miniature antennas affixed to products. RFID technology offers great potential for broadening access to library services and security in ways never before conceived. RFID plays a vital role in redefining the library processes to make everyone's job easier right from the users to library staff. It provides a platform to automate most of the processes performed by the library staff like check in-check out, sorting, stock management, etc.

Radio Frequency IDentification (RFID) is an exciting and fast growing technology for increasing efficiency, improving profitability and is an important area of study in today's information environment.

According to *Lindquist (2003)*:

[. . .] new technologies have always been of interest for libraries, both for the potential of increasing the quality of service and for improving efficiency of operations. At the present time, when libraries of all kinds [public, research, special] are facing economic hardships the overwhelming reason for considering new technologies is the potential for cost savings in the operations and the management of material flows.

Any library's priority is to add interpretive and educational value to its basic resources, and to highlight the importance of the library's contributions to the institution's well-being and future progress. The most significant time savings are attributable to the fact that information can be read from RFID tags much faster than from bar codes and that several items in a stack can be read at the same time.

The implementation of RFID technology certainly improves service efficiency for libraries and enables more diversified applications and service modes. However, as stated by *Yu (2008)* "regulating necessary standards, processes, and interfaces to fit in with current information systems and extend automatic library operations requires continuous effort". RFID technology promises to change our world. It has the capability of making our personal lives and our professional lives in the library more convenient.

2. COMPONENTS OF AN RFID SYSTEM

A comprehensive RFID system has following components:

2.1. RFID tag (or transponder)

The Chip and the antenna together are called RFID tag (or transponder). These are paper-thin smart labels which are electronically programmed with unique information. Tags are the electronic chips consisting of an integrated circuit and antenna coil that communicates with a reader by means of a radio frequency signal. These tags are available as labels with adhesive backings and ability to reel though a label printer. After sticking RFID label on the book, its vital bibliographical data including unique Accession Number is registered in the chip of the label. This function allows writing such information on chip either from the Library database or by scanning existing barcode labels and helps to identify each book.

Fig. 1. RFID Tag

(Courtesy-Central Library, IIT Delhi)

Two types of RFID tags are available viz. Active or Passive. Passive tags don't have their own power supply so the device is quite small. These have practical read ranges that vary from about 10 mm up to about 5 meters. Active RFID tags, on the other hand, must have a power source and may have longer ranges and larger memories than passive tags as well as the ability to store additional information sent by the transceiver. Active RFID tags can be about the size of a coin and have practical ranges of tens of meters, and a battery life up to several years. Many libraries are making use of passive tags because of their lower cost and appropriate size. The tags can be read at a distance of up to two feet by each of two parallel exit sensors. The devices used for circulation are usually called "readers" while the ones used at building exits are usually called "sensors".

There are three types of tags: "read only", "WORM," and "read/write" *(Boss, 2005).* "Tags are "read only" if the identification is encoded at the time of manufacture and not rewritable. "WORM" (Write-Once-Read-Many) tags are programmed by the using organization, but without the ability to rewrite them later. "Read/write tags," which are chosen by most libraries, can have information changed or added. In libraries that use RFID, it is common to have part of the read/write tag secured against rewriting, e.g., the identification number of the item.

2.2. RFID reader (or interrogator)

RFID reader consists of a transmitter, receiver, antenna and a decoder. They communicate with RFID tags, identify them and receive data stored on the tag. It provides a contact less data link which means books can be issued/ retuned without opening. A typical RFID system includes four different kinds of readers, also known as sensors or scanners. These devices are designed to detect and read tags to obtain the information stored thereon.

2.3. Staff workstations

For circulation desk charging and discharging. The equipment can easily be connected to a network or single workstation PC or notebook and the application can begin functioning thereon. It also supports all RFID functions like anti collision feature allowing to identify multiple labels simultaneously, present in the reader field and full read/write capability.

Fig. 2. RFID based Staff workstation
(Courtesy-Central Library, IIT Delhi)

It is used at the issue/return counters at the library and also for label personalization.

2.4. Self check-in/check-out stations

Fig. 3. RFID based Self check-in/ check-out stations
(Courtesy-Central Library, IIT Delhi)

For allowing users to borrow books without assistance from the library staff. It is an interactive station/kiosk with touch screen which prompts the user to enter library card. The validity of the library card is checked and user is prompts to place the books on to the deck of the Borrowing Station. The status of each book as checked-out is automatically updated on the Library Management database. The theft detection system of the RFID tag for that book is deactivated to enable smooth passage from the security gate. A receipt may be issued to the user confirming details of borrowed books along with due date.

2.4. Exit sensors

At exit are of two types; one reads the information on the tag(s) going by and communicates that information to a server. The server, after checking against the circulation database, activates an alarm if the material is not properly checked-out. Another type relies on a "theft" byte in the tag that is turned on or off to show that the item has been charged or not. It is then not necessary to communicate with the circulation database. The security system will work even though the online library server is

Fig. 4. Exit Gates (EAS Pedestal)
(Courtesy-Central Library, IIT Delhi)

not working. This gates security system composed of the desired number of pedestals i.e. generally 2 to 4. It may also be used to count the incoming/outgoing people with a facility to record their movement.

2.5. Shelf management system orPortable shelf scanner

It allows library staff to take inventory and find wrongly shelved books without having to pull the books off the stacks. It is very useful for stock verification purpose.

Fig. 5. Shelf / Inventory management system (Courtesy : Central Library, IIT Delhi)

2.6. Book Drop Kiosk

It checks in books when users drop them in the bookdrop. Libraries can offer a distinct service that is very useful for users, such as the ability to return books when the library is closed. An external book return is a machine with a slot with a chip RFID reader integrated into the wall. It works the same way as the self checkout station. The user identifies himself/herself (if required by the library), and then puts the book(s) in to the slot. Upon completing the return, the user will receive a receipt showing how many and which books were returned. The theft detection system into the smart labels is simultaneously activated. Since the books have already been checked in and RFID tags activated, they can go directly back onto the shelves.

Fig. 6. RFID based Book Drop Kiosk (Courtesy-Central Library, IIT Delhi)

2.7. Application software

It is used for the reader to transmit or receive data from a tag. Software integrates the reader hardware with the existing Library Automation Software for seamless functioning of Circulation Counter.

2.9. Server/Docking Station

It is one on which the software that interfaces with the integrated library software is loaded. The server is the heart of some comprehensive RFID systems. It is the communication gateway among the various components. It receives the information from one or more of the readers and exchanges information with the circulation database. Its software includes the APIs (Applications Programming Interface) necessary to interface it with the automated library system. The server typically includes a transaction database so that reports can be produced.

2.10. RFID Smart Card

This is used for RFID based library transactions. These cards can also be used for other purposes for the institute. RFID increasingly used with biometric technologies for security.

3. FEASIBILITY AND PLANNING

The initial task of any feasibility study is to establish the aims of the project, which need to be derived from some form of users' needs assessment in the beginning. *Vaishnaav and Bapat (1995)* have outlined three areas of feasibility study, namely: technical feasibility; social feasibility; and economic feasibility. The central endeavour of any feasibility study is a cost-benefit analysis of the various alternatives, although a full cost-benefit analysis is unlikely to be appropriate in a library situation, particularly when the system under analysis has not yet been instituted. However, a partial analysis can yield useful insights *(Rowley, 1980)*.

Before implementation of this technology in a library, it is necessary to study the feasibility of the system. A committee may be constituted with experts and administrators who may have knowledge in RFID systems and other administrative procedures. The committee may assess the requirements for the institution, budget availability, required hardware and software, cost effectiveness, availability of manpower, time line, etc. The methodology for implementation can be divided into many phases taking into consideration of budget provisions, the types of document holdings, number of volumes, types of items meant for circulation, status of present database/automation and the number and types of users that the institution has. To implement the RFID, gaining management commitment may be a big challenge as it may look into the Return On Investment (ROI) to assess RFID investment before it commits to its implementation. A challenge that institutions face with is the high cost of implementation. To justify the adoption of RFID technology, cost-benefit analysis is a must. Smooth implementation of any endeavor requires thorough planning. Since the technology is still not very common, the committee should see some demos and visit the libraries where the system is successfully running. Data validation is most important before actually starting the tagging work. A feasibility report on the basis of all this exercise may be prepared and finalized.

4. DEPLOYMENT PROCESS & RELATED ISSUES

Tendering is the most important and difficult process for the implementation of the system. A good tender document should look into all the minute details of the technical, administrative and functional aspects. If the tender document is full proof then there may not be any problem in its implementation. The feasibility report prepared by the committee may help in this regard. Some of the things which should be considered for the deployment of RFID system and for preparing the tender document and to select the vender may include:

i. Proven capability of vender to integrate the proposed solution with multiple LMS for future safety. The bidder should have sufficient successful practical experience of supply, installation, testing, commissioning and post commissioning.

ii. The items to be supplied should be of proven good quality with makes having globally accepted presence and compatible with global standards.

iii. Supplied equipments should allow forward compatibility with anticipated new standards.

iv. Robustness of the system (scalability, accuracy).

v. Judge vendors' technology know-how for products to be supplied.

vi. Ask for customer reference & arrange site visit and discuss your concerns with them.

vii. Librarians should compare overall benefits vs cost involved while adopting a particular automation technology.

viii. The tender may have two parts; Technical Bid and Financial Bid. The Financial bid should only be opened once the Bidder qualifies for the Technical bid.

ix. Incomplete, vague and conditionally submitted bids should not be considered.

x. The validity of the successful bid should clearly be desired by the institute with a clear delivery schedule. Payment should be made after satisfactory installation and commissioning.

xi. Issues related to onsite training, warranty, service and AMC should have been clearly mentioned.

xii. The institute may also think to retain some security money for the post commissioning period for a couple of years.

5. IMPACT OF RFID SYSTEM ON LIBRARY

The implementation of the RFID systems has impacted on the library in various ways.

5.1. Saving time at the circulation counter

The use of RFID reduces the amount of time required to perform circulation operations. This technology helps librarians eliminate valuable staff time spent scanning barcodes while checking out and checking in borrowed items. For the users, RFID speeds up the borrowing and return procedures. Library employees are released for more productive and interesting duties. Staff is relieved further when readers are installed in book drops.

Circulation includes check-out, check-in and renewal of the documents. It usually takes 1-2 min to complete a single transaction when the task is performed manually, while the same transaction takes place within 1-2 seconds with the RFID system. A further advantage is that if the user has five items to check-out or check-in the transaction can be easily completed within single stroke.

In the case of barcode systems the circulation staff have to scan the barcode of the user's card and then the barcode of every item to complete a single transaction, whereas using RFID five transactions are possible in one click. This has resulted in saving the time of the users at the circulation counter and also the time of the staff. After comparing the circulation using RFID with that of a manual and barcode system one can conclude that now the circulation system has become much faster than any previous system by implementing RFID.

5.2. Theft detection

The two security gates, i.e. theft detection pedestals, have been installed at the entrance and exit gates of the library. These gates are independent of each other and also have overlapping protection zones providing additional security. Before the implementation of RFID in the library many items were not traceable, and, apart from books being misplaced on the shelves, one of the main reasons was theft. Now, since most of the users know that the system is in place and is capable of detecting theft, none are trying to take items out of the library without charging them. The EAS exit gates have option to keep record of incoming and outgoing library users with recording.

5.3. Tracing missing books using RFID hand reader

Previously it was very difficult to trace misplaced books because of the size of the collection and also because of different classification scheme used by the Library to shelve items. To locate a book it sometimes used to take lot of time, however, using the RFID hand reader library staff are able to trace any item in a few minutes. The RFID hand reader allows accession numbers of missing books to be stored and when staff scan though the stacks with the hand reader an audible "beep" indicates the location of the missing item.

5.4. Shelving of books using RFID

Once the sequence of books is defined and stored in the software (IPAQ) installed on a Tablet PC/Note Book PC, it becomes very easy, with the RFID hand reader, to shelve books. Discharged books can easily be separated according to the rack number and location number.

5.5. Stock verification

Taking stock every year is an important function in all libraries and is a major challenge for those who have a large collection. Performing stock verification manually is practically impossible for this library. The PDA-based hand reader can scan thousands of books lying on shelves without even a single book being pulled out, as would be the case with a barcode reader. Data is then updated instantly on the server for stock verification with the database. At the end it shows a list of matched and unmatched items. This device also helps in sorting shelves and searching for specific items.

6. STEPWISE IMPLEMENTATION OF RFID SYSTEM IN LIBRARIES

6.1. Procurement of Hardware

Sourcing for the hardware required need to be done before anything else. Quotations/tenders may be called with detailed specification of each item required so as to compare the rates quoted for different items. The Libraries should procure the best hardware that includes Readers, Tags, Antenna, etc.

6.2. Retrospective conversion

This is already existing stack requires a "programmer" or "conversion station." The conversion of existing bar coded items, including affixing the tags to library materials, takes 15-30 seconds per item depending on the amount of information added to the tag and the skill of the person doing the tagging. Pre-programmed tags, which are used for new acquisitions in libraries that want only identification numbers on the tags, take even less time because they do not involve scanning existing barcodes. The speed of conversion can be increased by dividing responsibility for removing and replacing library materials, converting the barcodes, and inserting the tags among at least three people. It is essential that the tasks be rotated so that no one repeats the same motions over an extended period of time. Also, library might consider doing the tagging of new acquisitions at the time of receipt in Acquisition Section itself so as to avoid losses of unprocessed material from other sections of the library.

6.3. Tagging Books

Each document need to be tagged. The fixing of tags to documents can be initially outsourced then in house arrangement can be done after proper training. The tags can be over layered with the self adhesive sticker containing the logo of the library or the institution for longer life. It is also important to select a consistent location for book tags. The inside of the back cover is the recommended location because it is the fastest for right-handed tag installers to reach. One vendor recommends near the spine approximately three inches above the bottom. That avoids possible interference from metal shelves when inventorying. However, a library should consider placing the tags inside the front cover under a bookplate or with a bookplate printed on the tag. That may make the tag less apparent and, therefore, improve security.

6.4. Integration with Library Management Software

With the preset Library Management Software. Care should be taken to integrate the library automation package while detailed tender specifications are drawn.

6.5. Performing Test Cases

Predefined set of test cases will be performed in scenario based format to examine unit level and system level performance for accuracy and greater throughput. So that verification of hardware and software can be checked completely.

6.6. Training of Staff

Train the staff on various aspects of RFID technology. Since the technology is new to Indian library environment proper demonstration of the system can be arranged and librarian should visit the library where the system is successfully running. Each and every member of library should be well aware of the technology and the guidelines given for the entire process. Training Session should be organized to well understand the technology.

6.7. Process Improvement

The errors found out from the test cases will be revisited to make the system perform accurately. Until sufficient confidence is gained with the system, old system in practice can be continued.

7. BARRIERS FACED WHILE IMPLEMENTING THE TECHNOLOGY

7.1. Lack of technology experts

RFID being new technology lead to a situation of lack of expertise and professional advice as it has yet not been implemented in many libraries in India and sub continent. When any library implemented RFID technology it will be a new technology for the library staff. The lack of technology may be barrier in the implementation. In order to overcome this barrier the library can arrange various training programmes for the library staff.

7.2. Technology literate users

The technology literate users can also created many problems in the library. These users knew the function of the tags and so they removed the tags from the documents and tried to take the books from the library without charging them out in the proper way. Once the tags are removed from the documents the RFID gates were not able to detect the theft of the document and this helped some users to steal items from the library.

7.3 Moisture barrier

The moisture present in the atmosphere, especially on rainy days, affects the RFID tag. A tag, which contains moisture, does not respond to the RFID system. The users can take advantage of this by taking items out of the library without charging. Users can pass through the antennae without charging the book by putting their palm on the tag, because the RFID signal cannot pass through a liquid medium.

7.4. Problems of tagging and un-tagging

Tagging involves the coding of bibliographic data in the RFID tag attached to a particular book or item. Once data is entered in the database it is essential to perform the tagging function. For this the library application software tagging function is used to write, or feed, the accession number of the item on to the chip of the label. In some cases this tagging function may not perform correctly by the data-entry operators, as some wrong accession numbers may entered. This resulted in failure to retrieve the correct bibliographic details of the item at the circulation counter. Also, sometimes due to the moisture present on the tags it stops functioning. In such cases the library staff have to perform an "un-tagging" function first and then the tagging function or, in some cases, have had to replace the tag.

7.5. Problems encountered at the circulation counter

Staff at the circulation counter may encounter many problems while using the RFID technology. For instance, users may come to the counter with an item, which does not have an RFID tag, or the tag is removed due to heavy usage. In such cases the message such as "no book found" used to flash on the screen of the computer. Alternatively, when the bibliographic details of an item had not been entered correctly in the database the message "no accessioned book found" used to flash on the screen when a user wished to borrow the item. Staff should have sufficient knowledge about the problems and their solutions at circulation counter.

8. HURDLES IN RFID TECHNOLOGY

There are some hurdles in using the RFID technology.

8.1. RFID Tag

The RFID readers are fairly easy to use but the key failing is the lack of security of the tags themselves. RFID is a wireless technology and is therefore subject to third-party interception unless the signal is secured *(Hodgson, 2004).* Only a very restricted amount of security can be incorporated in current library RFID tags due to the limited amount of data they can hold and no library tags today employ password or read access control *(Molnar and Wagner, 2004).*

The tags used by library RFID vendors are not compatible even when they conform to the same standards because the current standards only seek electronic compatibility between tags and readers. The pattern of encoding information and the software that processes the information differs from vendor to vendor, therefore, a change from one vendor's system to the other would require retagging all items or modifying the software *(Boss, 2005)*.

When the distance among the tags is very close, interference between them may be made or erroneous access may occur. For example, if one patron is taking books to initiate the loan process under self-check in/out equipment (RFID reader), and another patron is standing too close to the first patron, the reader doing the self check in/out may detect the tags of books which are held by the other patron.

8.2. High cost

The major disadvantage of RFID technology is its cost. The readers and sensors used to read the information are comparable in cost to the components of a typical electro-mechanical or radio-frequency theft detection system *(Boss, 2005)*. The price of hardware (per unit) varies extensively from different suppliers, however, the infrastructure requirement also varies. While RFID tags are falling in price they are still more costly than barcodes, however they do offer long-term reliability. The cost is one of the major factors influencing acceptance of RFID system in libraries. At present, the cost of RFID adoption comprise the major investment in hardware, application software, middleware, tags, cost of integrating the RFID-based system with the legacy system, etc.

8.3. Patron privacy Concerns

Privacy concerns associated with item-level tagging is another significant barrier to library use of RFID tags.

The problem with today's library RFID system is that the tags contain static information that can be relatively easily read by unauthorized tag readers. This allows for privacy issues described as "tracking" and "hotlisting" *(Ayre, 2004)*. Tracking refers to the ability to track the movements of a book (or person carrying the book) by "correlating multiple observations of the book's bar code" *(Molnar and Wagner, 2004)* or RFID tag. Hotlisting refers to the process of building a database of books and their associated tag numbers (the hotlist) and then using an unauthorized reader to determine who is checking out items in the hotlist.

8.4. Accessibility to compromise

It is possible to compromise an RFID system by wrapping the protected material in two to three layers of ordinary household aluminum foil to block the radio signal*(Boss, 2005)*.The system may also be compromised by placing a normal coin on RFID tag or two items against one another so that one tag overlays another. That may cancel out the signals. Some interference from metallic material does occur and tag reading may not be correct. Physical damage to the tags removal by the library users is also un-avoidable. The moisture present in the atmosphere, especially on rainy days, affects the RFID tag. There may be some other factors as well that can influence the read/write efficiency of RFID as well like; metal, mist, distance and incorrect positioning of antennas.

8.5. Chances of Removal of exposed tags

RFID tags are typically affixed to the inside back cover and are exposed for removal. This means that there would be problems when users become more familiar with the role of the tags *(Boss, 2005)*. In Indian libraries, it is a major challenge to keep the tags intact.

8.6. Exit gate sensor (Reader) problems

While the short-range readers used for circulation charge and discharge and inventorying appear to read the tags 100 percent of the time *(Boss, 2005)*, the performance of the exit gate sensors is more problematic. They always don't read tags at up to twice the distance of the other readers. There is no library that has done a before and after inventory to determine the loss rate when RFID is used for security

8.7. Reader collision

The signal from one reader can interfere with the signal from another where coverage overlaps. This is called reader collision. One way to avoid the problem is to use a technique called time division multiple access, or TDMA. In simple terms, the readers are instructed to read at different times, rather than both trying to read at the same time. This ensures that they don't interfere with each other. But it means any RFID tag in an area where two readers overlap will be read twice *(Shahid, 2005)*.

8.8. Tag collision

Another problem readers have is reading a lot of chips in the same field. Tag clash occurs when more than one chip reflects back a signal at the same time, confusing the reader. Different vendors have developed different systems for having the tags respond to the reader one at a time. Since they can be read in milliseconds, it appears that all the tags are being read simultaneously *(Shahid, 2005)*.

8.9. Lack of Standard

The tags used by library RFID vendors are not compatible even when they conform to the same standards because the current standards only seek electronic compatibility between tags and readers. The pattern of encoding information and the software that processes the information differs from vendor to vendor, a change from one vendor's system to the other would require retagging all items or modifying the software *(Shahid, 2005)*. All existing RFID systems use proprietary technology which means that if Company A puts an RFID tag on a product, it can't be read by Company B unless they both use the same RFID system from the same vendor. Standards are emerging *(RFID Journal, 2003)*, but according to the industry watchers, the absence of a global standard for RFID deployment has resulted in interoperability issues and a technology that is still too expensive to acquire *(Yu, 2005)*.

9. LACK OF RFID COMPATIBLE SOFTWARE IN INDIA

Software that is available in the Indian market which is RFID compatible includes LibSys, LibSuite, New GenLib and VTLS. Libraries that are using other than these software solutions need to change their software or modify the software as per RFID requirements. In either case libraries need a lot of time and money, which is not economically feasible in an Indian scenario. Apart from the above listed Indian software there are some international products which are compatible with RFID namely: 3Me Detection System, BiblioChip RFID library system, ELiMSw and Civica.

Unlike default availability of free barcode integration module in premium LMS like VTLS, Alice, LibSys, etc, LMS vendors not only charge separately for allowing integration of RFID solution with their software using NCIP V2.0 or SIP2 protocol but also sometime integration is also difficult.

10. HOW LIBRARY RFID SYSTEM WORKS ?

Systems that make use of RFID technology are typically composed of three key elements:

i. An RFID tag, or transponder, that carries object-identifying data.

ii. An RFID tag reader, or transceiver, that reads and writes tag data.

iii. A back-end database, that stores records associated with tag contents.

The technology works through flexible, paper-thin smart labels (RFID tags), which allows it to be placed inconspicuously on the inside cover of each and every document in a library's collection and on the other collections like CDs. DVDs, etc. Complete information about each document is entered into the software installed in Server or Docking station. Now whenever a user brings the book for issue/return purpose. The RFID reader from the tag reads the information pertaining to that book and transmits the data into the software and book is smoothly issued in a few seconds with a minimum of manual intervention. As the user takes the book outside the library, the antenna placed at the exit gate automatically read the information contained on the RFID tag to verify whether the book is properly issued or not. In case the book is not issued to the user as per the library norms or it is being stolen from the library, the antenna senses it and give an instant alert. Thus the technology results in successful theft reduction of documents. The technology is also used for stock taking/inventory management purpose.

11. ROLE OF A LIBRARIAN

In this latest technology based library management system a librarian can play a vital role as he is the person who manages the library system and has to manage. The technology allows for greatly improved services for patrons especially in the area of self check out, it allows for more efficient use of professional staff, and may reduce repetitive stress to library workers. But the library using

RFID technology should serves to legitimize the technology in the eyes of the community. Therefore, it is incumbent on the library community to ensure that the technology is developed in concern with established privacy principles and that any library use of RFID follows best practices guidelines consistent with library values.

12. RFID STANDARDS FOR LIBRARY

The International Organization for Standardization (ISO) and EPC Global has been very active in developing RFID standards. The AutoID center and their commercial offshoot EPC Global have also defined specifications and standards. There are two important ISO standards pertinent to library RFID systems: ISO/IEC 15693 Standards & ISO/IEC 18000-3. These standards works on 13.56 Mhz (HF). The tags and the equipments used may carry the FCC certifications. They may follow the NCIP V2.0 or SIP2 protocol (*http://www.iso.org* ; *http://www.iec.ch*).

13. RFID IN INDIAN LIBRARIES

Several libraries have successfully installed the RFID solutions in India. The products of many manufactures of library RHO systems are available in India through their business associates or direct. RFID technology has been introduced in a number of Indian libraries like:

- Anna University, Chennai
- Bank of Baroda, Mumbai
- BCL, Chennai
- BCL, New Delhi
- IGCAR, Kalpakkam
- JIM, Indore
- IIM, Lucknow
- IISc, Bangalore

- IIT, Chennai
- IIT Delhi
- IIT Roorkee
- IIT, Kharagpur
- NASSDOC, New Delhi
- NCL, Pune
- Nirma University, Ahmedabad
- NIT, Rourkela
- NIT, Surat
- Parliament Library, New Delhi
- Punjab University, Chandigarh
- Sapru House, New Delhi
- University of Pune

14. RFID VENDORS IN INDIA

There are many vendors of RFID components all over the world and nowadays India is also producing RFID components. A list of some of the RFID vendors with presence in India and Indian sub-continent is given below (*Vasistha, 2009*; *http://libsys.co.in/customers.html*):

- 3M Library Systems, New Delhi
- Bartronics India, Hyderabad
- Capgemini India, Chennai
- Ecole Solutions, Bangalore
- Edutech, Chennai
- Gemini Traze, Chennai
- Grandeur Technologies, Chennai
- GreenFuturz Software Solutions, Chennai
- HCL Infosystems, Noida
- IDCUBE Identification Systems, Noida
- I-Tek, Pune
- LibSys Corporation, Gurgaon

- Modular Technologies India, Chennai
- Netlink Information Systems, Gurgaon
- R.S. Barcodes, New Delhi
- RapidRadio Solutions, Ahmedabad
- RFID lnfotek, Mumbai
- Total IT Solutions, New Delhi
- TS Informatics, Delhi
- VTLS Software, Noida

15. GLOBAL SCENARIO

The RFID in libraries was first proposed in the 1990s as a technology that would enhance workflow in the library settings. Singapore was certainly one of the first to introduce RFID in libraries and Rockefeller University in New York may have been the first academic library in the United States to utilize this technology, whereas Farmington Community Library in Michigan may have been the first public institution, both of which began using RFID in 1999. In Europe, the first public library to use RHO was the one in Hoogezand-Sappemeer, the Netherlands, in 2001. The University of Connecticut Library; University of NevadalLas Vegas Library, the Vienna Public Library in Austria, the Catholic University of Leuven in Belgium, and the National University of Singapore Library are among the few sites that appear to have tagged more than 500,000 items each. The most ambitious RFID program is that of the Nederlandse Bibliothek Dienst (Netherlands Library Service). It envisions implementing RFID in all of the public libraries of the country, with an item able to travel among libraries that are equipped to read the tags of all of the books, not just their own. Worldwide, RFID is used most in the United States, followed by the United Kingdom and Japan. The largest RFID implementation in academic libraries is in the University of Hong Kong Libraries which has over 1.20 million libraryitems tagged; whereas the largest implementation for public institutions is in Seattle Public Library in the United States.

16. CONCLUSION/THE FUTURE

RFID is a technology that is booming in libraries due to increased productivity in library processes. It is quite clear from the above discussion that an RFID system may be a comprehensive system that addresses both the security and materials tracking needs of a library. RFID in the library is not a threat if best practices guidelines followed religiously, that it speeds up book borrowing and inventories and frees staff to do more user-service tasks. The technology saves money too and quickly gives a return on investment.

Implementing RFID technology provides major benefits for libraries. Because of the growth of collections the functions like stock verification and tracking of missing books was becoming almost impossible for the library. This library serves a large clientele, and RFID technology has enabled the library to provide a quick, accurate and timely service to the users. Quick circulation of books means no queuing in front of the circulation counter, and tracking and shelving of the books has become much easier. The manpower required to perform all these functions is now being reduced and is being utilised for providing some extra services. Most importantly the system has already put a check on the theft and misuse of documents, as users understand that the system is in place and capable of detecting theft.

Although, the RFID technology is quite expensive, still it has yielded excellent results for many libraries throughout the world. It is taking off in libraries at an increasingly rapid pace. It has the capability of making the management processes in the library more convenient. The only barrier in the journey is the high cost of it, but every new technology implementation is somewhat dearer. Moreover, RFID applications lead to significant savings in staff costs, enhance services and provide efficient results, which leads to almost fool proof security and access control. It not only provides a constant update of library collections, proper holding management, but also accomplishes real-time services. The bottom line is that the synergy between the latest technology like RFID and libraries can create wonders resulting in empowerment of both users as well as librarians. Also, it is recommended that smaller and new libraries should adopt RFID at an early stage since initially costs and resources involved in adopting & implementing the technology are lower compared to significant benefits it provides. Now-a-days, there are book distributors who supply new books tagged with RFID tags at no extra cost, saving recurring expenses to the institution. In nutshell, RFID can be taken as a boon because of its benefits over other technologies in libraries.

The traditional security systems have proved to be less effective than libraries desire them to be and RFID is more effective in material management. RFID is one of the most demanded and employed technologies in large successful enterprises such as Wal-Mart, Dell, automobile part makers, airlines, supermarkets, computer stores, bookshops, etc. The types of operations that can be done by RFID technology and the benefits offered by that match the needs of libraries as well. Currently, only about 8 percent of libraries world-wide are using RFID, but this figure is rapidly increasing as libraries understand the benefits and convenience of incorporating RFID into their system *(Mehrjerdi, 2011)*.

The library of the not too distant future may be assumed to be very different with what we have today. It may work with a combination of computer hardware/ software, RFID technology, robots, conveyor belts, computer experts, and few librarians. This is a big picture of the RFID-based system for large libraries where a combination of technologies may be used for wisely managing situations better and more efficiently using the robots to take books off for patron or librarian; and use conveyor belt to send book down the line. A good Material Handling System (MHS) as it is used in large warehouses can be tremendously helpful in RFID based libraries. Since the use of MHS can be quite expensive for large libraries, it is possible to set-up such systems in a portion of the library having large demands on the hourly and daily basis. Using RFID-based systems, it is possible to determine where the material is currently located and then with the help of robots, the material can be brought to the conveyor belt and routed easily to the patron or circulation desk. This is quite possible with the aid of the current technology if the working system at the library is an RFID- based system. In addition to that, it must include a dynamic automated moving robot that can go in search of materials somewhere in the shelves in the limited surrounding that it has authority to work *(Patil, 2008)*.

Since RFID technology for the libraries in India is new and the future of Indian libraries depends on this technology, there is an urgent need to develop Indian libraries with RFID enabled technologies, to face global competition. The only barrier in the journey is high cost, but, "every new technology comes at a cost" *(Ayre, 2006)*. As *Mossop (2008)* rightly said, "there's never a 'best time' to adopt any new technology – today's facilities are always better, cheaper and faster than yesterday's, but whatever you buy today is almost guaranteed to have been superseded by something even more ideal by the time tomorrow comes". To conclude, the future of libraries lies in RFID technology and it is expected that in the coming years the cost will come down further and soon we will see mass adoption of this technology in many libraries in India. Regardless of these potential future developments, and of existing problems, the rate of growth in the use of RFID technology by libraries in India continues to increase rapidly, to the extent that, while still clearly developing and adapting to the demands made of it, "it is no longer seen as a novelty, but much more as a significant tool that enables library managers to transform and modernize their services in a way that meets the needs of their 21st century customers" *(Palmer, 2009, p. 135)*. Therefore, despite its limitations, it has become imperative for libraries to use it as it would give definite benefits and solve many tedious, mundane and complex problems easily. The benefits of RFID technology cannot be ignored in today's tight staffing and funding climate in recession.

Finally, we can say that despite all its limitations, the RFID technology is the future of libraries but we should also remember that it is a supporting technology and not a competing one.

REFERENCES

1. Bhuptani, M. and Moradpour, S. (2005). RFID Field Guide: Deploying Radio Frequency Identification Systems, Sun MicroSystems, Prentice-Hall PTR, Upper Saddle River, NJ.
2. Boss, R.W. (2005). RFID technology for libraries. Available at: *www.ftrf.org/ala/mgrps/divs/pla/plapublications/platechnotes/RFID-2007.pdf* (Accessed 24 April 2014).
3. Butters, A. (2007). RFID systems, standards and privacy within libraries. *The Electronic Library, Vol. 25 No. 4*, pp. 430-9.
4. Coyle, K. (2005). Management of RFID in libraries. *Journal of Academic Librarianship, Vol. 31, No. 5*, pp. 486-9.
5. Galhotra, M.K. and Galhotra, A.M. (2009). Application of Radio Frequency Identification technology in libraries. *DESIDOC Journal of Library and Information Technology, Vol. 29*, pp. 59-64.
6. Hodgson, C. (2004). RFID in libraries: are we ready. *Information Standards Quarterly, Vol. 16, No. 4*, pp. 1-4.
7. Lindquist, M.G. (2003). RFID in libraries : Introduction to the issues. Paper presented at 69th IFLA Conference, 1-9 August, Berlin. Available at: *www.ifla.org/IV/ifla69/papers/161e-*Lindquist.pdf (Accessed 24 April 2014).
8. Mehrjerdi, Yahia Zare (2011). RFID: the big player in the

libraries of the future. *The Electronic Library, Vol. 29*, pp. 36-51.

9. Mittal, A., et al. (2010). RFID: a complete security system for libraries. In Proceedings of 2nd International Symposium on *"Emerging Trends and Technologies in Libraries and Information Services"*. (ETTLIS-2010). Solan: JUIT: 327- 331.

10. Molnar, D. and Wagner, D. (2004). Privacy and security in library RFID issues, practices, and architectures. In, Atluri, V., Pfitzmann, B. and McDaniel, P.D. (Eds), Proceedings of the 11th ACM Conference on Computer and Communications Security, Washington, DC, USA, pp. 210-9. Available at: *www.cs.berkeley.edu/,dmolnar/library.pdf*

11. Mulla, K.R. and Chandrashekara, M. (2006). Application of RFID in libraries for physical information security – a view. In, Murthy, T.A.V. et al. (Eds), Dynamic Interoperable Web Based Information System, INFLIBNET, Gulbarga, pp. 500-6.

12. Nagalakshmi, L. Rasha (2011). Development of RFID (Radio Frequency Identification) at Indian academic libraries: issues and best practice. *International Journal of Library and Information Science, Vol. 3.* pp.34-37.

13. Patil, A., et al. (2008). Bluebot: asset tracking via robotic location crawling. *Computer Communications, Vol. 31,* pp.1067-77.

14. Radio-frequency Identification *http://en.wikipedia.orglwikil Radio-frequency_identification#Libraries* (online) (Accessed on April 25, 2014).

15. RFID Journal (2003). ISO moves on RFID standards. *RFID Journal.* Available at : *www.rfidjournal.com/article/articleprint/297/-1/1/* (Accessed on 24 April 2014).

16. RFID library solutions *http://www.tagsysrfid.com/MarketsfTndustries/Library* (online) (Accessed on April 8, 2014).

17. Rowley, J.E. (1980). Computers For Libraries. Clive Bingley, London.

18. Shahid, S. (2005). Use of RFID technology in libraries: a new approach to circulation, tracking, inventorying, and security of library materials. *Library Philosophy and Practice, Vol. 8 No. 1.* Available at: *www.webpages.uidaho.edu/,mbolin/shahid.pdf* (Accessed on 24 April 2014).

19. Strickland, L. and Hunt, L. (2005). Technology, security, and individual privacy: new tools, new threats, and new public perceptions. *Journal of the American Society for Information Science and Technology, Vol. 56 No. 3,* pp. 221-34.

20. Tagsys (2008). RFID tags. Available at: *www.tagsysrfid.com/systems/flexible-hf-tags.cfm*

21. Vaishnaav, A.A. and Bapat, N.G. (1995). Library automation – a feasibility study. DESIDOC *Bulletin of Information Technology, Vol. 15 No. 2,* pp. 11-16.

22. Vasistha, Seema (2009). Roadmap for RFID implementation in central library, PEC University of Chandigarh. In Proceeding of *"International Conference on Academic Libraries"*. (ICAL-2009). New Delhi: University of Delhii, pp. 300-306.

23. Yu,E.(2005). RFID interoperability still problematic. p.3.Available at: *www.news.cnet.com/*

24. Yu, S.C. (2008). Implementation of an innovative RFID application in libraries. *Library Hi Tech, Vol. 26 No. 3,* pp. 398-410.

10

Web 3.0 : Emerging Technology for Libraries

1. INTRODUCTION

A web service is a software system designed to support computer-to-computer interaction overthe Internet. Web services are not new and usually take the form of an Application ProgrammingInterface (API). In today's world of extreme competition on the business front, informationexchange and efficient communication is the need of the day. The web is an increasingly importantresource in many aspects of life: education, employment, government, commerce, health care, recreation, and more. The web is a system of interlinked, hypertext documents accessed via theInternet. With a web browser, a user views web pages that may contain text, images, videos,other multimedia and navigates between them using hyperlinks.

The web was created in 1989 by Sir Tim Berners-Lee, working at CERN (The European Organizationfor Nuclear Research) in Geneva, Switzerland. Since then, Berners-Lee has played an active rolein guiding the development of web standards (such as the markup languages in which web pagesare composed), in recent years has advocated his vision of a Semantic web.

The term web 2.0 was coined by Dale Dougherty of O'Reilly Media. Web 2.0 is a term referring to ongoing transactions on web in a two ways medium where a people can read and write with the help of software and communicate among the society. Web 2.0 opened up the doors for us to create to read and to write documents, where publisher could publish data and user could interact with the data by commenting with text, voice or video (Blogs, You Tube, Twitter, Face book). Web 2.0 is the era when people have come to realize that it's not the software that enables the web that matters so much as the services that are delivered over the web. New technologies will make online search more intelligent and may even lead to a web 3.0. Enter web 2.0, a vision of the web in which information is broken up into "microcontent" units that can be distributed over dozens of domains. The web of documents has morphed into a web of data.In the changing technology Web 3.0 is creating a more intelligent web. Web 3.0 promises to take away the repetitive tasks that machines can do at a fraction of the speed, and enable people to do what is uniquely human as it simplify and humanize our online experience. The third generation of web is about giving everything we have out there meaning. Web 3.0 will make tasks easier and faster. Instead of multiple searches, you might type complex sentences or two in your web 3.0 browsers and the web will do the rest.

2. WEB 3.0

Web 3.0 is a term that has been coined to describe the evolution of Web usage and interaction thatincludes transforming the Web into a database. Web 3.0 is an era in which we will upgrade theback-end of the Web, after a decade of focus on the front-end (Web 2.0 has mainly been aboutAJAX, tagging, and other front-end user-experience innovations.) This in turn leads us to the rumblingsand mumblings we have begun to hear about

Web 3.0, which seems to provide us with a guaranteethat vague web-versioning nomenclature is here to stay. By extending Tim Berners-Lee's explanations,the Web 3.0 would be something akin to a "read-write-execute" web. Web 3.0 is defined as thecreation of high-quality content and services produced by gifted individuals using web 2.0 technologiesas an enabling platform.

Web 3.0 is also called the semantic web, this version is when the web gets smart and begins to understand what you want and thus creating a more "intelligent" web. It is a way for us to tell computers how to take the enormous amount of data that already exists and each of us generate on a daily basis and deliver it to us in a more meaningful and usable way. Web 3.0 promises to take away the repetitive tasks that machines can do at a fraction of the speed, and enable people to do what is uniquely human. Web 3.0 needs different technology. Web 3.0 is a term that is used to describe various evolutions of Web usage and interaction among several paths. These include transforming the Web into a database, a move towards making contentaccessible by multiple non-browser applications, the leveraging of artificial intelligence technologies,the Semantic web, the Geospatial Web, or the 3D web.

Web 3.0 could mean many things,a web where the concept of website or webpagedisappears, where data isn't owned but insteadshared, where services show different views for thesame web. Those services can be applications,devices or other, and have to be focused on context and personalization, and both will be reached byusing vertical search. Web 3.0 technologies maytransform the web into a database, a move towardsmaking content accessible by multiple non-browserapplications, the leveraging of artificial intelligencetechnologies etc. *Web 3.0 is a collection of technologies that consist of:*

- The Semantic Web
- The 3D Web,
- Real World Web
- Linked Data
- Natural Language Processing
- Artificial Intelligence

The term 'Web 3.0' reflects an equally momentous change in the way we view the web. Some of the possible avenues for the future include the 3D web, the semantic web, and the real world web. All have gained a lot of interest among library and information professionals. Virtual 3D worlds such as Second Life provide new places and ways to offer information and services. An increasingly semantic web offers the opportunity for access to increasing amounts of information from disparate sources. Meanwhile the real world web offers to integrate the web with the world around us. We are yet to see which of these will capture the imagination of library stakeholders to such an extent that it will reflect a new perspective in the way they see the web.

2.1. The semantic web

Web 3.0 or Semantic web is "an extension of thecurrent web in which information is given welldefinedmeaning, better enabling computers andpeople to work in cooperation". The word'semantic' stands for 'the meaning of', andtherefore the semantic web is one that is able todescribe things in a way that computers can betterunderstand.

The semantic web is a vision: the idea of having data on the web defined and linked in a way that it can be used by machines not just for display purposes, but for automation and integration of data for various applications.

In comparison to the excessive hype surrounding sites like Second Life, there is relatively little widespread understanding of the semantic web – a web of information that is meaningful to computers. The specialist terminology of the semantic web has created a barrier to most people engaging with the topic. And those that do engage with the semantic web fail to get the same sense of discernable contrast that people notice with the 3D web. Whilst O'Reilly identified data as "the next Intel inside", much of the data that is currently hosted is in information silos. Accessing the data from a specific information resource requires learning the quirks and format of each specific application programme interface (API).

Nonetheless, access to APIs has encouraged an increasing number of users to start thinking about the web of data, and there is increased interest in the possibilities of both Linked Data and microformats for the embedding of semantic information. Linked Data is about publishing and connecting related data from different websites in a way that the relationships are meaningful to computers. Microformats focus on embedding semantic attributes into web pages through the application of agreed standards (for example, marking up contact information in the hCard format).

Embracing the semantic web requires librarians and information professionals to not only move beyond the physical and virtual document, which has been the focus of much of their attention up until now. It also requires them to start thinking of interacting with the data on the web as a large information resource, rather than in individual data repositories. When discussing the potential of a semantic web to bring together previously disparate information resources in as yet unthought-of ways, it is difficult not to slip into hyperbole – assigning increasing amounts of our daily online activity to automated agents that could carry out the tasks on our behalf.

2.2. The 3D web

The potential of a 3D web and a far richer web experience have been enabled by increases in computer processing power and higher bandwidth capabilities. Complex virtual worlds offer the opportunity for 3D virtual representations of users to interact with one another in real time and explore information and virtual objects in new ways. The potential of such virtual worlds for the provision of information services has been recognised by many information professionals.

2.3. Real world web

While the incremental changes of the semantic web may not be immediately discernable, or beneficial, this is not the case with the real world web. Small-scale applications incorporating the web into the world around us can have an immediate impact. Connections between the web and the real world are not only possible through the increased sophistication of mobile phones, but also platforms that enable real-time updates from real world objects.

The Semantic Web (Web 3.0) promises to "organize the world's information" in a dramatically more logical way than Google can ever achieve with their current engine design. This is especially true from the point of view of machine comprehension as opposed to human comprehension.The Semantic Web requires the use of a declarative ontological language like OWL to produce domain-specific ontologies that machines can use to reason about information and make new conclusions, not simply match keywords. The effects of Web 2.0 are far-reaching. Like all paradigm shifts, it affects the people who use it socially, culturally, and even politically. One of the most affected groups is the social networks and Wikis are all products of Web 2.0 designers and developers who will be building it—not just because their technical skills will change, but also because they will need to treat content as part of a unified whole, an ecosystem if you will, and not just an island. First, knowledge of all kinds gets represented in a form that is interpretable both by people and machines. Second, different forms of language in which knowledge is expressed begin to be interrelated and made interchangeable with each other. Third, when knowledge is encoded in a semantic form, it becomes transparent and accessible at any time to a variety of reasoning engines.

3. CONCLUSION

Web 2.0 Development is a conclusion of an open source community efforts where business can capture a new-fangled character of all its users. Web 2.0 Development standards are being acknowledged across the globe to smooth the progress of inventiveness, information sharing, and collaboration amongst web users in the World Wide Web. The best conception of web 2.0 at this point in time would be a social network interface that the user designs. It is a personalized OPAC that includes access to IM, RSS feeds, blogs, wikis, tags, and public and private profiles within the library's network. It is virtual reality of the library, a place where one can not only search for books and journals, but interact with a community, a librarian, and share knowledge and understanding with them. Web 1.0 moved collections and sparse services into the online environment, and Web 2.0 will move the full suite of library services into this electronic medium. The data you'll get from Web 3.0 will no longer be random and a mess of search results but it will search only you want it needs different technologies and thinking to organize and access information on the web in a way that moves from lists and pages of data to meaningful content. In short concept Web 3.0 is a medium for data, information and knowledge sharing.

REFERENCES

1. Jennifer Lang. Libraries and the Social Web: Using Web 2.0 Applications to Deliver Information in the 21st Century. Available at http://jenniferlang.net/lib20/ (Accessed on 05/01/2014)

2. Brian Getting. Basic Definitions: Web 1.0, Web. 2.0, Web 3.0. Available at http://

3. Chris. Unlock knowledge with Enterprise Search. Available at http://blog.devnet.com.au/(Accessed on 04/01/2014)

4. Jason Vallery. What is Web 3.0?: A review of the ICWSM. Available at http://vallery.net/2007/03/27/what-is-web-30-a-review-of-the-icwsm/ (Accessed on 05/01/2014)

5. Jeffrey Zeldman. Web 3.0. Available at http://www.alistapart.com/articles/web3point0

6. Miller, P. Web 2.0: Building the New Library. Available at http://www.ariadne.ac.uk/issue45/miller/ (Accessed on 05/01/2014)

7. Mills Davis. Semantic Wave 2014. Available at http://www.project10x.com/about.html

8. Mind Booster Noori. What is Web 3.0?. Available at http://mindboosternoori.blogspot.com/2007/08/what-is-web-30.html (Accessed on 05/01/2014)

9. O'Reilly, T. What Is Web 2.0: Design Patterns and Business Models for the Next Generation of Software. Available at http://www.oreillynet.com/pub/a/oreilly/tim/news/2005/09/30/whatis-web-20.html (Accessed on 07/01/2014)

10. Paul Miller. Thinking about this Web 2.0 thing. Available at http://paulmiller.typepad.com/thinking_about_the_future/2005/08/thinking_about_.html (Accessed on 06/01/2014)

11. Really Simple Syndication and Rich Site Summary. What is Web 2.0. Available at http://www.rss-specifications.com/what-is-web-2.htm (Accessed on 04/01/2014)

12. Sourav Sharma Dot Com. Web 1.0, Web 2.0, Web 3.0, Web N.0. Available at http://souravshaıma.com/blog/webnpointzero.html (Accessed on 05/01/2014)

13. Steve Spalding. How to Define Web 3.0. Available at http://howtosplitanatom.com/news/howto-define-web-30-2/ (Accessed on 04/01/2014)

14. Wikipedia. Web 2.0. Available at http://en.wikipedia.org/wiki/Web_2 (Accessed on 06/01/2014)

15. World Wide Web Consortium (W3C). Introduction to Web Accessibility. Available at http://www.w3.org/WAI/intro/accessibility.php (Accessed on 04/01/2014)

11

Electronic Books (E-Books) : Latest Trends and Future Directions

1. INTRODUCTION

The libraries have witnessed the emergence of e-books in recent years by major publishers and content providers. With the expansion of electronic publishing, researchand academic libraries have started to complement their print holdings with electronic publications. Themarket for electronic publication seems to be in constant change and collection developers and acquisitionmanagers, especially in libraries, find themselves disillusioned as new methods of electronic publishing andaccessing are emerging. Libraries are in a transition period from conventional to digital formats and have notyet developed common practices and traditions on policy for digital material.

The purpose of this paper is to find out whether E-Books are cannibalizing print books, as well as an assessment of factors that are influencing E-Book usage. Traditional book publishing, especially in the academic world, is changing at a rapid pace. The question on everybody's mind is what direction book publishing will take? Will print survive in the next generation, or is it destined to be totally replaced by E-Book or something else?

Today there are an increasing number of web sites, news groups, discussion boards, and email newsletters dedicated solely to the promotion of books. More importantly, one will find web sites that provide information on very specific and narrow genres. These web sites will address audiences and topics that are considered to small or narrow to be addressed by traditional means today.

These web sites will address audiences and topics that are considered to small or narrow to be addressed by traditional means today. As a greater number of electronic resources become available, retrieving relevant and authoritative information has become progressively more challenging and time consuming. Locating relevant information in a timely manner is critical for both the researcher and the information professional. Electronic books (E-Books) are one way to enhance the digital library with global 24-hours-a-day and 7-days-a-week access to authoritative information, and they enable users to quickly retrieve and access specific research material easily, quickly, and effectively. It is crucial to not only provide these electronic resources, but to integrate them into library systems to streamline library operations, as well as promote user adoption. As with any new opportunity, new challenges emerge and utilising the internet to deliver book content is no exception. Integrating E-Book into the digital library has created challenges and opportunities for librarians, publishers, and E-Book providers.

An E-Book collection should be accessible anytime, anywhere via the internet, requiring no device but a personal computer to access the content. An ideal E-Book should provide content of value, the ability to view online, the ability to download to a PC or view offline, and the ability to view on a handheld device or personal digital assistant. Users should be guaranteed privacy for the content they access and use and should be able to aggregate and customize items and content regardless of format. An E-Book is based both on emulating the basic characteristics of traditional books in an electronic format, as well as leveraging internet technology to make an E-Book easy and efficient to use.

An E-Book can take the form of a single monograph or/a multi-volume set of books in a digital format that allows for viewing on various types of monitors, devices, and personal computers. It should allow searching for specific information across a collection of books and within a book. An E-Book should utilize the benefits of the internet by providing the ability to embed multimedia data, to link to other electronic resources, and to cross reference information across multiple resources.

An E-Book is quite similar to a print book; basically the medium is different. It is the digital representation of the printed material; the medium may vary from a computer to a digital E-Book reader like PDA, KINDLE, iPAD, mobile phone, etc. Usually the content is available in PDF or HTML format, but also plain text or XML formats. This makes the content much more versatile and flexible than the traditional print book. An E-Book is a digital object with textual and/or other content, which arises as a result of integrating the concept of a book with features that can be provided in an electronic environment; and E-Books typically have in-use features such as search and cross reference functions, hypertext links, bookmarks, annotations, highlights, multimedia objects and interactive tools.

While any book-length electronic document could be considered an E-Book, a true E-Book reader and software is optimized for reading rather than developing contents, and most E-Book readers attempts in some way to simulate the experience of reading a paper book. The E-Book makes it possible to take reading with you, without the mess of lugging dozens of books around with you. Perfect for traveling, trips or even the long commute to work. All these features enable an E-Book to be fully indexed. Readers can also find these books through search engines (such as Google), the library catalog (OPAC) or the publisher platform.

2. DEFINITION OF THE E-BOOK

An E-Book is essentially the contents of a book distributed in the form of an electronic (hence the 'e') file. Any file that holds text can be in theory used as an E-Book. However, there are a number of specialized formats and reading programs designed with E-Book reading in mind. E-Books are exactly like print or paper books except that they are bound electronically. E-Books come in a variety of formats as well. They can be downloaded in .pdf, .html, plain text and rich text formats for example, and they can also be purchased in CD-ROM and floppy disc formats.

An E-Book collection should be accessible anytime, anywhere via the internet, requiring no device but a personal computer to access the content. An ideal E-Book should provide content of value, the ability to view online, the ability to download to a PC or view offline, and the ability to view on a handheld device or personal digital assistant. Users should be guaranteed privacy for the content they access and use and should be able to aggregate and customize items and content regardless of format. An E-Book is based both on emulating the basic characteristics of traditional books in an electronic format, as well as leveraging internet technology to make an E-Book easy and efficient to use.

An E-Book can take the form of a single monograph or/a multi-volume set of books in a digital format that allows for viewing on various types of monitors, devices, and personal computers. It should allow searching for specific information across a collection of books and within a book. An E-Book should utilize the benefits of the internet by providing the ability to embed multimedia data, to link to other electronic resources, and to cross reference information across multiple resources.

Various definitions have been propounded by various information experts, to define the concept of E-Books. Here we would like to move from simple to complex definition, so that we can understand the E-Books arena in its various facets.

Jan O. Borchers defines E-Books as "An electronic book or E-Book, is a portable hardware and software system that can display large quantities of readable textual information to the user and that lets the user navigate through this information"

Ana Arias Terry defines "At its simplest level, an E-Book consists of electronic concept "Originating from traditional books, reference material, or magazines" that is downloaded from the internet and viewed through any number of hardware devices. These include PC's or palmtops or dedicated E-Book readers."

Nelson (2008) has defined an e-book as, 'an electronic book that can be read digitally on a computer screen, a special e-book reader, a personal digital assistant (PDA), or even a mobile phone. In other words, e-books are consumed on a screen rather than on paper'.

Wikipedia defines e-book as 'An e-book is an e-text that forms the digital media equivalent of a conventional printed book, often protected with a digital rights management system'. General and specialized are two kinds of e-books. The examples of these two are 'netLibrary' or 'ebrary' and 'Books 24X7', 'Knovel'.

Copy and print capabilities for portions of the E-Book should be permitted within copyright and fair use guidelines. Copyright protection must be ensured regardless of whether the content is accessed via the internet or via a downloadable reader that allows access to the book offline.

3. SPECIAL FEATURES OF E-BOOKS

Simply put an E-Book is a special computer file, which contains the text of a printed book. The file may be read on a personal computer (PC), a personal digital assistant (PDA), or an electronic device designed specifically for reading E-Books (E-Book reader). E-Book readers have many features that are simply not available with standard printed text. Following are some special features of E-Books :

- E-Books cost less than traditional books,
- Books never go out of print,
- Economically feasible to publish low demand titles,
- No shipping and handling charges when purchased online,
- Search for specific text - find that quote in seconds,
- Ability to self publish and distribute own books inexpensively,
- Look up words with dictionary software (included with most E-Book readers),
- Annotate or highlight text,
- Enjoy content which includes audio and full motion video,
- Choose different fonts (text) sizes in which to read,
- Teachers may prepare customized e-Textbooks for their students,
- Read in the dark or low light conditions,
- Carry several books in one small package.
- E-Books may be customized to suit an individual's specific interests and tastes.
- Save E-Books on the Internet or Personal Computer (create your own virtual library).

- Copyright protected through software (prevent unauthorized duplication of E-Book content).
- Create links between multiple E-Books.
- The visually impaired may switch to audio mode and have en E-Book read to them.
- Reduce environmental waste (save trees, and reduce pollution from delivery trucks).
- Reference material in E-Book format may be easily updated.
- Libraries may "Loan" E-Books by setting a time period in which an E-Book may be read.
- No expense for overstocking or missed sales from out of stock books

Before E-Books can create literary nirvana and truly benefit the general public, five things must continue to develop and improve; Content creation and publication;

i. E-Book software;

ii. E-Book reader hardware;

iii. E-Book standards formation; and

iv. E-Book education, distribution and promotion.

4. HOW DOES AN E-BOOK WORK?

An electronic book is book content that exists in digital form. Electronic books may be in any number of digital formats, and, depending on the format, any number of different software applications and computer hardware may be required to view them. To understand the workings of E-Books, it is useful to distinguish between an "electronic book" (i.e. book content in digital form) and a "book-reading appliance" (tool for reading the book). A book-reading device is a specialized device (other than a personal computer) required to display an electronic book. Electronic books created for use with a digital device are usually produced in such a way that they can only be viewed using the respective product's specialized software or hardware.

5. E-BOOK READERS - THE FUTURE OF READING?

An *E-Book reader,* also called an *E-Book device* or *e-reader,* is an electronic device that is designed primarily for the purpose of reading digital books and periodicals and uses e-ink technology to display content to readers. The main advantages of these devices are portability, readability of their screens in bright sunlight, and long battery life.

A pragmatic factor in using E-Book is the ease of reading and using them, yet E-Book hardware devices are still not quite practical or cost effective enough to penetrate very deeply into the market. A variety of devices are being developed to replicate some of the virtues of printed monographs, including portability and network-independence, so that E-Book themselves will function on a variety of platforms. The two basic kinds of e-book readers on the market today are the full-sized reader and the palm-sized reader. Currently, all readers use proprietary file formats. (Brochers, 2009).

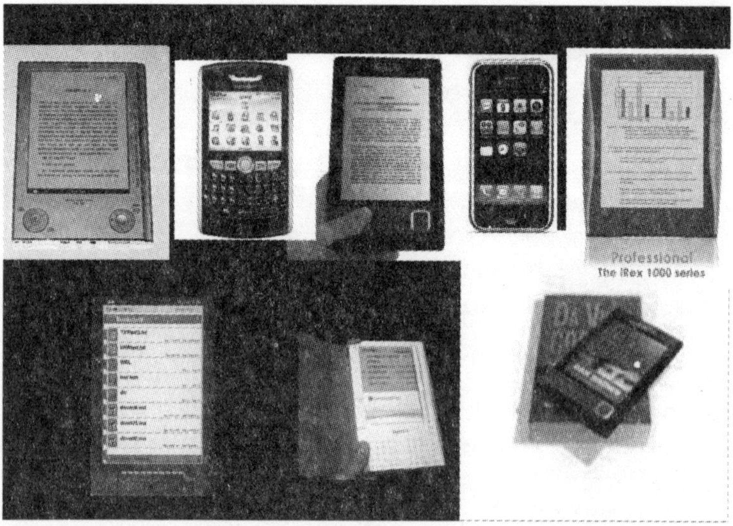

6. E-BOOK BUSINESS MODELS AND LICENSING:

The variance amongst access models affected the pricing and purchasing of E-Books. There is absence of standard pricing model for E-Books. Libraries should be aware of various business models offered by different publishers of E-Books. Following are various available business model and content type available in the market which would throw more clarity on the decision of moving to E-Book:

6.1. E-Book vendors fall into two categories:

a. Aggregators : they provide a common platform for multiple publishers and aggregateE-Book contents in either PDF or HTML formats and make available thousands of E-Book.

b. Primary publishers : they provide on their proprietary platform the E-Book contents published by them.

6.2. E-Book content available from various publishers also fall under two categories

a. Reference books like encyclopedia and handbook largely used by libraries and

b. Research books and scholarly book contents available in electronic form not many text books are available in electronic form however some aggregators and primary publishers are moving their focus to make available text book contents.

6.3. E-Book selections for use by the library can also be categorized into two methods depending upon the publishers

a. Some publishers offer pick and choose model - they allow the library to pick up the books of their choice subject to a certain minimum and

b. Some publishers expect the libraries to buy/

subscribe the complete subject collections. The library will have no choice but take the entire collection of E-Book whether they are interested in some books or not.

6.4. E-Book licensing models are also of two kinds;

a. Some publishers offer purchase models where the library can purchase the latest edition of the books in a pick and choose or subject collection model. They will have to keep on purchasing these books as and when the new editions are released. The cost of the books is slightly higher than the print book. In pick and choose models some of the publisher charge a platform access fees to maintain the book lifelong for the library on their site.

b. A few of the publisher offer E-Book on subscription license. The library subscribes to the selected books or collection at a price which is lower than the print books and gets the libraries do not have perpetual access to the content and loose the right of access in the event of non renewal.

6.5. E-Book swapping models

Some publishers offer E-Book swapping models during the period of subscription the library can swap the book of their choice of the same value during the course of subscription .the swapping feature is normally available in subscription license models; however some publishers that offer purchase models also offer swapping features by some additional payment.

6.6. Download option

Another important criterion for E-Book evaluation is the download options. Some publisher allow download of only chapters, some allow download of complete books and some publishers do not allow any downloads.

7. E-BOOKS: CHALLENGES FOR THE LIBRARY PROFESSIONALS

To enhance the use of E-Books, libraries have to advertise their E-Book collections and made awareness in their members about E-Book holdings and findings. The acceptance of E-Book by the education community will be directly proportional to ease of access in terms of find, buy, obtain and use. With a seamless, one-click E-Book purchasing or lending experience, students may switch to digital mode. Librarians must develop innovative policies, procedures, and technologies to accommodate the publication of and access to E-Books.(Cox, 2004). E-Book challenges for librarians can be divided into three categories:

i. Acquisition and collection development

Acquisition and collection development challenges include budget allocations; usage and distribution models; purchase models; and collection development strategies;

ii. Standards and technology

Standards and technology challenges include, not only cataloging and metadata standards and schemes, but also E-Book hardware and software technologies, digital rights management software, and user and staff training;

iii. Access

Access challenges include the cataloguing and indexing of E-Books, circulation models for the electronic environment, and preservation and archiving of E-Book and the resources linked to them.

The integration of E-Book into the digital library has not only created opportunities for librarians, but also created several challenges. Full-text access and retrieval of E-Book combine library-based theories and principles with web search and retrieval techniques.

8. E-BOOK VS PRINTED BOOKS

The reason for E-Book success, survival and facility is because of its advantages over its print counterparts. It is not only the users who is going to be benefited, but different target group such as libraries; publisher and authors can easily examine their specific advantage. In my opinion, in every aspect, E-Book offer more positive attributes, features and benefits to academic and professional users than print formats.(Pastore, 2008). The benefits of E-Book over print are :

- E-Book users can access book contents concurrently, and search the full text of any title. Multiple libraries can share in a small number of copies. E-Book offers users remote access outside to traditional library hours.
- The E-Book offers readers even more benefits over traditional paper books. E-Book can be read in a variety of lighting situations, and due to the back-lighted screens readers can read an E-Book in most low or no light situations. An E-Book may be more comfortable for some to hold because it need not be held open like a physical book and can also be set down and read without needing to be held open.
- Readers who have difficulty reading printed books can benefit from the adjustment of text size and font face.
- E-Book are subject to no transportation, storage, or processing costs, nor do they suffer from physical degradation or damage.
- The readability of an E-Book won't degrade over time. The pages won't crumble because of high acid content, the binding can never break, and there can be no variations in the ink. Despite being criticized for their inconvenience and for being hard

to read, E-Book are often more convenient than their paper based counterparts.

- The production of E-Book does not consume the paper, ink, and other resources that are used to produce print books.
- E-Book may allow animated images or multimedia clips to be embedded. Users can easily add and save their own notes to the contents and cut and paste selected texts, illustrations and diagrams.
- Multiple libraries can easily negotiate and manage shared use of E-Books, rather than engaging in the costly and time-consuming inter-library loan programs required for print.
- A single E-Book reader containing several books is easier to carry around than several print books.
- Text can be searched automatically and cross-referenced using hyperlinks, making the E-Book format ideal for works that benefit from such functions.
- It costs little to reproduce or copy an E-Book, which makes it ideal for archival and backup purposes.
- Direct contact of author and readers facilitates easy feedback and thus improves the quality of product.
- It is easier for authors to self-publish E-Books.
- Ease of distributing e-texts means that they can be used to stimulate higher sales of printed copies of books.

The benefits of E-Book over print are summarized below:

Attribute	E-Book	Print
Concurrent users	YES	NO
Full text searchable	YES	NO
Shared access	YES	NO
Remote access	YES	NO
24/7 access	YES	NO
User can add notes	YES	NO
Cut and Paste function	YES	NO
Cost of transportation	NO	YES
Cost of storage	NO	YES
Processing cost	NO	YES
Risk of damage	NO	YES
Inter-library loan cost	NO	YES

9. BENEFITS OF BUYING FROM AGGREGATED E-BOOK PLATFORM VS DIRECT FROM PUBLISHERS:

Many publishers are offering libraries direct purchase of their E-Book titles but it makes more sense for libraries to buy an aggregated E-Book platform. Most of the publishers offer access to their E-Books only on subscription basis – In this option the library only has the access to the content as long as they keep paying the subscription and may end up paying many times the cost of the book overtime. Aggregated E-Book platform offers a perpetual purchase model which gives the library ownership of access to the content in the same way that a book does, with the much more functionalities.

Most of the publishers selling their E-Book content in the form of large packages which often contain high proportion of backlist. With aggregated model the entry fee is lower and customer can buy single copy or multiple copies from different publishers with a single transaction.

An aggregated E-Book platform offers users a single point of access to a vast array of content from different publishers, whereas buying different platform from individual publishers means that the users have to go in and out of several platforms to search for and use the content. Many federated search engines are available to overcome this issue, but these are not yet an effective solution. The aggregated E-Book platform offers many more features to the librarians as well as to the library users than publishers' platforms, including:

- Secure Digital Rights Management (DRM) features to ensure that libraries and their users stay within copyright laws.
- Comprehensive reporting on E-Book usage.
- Integration into OPAC systems, making it easy to find and view E-Book alongside other information resources.

10. DIGITAL RIGHTS MANAGEMENT (DRM) AND LEGAL ISSUES

One of the most critical elements in the development of electronic publishing that will impact libraries involves Digital Rights Management Systems (DRMS). As with digital rights management in other media, E-Book are more like rental or leasing than purchase. The restricted book comes with a number of restrictions, and eventually access to the purchase can be removed by a number of different parties involved. These include the publisher of the book, the provider of the DRM scheme, and the publisher of the reader software. These are all things that are significantly different from the realm of experiences anyone has had with a physical copy of the book. Still being developed, DRMS are either hardware or software (or both) that enforce control over intellectual property, such as limit by user, time, fee, and/or extent of content. Although similar controls have existed in the licensing of electronic journals, the length of book content and the concerted effort by publishers to establish such software for E-Book make this issue more pressing. Due to publishers' concerns about rights, to date E-Book vendors are normally able to offer only limited usage rights for printing, downloading and copying. Normally, interlibrary loan is not allowed, and classroom use is not always allowed.(Falk, 2001).

Legal issues worry E-Book users as well as publishers. Users feel that fair use should apply to E-Book just as it does with printed books. An owner of a printed book is free to give it away, lend, or sell it at any time. Many E-Book licenses forbid such activities. The publisher concludes a contract with an author who undertakes to produce a satisfactory completed work within a specified period of time. The author certifies in the contract the work's originally, the royalty of sale, etc. Marketing and distribution includes sales promotion, advertising, publishing and selling in what is considered a largely integrated process.

Legal issues continue to bedevil the E-Book market. Publishers resist distributing their products in electronic form because of the potential for piracy. Copy and print capabilities for portions of the E-Book should be permitted within copyright and fair use guidelines. Copyright protection must be ensured regardless of whether the content is accessed via the internet or via a downloadable reader that allows access to the book offline.

11. USAGE OF E-BOOKS IN THE LIBRARIES

In this section I will focus on my experiences with E-book usage both at Indian Institute of Technology Delhi and E-book use in general. As of yet E-books are not as established as e-journals in libraries, there are great variations both in access models and user friendliness of the offered services. Also, E-books tend to be more practical in some contexts, for example for literature research or looking up definitions etc. Still the digital media, mainly because of problems with user friendliness of reading screens, makes it challenging to read longer texts from cover to cover.

The everyday environment of faculty and students is to a great extent digital, and learning and teaching is simplified by making information electronically accessible. Those who are digitally literate are able to utilise the facilities of the digital resources and have good chances to succeed with their work. E-books are part of this, assuming one has access to these digital resources, which depends upon many factors:

- Electronic resources are, in general, expensive, and every subscription renewal or new purchase by the library has to be thoroughly discussed.
- Many vendors only sell access to a limited number of users, sometimes as few as one at a time. This means that users may be turned away from important resources, which can be frustrating when information is urgent.
- Vendors generally control access either by checking that the user belongs to a valid Institute IP-address. To gain access from outside of Institute one has to access the digital resources by using a proxy server. This can be technically challenging and therefore limits the flexibility of accessing the services outside the Institute.
- In the case of Ebrary, readers must install separate reading software. This is free, but requires an extra effort which could be avoided if for example standard reading software had been used.
- For some users the various user interfaces of the E-book services can be confusing and therefore be restraining for their use.

12. WHAT DRIVE AN E-BOOK USAGE?

Several factors drive an E-Book usage. Obviously the usage of online contents is driven by visibility and discoverability of the contents in major search engines such as Google. Also, the library websites, blogs and catalogs and ofcourse the contents themselves are huge drivers of traffic to the E-Books. Libraries play a very important role in making contents visible and findable for their patrons.

13. E-BOOK USAGE BARRIERS:

Some of the barriers in the E-Book usage may be enumerated as below:

- Contents/Books of choice are not available in e-format, especially the text and popular books
- Screen resolution, contrast and brightness
- Harmful for eyes, brain and health?
- Hardware for E-Books is fragile, non-flexible
- There is no compatibility across different hardware/ software for using titles
- User's current reliance on prints neglects the benefits of E-Book
- Purchase/subscription policies are different and difficult to understand. Pricing models are varied from publisher to publisher and vendor-to-vendor
- The cost of E-Books for single use is very high
- Many publishers are reluctant to produce E-Books/ make their products available in E-Book format simultaneously

14. USAGE STATISTICS ISSUES

In the current state of E-Book statistics, there is still a great deal of difficulty in comparing usage on different platforms as many platforms still do not offer COUNTER book reports. There are also E-Book platforms offering usage counts for activities not necessarily counted from all platforms, such as table of content views. However, the library finds patterns of interest and activity here that we intend to watch closely in the near term. It is difficult to evaluate the way as the usage of E-Books is counted because the publishers of the E-Books hardly provide details as how they have generated the E-Book usage details. The authors recommend that E-Book vendors should adopt consistent, comparable usage data, such as that advocated by Project COUNTER. Librarians need to encourage vendors and publishers to adopt standard usage statistics and become COUNTER compliant. Looking at raw usage statistics only provides a part of thc overall picture. While we have found that our E-Books have not been heavily used, the question is now "why?" Is it the interface? Is it the selection of titles? Is it a need for us as librarians to build a greater awareness of this resource in our user community? As next steps in assessing our E-Book collection, we will need to collect qualitative data from our users to help explain the quantitative.

When we initially purchase our E-Book packages, we assume that the convenience of anytime, anywhere, simultaneous and full-text searching would be very popular with our users, particularly our numerous campus locations. But experience show that this initial assumption does not appear to have been correct. We may look forward to going forth and speaking to our users about E-Books to gather comments and gauge awareness and hopefully begin to understand why these resources have not been as popular as anticipated?

15. E-BOOKS RECENT TRENDS AND TRENDS TO MONITOR

By removing the costs of printing, warehousing and the physical distribution of paper books, publishers will realize a dramatic improvement in profit per sale by using E-Book. Furthermore, they will substantially reduce the risk involved in releasing new titles. E-Book provides publishers a turnkey e-business solution that allows them to focus on traditional sales channels. Publishers are forced to pay for all aspects of publication and absorb all of the risk of failure, before the possibility of payment, which is further delayed after the sale of the publication by their distribution agreements. E-Book has become more popular with publishers, vendors and librarians within the past few years. This is evident by the number of E-Book initiatives.

Libraries should monitor the ongoing development of E-Book industry standards and intellectual property and privacy issues so that the principles and operations of libraries are not restricted or jeopardized in the future. Libraries should also monitor the cost of E-Book appliances and services. However, if the price drops over time, E-Book may become more popular and accessible. Trends to watch include:

- Standards and compatibility for appliances and software book readers.
- Ownership vs. licensing of E-Book content.
- Copyright controls and the ability to loan E-Book to library patrons.
- Possible development of encoded rights management systems that technologically prevent copying or transmission of E-Book content.
- Relationships between authors and publishers.
- Book distribution practices.
- Potential for E-Book sellers to attach data mining technologies to their products that will monitor the book reading habits of purchasers.
- Convergence of newspaper, magazine and other content with E-Book technology.

16. FUTURE DIRECTION AND FURTHER AREAS FOR RESEARCH

Library users' expectations are changing as they

become more wired and more dependent upon technology as wireless technologies have become more advanced and readily available. The librarians must think beyond the paper book and utilise the capabilities of the E-Book. It is more than an alternative to a paper book. We should include links from the E-Book to dictionaries, thesauri, related images, photographs, electronic text, and, audio and video segments. Now is the time to enhance the bibliographic record. Librarians should utilise the table of contents and book indices in the bibliographic record since these are already digitized in the E-Book format. We should also include links to book reviews, electronic resources that are referenced in the book, and book summaries. The full-text search capabilities of E-Books should be integrated into our library OPACs to enable users to search within the library's electronic collection, as well as across other electronic materials available on the web. Library systems should also enable the integration of semantic searches that map and retrieve concepts and ideas in addition to keyword and known-item searches. These advances will move libraries into the digital world. People are becoming more comfortable using technology and the internet for meeting their information needs. Several internet use studies have been completed and recently made available for review. Despite of slower than expected evolution and adaptability, E-Book will continue to prevail. Students demand will grow. Distance mode of education and off campus universities will demand more E-Book than printed books.(Cox, 2004).

If we, as librarians, do not provide new methods for library users to access electronic resources, we may become obsolete. As stated by Toffler, 'Tomorrow's illiterate will not be the man who can't read; he will be the man who has not learned how to learn.'(Nelsion, 2008).

Future of E-Book is very good as per Faculty, Librarian and Publisher Surveys however Printed books are still preferred for cover to cover reading. E-Book exists next to print books. It is believed that there will always be a place for traditional publishing with paper books. Print books are here to stay - E-Book will enhance access to more science and research. E-Book has many advantages to offer, however print will not disappear.

There is considerable development of standards, technologies and pricing models needed to make the market for E-Book viable and sustainable. Technologies for reading and using E-Book are not yet convenient enough for the longer text format to have made much market penetration. There are still concerns about adequate rights to information to support the academic mission of open scholarly communication. Despite the considerable promise of E-Books, it is concluded that all the elements that would make the e-book market viable are not quite in place. The partnerships in the market, development of standards, software and hardware features, and business models are still regularly changing. So, in my opinion the future directions for research in E-Book may fall into three major Categories: Technology, Content and Business models. The Content, Digital Rights Management, Access, Archiving and Privacy of E-Books features are also very important elements to study regarding academic use of E-Book.

The development of the electronic book is still in its early stages. Formatting and other issues are unresolved with competing and commercial products on the market. Still, electronic book technology is already beginning to have an effect on libraries, book publishing, copyright, and the future of communication in our world. Today India will match the world as far as E-Book is concerned.

17. CONCLUSION

Will the E-Books eventually become a transformational digital Content technology? Certainly they should, given that there is such a strong preference for digital provision in today's information world. However, a number of problems must be resolved before such a transformational change can take place. The arrival of E-Books presents many opportunities for users in new, convenient and cost-effective ways. At the moment, viewing technology, contents and pricing models are important limiting factors but in future, contents will become paramount. The success or failure of E-Books depends not only on their acceptance by users, but also on the publishing industry's ability to see beyond traditional business models and recognize that E-Books are not just a replacement for paper-based books. They are a new medium with their own potential. E-Book readers are still even now at an early stage of development and the hope is that generally accepted industry standards will soon be adopted; creating a more homogenous product for a market whose potential is yet to be fully explored.

E-Books are yet to become a major form of publication, even for students to consume and enjoy. In addition to improving the quality and reducing the cost, the E-Book industry should make more relevant, popular and interesting titles available, along with wider and more effective publicity. Printed books are still preferred for cover to cover reading. E-Books exists next to print books. Print books are here to stay - E-Books will enhance access to more science and research. E-Books have many advantages to offer, however print will not disappear.

Thus E-Books are future of printed books as printed books were future of manuscripts.

Some Renowned E-Book providers

Access on Payment

There are so many publishers/vendors/aggregators who are providing ebooks subscription, some are listed below :

Bernes and Noble.com (http://www.barnesandnoble.com) : Barnes & Noble, Inc. is the largest book retailer in the United States, operating mainly through its Barnes & Noble Booksellers chain of bookstores. It carries downloadable e-books in their E-Book section apart from the book in the form of CD-ROM and DVD-ROM. On January 8, 2014 it was announced that Michael P. Huesby would become the new CEO of Barnes and Noble.

Cambridge University Press (http://ebooks.cambridge.org/): Cambridge University Press is one of the largest and most prestigious academic publishers in the world widely respected as a world leader in publishing for subjects as diverse as astronomy, Shakespeare studies, economics, mathematics and politics. The Key Features are: Dynamic content and feature set, frequent addition of new titles and regular functionality enhancements, titles from across all Cambridge world renowned subject areas, powerful quick search, advanced search and browse capabilities.

Palm digital media (http://www.peanutpress.com): Palm Digital Media is the first electronic book publisher to offer contemporary fiction and non-fiction books for reading on handheld computers or Palm handheld platform. Palm Digital Media has relationships with more than 75 publishers, including industry leaders HarperCollins, Penguin Group (USA), Random House, St. Martin's Press, Simon & Schuster and Time Warner Book Group. It offers more than 10,000 e-book titles.

Questia (http://www.questia.com) : Questia is an online commercial digital library of books and articles with an academic orientation, with a particular emphasis on books on humanities and social sciences. The great majority of items are under copyright, for which Questia has paid a fee to the copyright owners. All the text in all the Questia books is available to subscribers. Questia does not sell ownership to books or e-books, but rather sells monthly or annual subscriptions that allows temporary online reading access to more than 78,000 online books from reputable commercial and academic presses. This rich, scholarly content selected by professional collection development librarians is not available elsewhere on the Internet.

Sage e-books (http://knowledge.sagepub.com/): SAGE Knowledge is the ultimate social sciences digital library hosting 3332 titles, it includes an expansive range of SAGE eBook and e-Reference content, including scholarly monographs, reference works, handbooks, series, professional development titles, and more. The platform allows researchers to cross-search and seamlessly access a wide breadth of SAGE book and reference content from one source.

Springer e-books (http://link.springer.com/): Springer e-book platform makes the accessibility of its online e-book collection easier and more convenient for subscribing institutions. The subscription requires IP based authentication. Springer e-books currently includes books in mathematics and statistics (11579), Physics (8745), computer science (11370) Life science (9904), engineering (6746) and reference books (194) totaling 48344 e-books.

Taylor & Francis (http://www.crcnetbase.com/): This site offers instant access to the world's premier Humanities, Social Sciences, Behavioral Sciences, Built Environment, STM and Law content -from renowned imprints such as Routledge, Psychology Press and Focal Press. They have more than 40,000 titles available for institutions via their eBook collections - from general subject areas to interdisciplinary selections. The broad subjects includes : Business & Management, Communication and Media Studies, Counseling and Psychotherapy, Criminology & Criminal Justice, Education, Engineering & Materials Science, Geography,

Earth & Environmental Science, Health and Social Care, History, Life & Biomedical.

Word Wrangler (http://www.wordwrangler.com): Known for providing excellence in eBooks, Word Wrangler publishes in all genres, traditional and non-traditional, other than works which contain deprecatory material concerning gender, race, or religion, Children's, Fantasy, Historical, Mainstream, Media, Mystery, Poetry, Romance, Science Fiction, Speculative Fiction, Western, Young Adult, Non-fiction. It also lists eBooks for self-publishing authors and other publishers in its bookstore. Word Wrangler offers a POD (print on demand) option separate from their e-publishing sector and also a cover-design service.

Free Access of e-books

Bartleby.com (http://www.bartleby.com/): It was founded under the name "Project Bartleby" in January 1993 by Steven H. van Leeuwen as a personal, non-profit collection of classic literature on the website of Columbia University. It is a comprehensive, searchable database of reference, verse and classic literature, summaries of each book, and author biographies, having enhanced navigational tools and extensive cross-referencing. No access fee is charged.

Digital book Index (http://www.digitalbookindex.com): Digital Book Index provides links to more than 165,000 full-text digital books from more than 1800 commercial and non-commercial publishers, universities, and various private sites. More than 140,000 of these books, texts, and documents are available free. The coverage includes : Reference Books, Literature & Languages, History, Social Sciences, Medicine & Health, Math & Sciences, Philosophy & Religion, Law, Children eBooks etc.

National Academic press (http://www.nap.edu): National Academies Press was created by the United

States National Academies, to publish the reports issued by the National Academy of Sciences, the National Academy of Engineering, the Institute of Medicine, and the National Research Council. It publishes nearly 200 books a year on a wide range of topics in the science, engineering, health including the most authoritative view on important issues in science and health policy. The institutions represented by NAP are unique in the sense that they attract the leading experts in every field to serve their important panels and committees. Presently more than three thousand online books are available free.

Project Gutenberg (http://www.gutenberg.org/): Project Gutenberg (PG) is a volunteer effort to digitize and archive cultural works, to encourage the creation and distribution of eBooks. It was started by Michael Hart in 1971 and is the oldest digital library. Most of the items in its collection are the full texts of public domain books. The project tries to make these as free as possible, in longlasting, open formats that can be used on almost any computer. As of March 2013, Project Gutenbergclaimed to have over 42,000 items in its collection. The site has browsing facility by Author and by Title. Author wise list of e-books are available at http://www.promo.net/pg/authors.zip and Titlewise list of e-books are available at http://www.promo.net/pg/titles.zip.

This site includes different sections like books online, news, features, Archives. It includes more than twenty thousand free e-books on the web in various formats. All of the books are free for personal and noncommercial use. Users can search the book through author, title, subject and serial archive.

University of Illinois E-Book (http://www.press/illinois.edu/epub/books.html): The University of Illinois Library has thousands of free eBooks mostly with full content that can be accessed anytime.The books can be accessed through author, title and subject. It also provide facility of keyword searching to enable user to locate specific information.

University of Pennsylvania online book (http://online books.library.upenn.edu): The University of Pennsylvania online book page facilitates access to e-books that are freely readable over the Internet.

University of Virginia e-book library: On this site more than 1800 publicly available e-books including classic British and American fiction, renowned authors, children's literature, the Bible, Shakespeare, American history, Afro-American documents, and much more are freely available.(http://etext.lib.virginia.edu/ebooks/ebooklist.html)

Web Book Publications (http://www.web-books.com): All the titles on this website are free for online reading and can be downloaded in EXE or ZIP formats. The EXE format can be read by Internet Explorer on Windows 95/98/XP. The ZIP format is a collection of HTML files which can be read by any web browser on any device, such as notebook, Smartphone etc. Currently more than seven hundred titles are available free.

REFERENCES

1. Armstrong, C and Lonsdale, Ray (2005). Challenges in managing e-books in UK academic libraries. *Library Collections Acquisition & Technical Services*, 29 (33-50).
2. Borchers, Jan O.(2009). Electronic books: definition, genres, and interaction design patterns. Available at *http://readingonline.org* (Accessed on 19 Dec. 2009).
3. Bry, Francois and Kraus, Michael (2002). Perspectives for Electronic Books in the World Wide Web age. *The Electronic Library*, 20(4), pp.275-87.
4. Bry, Francois and Kraus, Michael (2002). Perspectives for Electronic Books in the World Wide Web age. *The Electronic Library*, 20(4), 275-87.
5. Chakaravarti, A.K. and Arora, Jagdish. (1999). Internet-based online interactive courseware in IT : effective delivery of IT

education in a networked society. In NACLIN 99 : National Convention on Library and Information Networking. New Delhi, DELNET, pp. 26-37.

6. Chaurasia, Neeraj Kumar (2004). Electronic Books : An overview. Proceedings of 22nd Annual Convention and Conference of Society for Information Science (SIS) on Digital Information Exchange : Pathways to Build Global Information Society, Madras: Central Library, Indian Institute of Technology, 21-23 Jan. 2004. pp.1-7.
7. Cox, J. (2004). E-books: Challenges and Opportunities. *D-Lib Magazine*, 10(10).
8. Dinkelman, A. et al., (2007). Accessing E-books through Academic Library Web Sites. *College & ResearchLibraries*, 68(1), pp.45-48
9. Falk, Howard (2001). What Is Fair Use of E-Books? *The Electronic Library*, pp. 349-351.
10. Gibbons, Susan (2001). E-books: Some Concerns and Surprises. *Portal: Libraries and the Academy*, 1, pp.71-75.
11. Helfer, Doris Small (2000). E-Book in Libraries: Some Early Experiences and Reactions. *Searcher*, 8, pp.63-5.
12. Nelson, M. R. (2008). E-Books in higher education: Nearing the end of the era of hype? *EDUCASE Review*,43(2).
13. O'Leary, Mick (2001).E-Book Scenarios, ONLINE, pp. 62-64.
14. Pastore, M. (2008). 30 Benefits of E-books. Available at: *http://epublishersweekly.blogspot.com/2008/02/30- benefits-of-E-Books.html*
15. Pope, Barbara Kline (1999). National Academy Press : a case study. Journal of Electronic Publishing, 4(4).
16. Quint, B. (2005) Books Online: The Fee versus Free Battle Begins. *Information Today*.
17. Rosy, R. L. (2002) E-Book for Libraries and Patrons: Two Years of Experience. *LiberQuarterly*, 12(2/3), pp. 228-233.
18. Safley, E. (2006). Demand for E-books in an Academic Library. *Journal of Library Administration*, 45(3/4), pp.445-457
19. Sinha, Reeta (2008). Electronic book collection development and acquisitions: Key issues for libraries andvendors. In, Shaping the future of special libraries / edited by Dhawan, S.M. et al. New Delhi: Ane Books.
20. Sottong, Stephen (2008). The Elusive E-book, Ready for Prime

Time?. *American Libraries,* 39(5), pp. 44-48.

21. Tedd, L. A. (2005) E-Book in academic libraries: an international overview. *NewReview of Academic Librarianship,* 11(1), pp.57 - 79.
22. Twiss-Brooks, Andrea (2007). Challenges in building e-books collections. Paper presented at the 23rd National American Chemical Society Meeting August 25-29, 2007.
23. Wikipedia (2009). E-book, from *http://en.wikipedia.org/wiki/E-Book#cite_note-0*

12

Federated Search Technology and Discovery Tools

1. INTRODUCTION

The universe of libraries has evolved and expanded from repository of books, journals and other non-print materials in physical format to knowledge repositories that contain collections in physical well as electronic and multimedia format. With this changing environment of collection of library resources, the greatest challenge in front of libraries is to find out the best way to present, promote and make accessible the growing collections of heterogeneous resources. Libraries are required to look for search and discovering tools to provide seamless access to their resources. Internet content is considerably more diverse and the volume certainly much larger than commonly understood. In the early days of the Internet, it was reasonably easy to find information or data files using a variety of software that were usually command driven. In order to overcome the lack of retrieval facilities, a number of search engines came which prove to be of great assistance in allowing the information seeker to quickly find the piece of data that they require. But, the search engines all have their own shortcomings.

With remarkable increase in availability of content in electronic format, libraries are increasingly committing their funds for purchase and subscription to full-text e-journal and e-journal databases, bibliographic databases, e-books, etc. Moreover, libraries are also developing their own electronic content through institutional repositories consisting of e-prints of research articles, manuscripts, electronic theses and dissertations, institutional publications, digital images, photographs and images and artifacts of cultural heritage. Broadly, the collection in a library may include items that the library acquires and manages, items that are managed by third parties and are available for access from remote locations, items that are held locally, items that are subscribed or are available for a fee and items that are free at their point of use.

Today's libraries offer more information than ever before. From traditional books to categorized websites to online databases, students and teachers can access thousands of resources with just a few keystrokes. Federated Searching (also known as meta-searching or cross-database searching) is a technology that allows users to search many networked information sources from one interface. When students conduct a federated search, they simply enter a word or phrase into the computer and receive results from multiple targets. These targets include the library's collection of books, software, databases and online public access catalogs. Federated searching allows users to search across a number of information resources simultaneously.

2. FEDERATED SEARCH TECHNOLOGY

With the multiple numbers of open access and subscribed electronic resources available to users in research and education organizations, searching for relevant literature becomes a challenging task for a user. A user has to visit a number of individual databases, understand different types of user interface and retrieve results. If a users gets sufficient number of results from first few preferred databases, he / she tends to ignore remaining databases at the risk of missing out on important research work published in them. The new-generation web-savvy users prefer single search box approach offered by search engines like Google, Yahoo, Bing, etc that serve as a single-window access interface for all web-based resources. Design and approach of federated search and discovery tools are essentially inspired by the Web search engines. The federated search solutions facilitate users to search multiple full-text and bibliographic databases subscribed by the library as well as open access e-resources, library OPAC, IRs, and other library resources through a single search box. Terminology found in current library automation literature associated with single-search interface technology includes the following:

- Broadcast searching
- Consolidated searching
- Cross-database searching
- Distributed searching
- Federated searching
- Integrated searching
- Metasearch searching
- Portal searching

Federated search is the simultaneous search of multiple online databases or web resources and is an emerging feature of automated, web-based library and information retrieval systems. Library federated search (or metasearch) engines have become increasingly popular for libraries to improve services. The benefits to the library user are obvious – not having to repeat searches across several different resources, by carrying out a simultaneous search and receiving blended results. Although aspects of this kind of shared searching has existed for some time (especially with Z39.50 catalogue searching), the explosion of online content and the rise of Google as the dominant web-based search tool has made the development of this kind of searching more important than ever.

Within the world of computer technologists, these terms have meanings that differentiate one technology from another. When referenced for library automation systems, these terms imply the ability to search multiple databases through a system's interface. Federated searching in this sense primarily utilizes the Z39.50 protocol in order to search local and remote databases. Paul Miller, in his 1999 article about Z39.50, states, "[federated searching] is designed to enable communication between computer systems such as those used to manage library catalogues." Some vendors are working at adding XML (eXtensible Markup Language) to Z39.50 in order to take advantage of existing Web clients, protocols, and tools. Dorman (2003) explains, in easy-to-understand language, the work being done in this area. As it is a technology in its infancy, library media specialists and technology coordinators should see rapid improvements to federated searching as it exists today.

3. PURPOSE OF FEDERATED SEARCH TECHNOLOGY

Federated search helps users find resources across library collections. Federated search applications excel at finding scientific, technical, and legal documents whether they live in free public sites or in subscription sites. This makes federated search a vital technology for students and professional researchers. For this reason, many libraries and corporate research departments provide federated search applications to their students and staff. The user does not need to know of the existence of particular databases, nor does he/she need to know how each individual search interface works. In the basic search mode, federated search provides a single search box offering a Google-like experience.

In recent years, libraries of all types have been spending an increasing portion of their budgets on electronic resources. These resources provide access to a rich body of information via an array of disparate packages: multidisciplinary databases, subject-specific databases, journal packages from major publishers, individual electronic journal subscriptions, electronic books, and online reference works. To address the growing complexity of online research, many libraries have implemented federated search products. Federated search provides a single search interface that allows users to search multiple online resources simultaneously—subscription databases, library catalogs, and other electronic resources—with one query, that returns one list of results.

4. DISCOVERY TOOLS

Web search engine approach, wherein discovery services maintain a database of structured and standardized metadata obtained directly from the publishers with link to respective full-text databases. The Meaning of "Discovery" as per Dictionary.com is to see, get knowledge of, learn of, find, or find out; gain sight or knowledge of (something previously unseen or unknown). According to Eddie Clarke, resource discovery in libraries means the process of identifying and accessing the information relevant to the user. As defined by Andrew Nagy, a "Resource Discovery" system implies the discovery of resources that might be unknown or new to the user. It may be noted that the scope of the library collection has been widened from resources available in the library to the resources available on web. As such, discovery tools available in conventional environment have to be reoriented and repurposed not only to include conventional content but also the contents that are available on the web.

A discovery tool is often referred to as a stand-alone OPAC, a discovery layer, a discovery layer interface, an OPAC replacement, or the next generation catalog (NGC). Unlike the front end of an integrated library system or ILS OPAC, a discovery tool is defined as a third party component whose purpose is to "provide search and discovery functionality and may include features such as relevance ranking, spell checking, tagging, enhanced content, search facets". Discovery tools should not be confused with federated search products. The former "promise to provide a single interface to multiple resources based on using a centralized consolidated index to provide faster and better search results", while the latter search remotely, rely on connectors, and provide "only partial and limited solutions". In addition, a federated search tool usually requires user logon and works in a protected environment, while a discovery layer is open to the public. A federated search tool is dedicated to finding articles across a number of subscribed databases and as such is not within the scope of this paper. Libraries are disappointed with commercial ILS OPACs. Developed as a part of an integrated library system, they have remained relatively static over the years and have not evolved in pace with the discovery and search tools now commonplace at commercial sites such as Amazon. Most of them cannot and will never be able to provide advanced functionalities in order to meet current expectations. It is more practical for vendors and developers to field new OPAC systems that run alongside the older ones than to attempt to alter the proprietary code of ILS OPACs. Most current ILS OPACs do not offer the features of these standalone, next generation catalogs.

Until recently, libraries could do nothing about their outdated OPAC. Proprietary ILS OPACs offered only limited customization. Today, libraries using some of the ILS OPACS can add patches and a limited number of functional improvements by acquiring both free and commercially available plug-ins or add-on modules, but this solution will not completely transform an old OPAC into a next generation catalog. Additionally, libraries may adopt a "Web OPAC wrapper" solution to embed their existing OPAC within another user interface layer. The current trend some libraries seem to favor is to simply abandon their current OPAC in favor of one of the new standalone, next-generation discovery tools.

5. FEDERATED SEARCH & NEXT GENERATION LIBRARY CATALOGUE

The biggest advantage of Search engines over the federated search is the speed with which it retrieves the results. The reason behind the first retrieval is that the search engines search the indexes instead of the databases. To overcome this alternate approach for federated searching is the harvesting service or maintaining a centralized index of relevant sources of information with a normalized metadata schema. OAI-PMH and METS are major standards for harvesting of metadata. Open Archives Initiative Protocol for Metadata Harvesting (OAI-PMH) provides a mechanism for repository interoperability. Using OAI-PMH, the service providers can make request to the repositories to harvest metadata. This is mostly used by the repositories and some e-journals providers also expose their content using it. Similar to OAI-PMH in purpose and function, METS supports XML-encoded metadata harvesting, but unlike OAI-PMH, METS can harvest both metadata and object. The foremost product in Web Scale Discovery is the Worldcat Local followed by Summon from Serials solution and later on other competitors in library software & services like, EBSCO Discovery Service, Primo Central from ExLibris have launched their products.

5.1. EBSCO Discovery Services

EBSCO Discovery Service™ (EDS) launched in early 2010 provides web-scale discovery through creating a unified, customized index of an institution's information resources, and an easy, yet powerful means of accessing all of that content from a single search box. It is offered as a hosted service and required user authentication for searching the index. Later it released a guest mode with limited search capabilities for unauthorized users. The EDS content include metadata from Journal & magazines, index of all the EBSCO host databases that the library subscribes to, other databases that library subscribes like Alexander Street Press, LexisNexis, Cambridge Unviersity Press, IEEE, Ingenta, Springer, Elsevier, Taylor & Francis, Wiley, NewsBank, Readex etc. It also indexes institutional archives/repositories, catalogue records of the library and other additional contents like book jacket images, book records, entertainment records, annotations, family keys, subject headings, demand information, awards, review citations, etc. It also indexes content from various open access repositories like DOAJ, OAISTER, and arXiv.org.

The EDS platform users the institute's link resolver for resolution to the full-text of the articles that library subscribes. The search results are ranked by relevancy based on the frequency of term in document, which field the term appears in and the uniqueness of a word in the overall index. The relevancy is also determined based on the currency, number of times cited, type of document etc. The EDS provides an administrative interface for customization of the interface as per the library requirement, like layout, colour, logo of the library etc. The interface also provides faceted navigation, search refinement, export to various citation formats, printing, e-mailing and adding to cart, RSS feeds, spelling suggestions, option for adding widgets and also a mobile interface for searching on mobile devices.

5.2. ExLibris Primo Central

The ExLibris Primo which is its next generation discovery layer product by Ex Libris provides a common platform to search the local library collections, such as bibliographic records, digital collection materials, and items within institutional repositories by harvesting the contents into a single index. It also provides an option to configure for searching remote resources and provide results blended with local library collection.

The Primo Central Index is just an extension of the Primo discovery layer and the discoverylayer is offered as a hosted service as well as local installation and the Central index is hosted and maintained by the Ex Libris Group in a cloud environment. The search results in Primo are listed by relevance which calculated based on Primo's proprietary relevancy- ranking algorithm that includes but is not limited to factors such as term frequency, field weighting, number of times a record has been accessed, and currency. It also considers peer-review status of journal articles for giving relevance.

5.3. Google Scholar

While libraries and other scholarly resources are trying to provide Google-like single user interface to encourage usage of resources subscribed by the libraries, Google has started providing scholarly content to the users through the Google Scholar that searches through scholarly full-text databases, theses, books, pre-prints and other grey literature available in open access. Since Google Scholar searches through a precompiled database of scholarly content, users get the results within a fraction of seconds. Google uses its link analysis algorithms for relevance ranking of the results. Recognizing potential and perception of the new generation users, several publishers have signed agreement with Google to supply metadata of their scholarly resources including books and journals to Google for enabling better discovery and usage of their resources through Google Scholar. With integration of online databases and online books in Google books programme with other information resources, Google Scholar provides almost 100% discovery of the resources. However, discovery of resources is only half of the process and the users have to return to the library / library catalogue to gain access to resources in full-text found through search engines like Google Scholar. This is where; libraries need to position themselves as a critical part of the information-seeking process. Search engines may enable users to discover information resources, but it is the library that provides the "last mile" service, enabling users to gain access to full-text resources. To minimize the intermediate interface of library OPACs or any other gateways, Google Scholar has come up with its Library linking programme that provides direct full-text linking to the library resources through the OpenURL resolver. However, there are a number of apprehensions regarding Google scholar, its scope, coverage, and accuracy of the content, completeness of the data, focus on specific disciplines and the lack of control over it, which is perhaps the most important concern of all.

5.4. Serial Solutions Summon

The Summon™ by Serial Solutions, which is one of the early entrants in the library web-scale discovery services, with its general release in the mid 2009. It is offered as a hosted software-as-a service solution providing the Summon service and index. The items in Summon include library catalog records, e-journal articles, databases, newspaper articles, e-books, dissertations, institutional repositories, conference proceedings, grey literature, cited references, reports, digital library, etc. It has made agreements with major content providers and aggregators like ProQuest, LexisNexis Academic and Gale. The academic publishers include Springer, IEEE, Emerald, Ingentaconnect, Sage,

Taylor & Francis and ScienceDirect freedom collection. It also includes content from Web of Science and ABC-CLIO. The index also covers content from many open access repositories which include DOAJ, Hindawi Publishing, arXiv.org e-Prints, and the HathiTrust materials. The index is updated through an automated process and the content providers provide the content on a regular basis varied on the content publication, like daily for a newspaper and on monthly basis for a monthly journal.

One of the interesting things is that it is open to all on the web and does not require any user authentication for searching as in case of most federated search solutions. It works with the library's link resolver to guide the user to the relevant content subscribed by the library. By default the users get search results for the content accessible in the library which includes the subscribed content of the library and the local holding available in the catalogue of the library. The search results can also be expanded to include all the content from the Summon index. The search results are sorted by relevance ranking based on various parameters like peer-reviewed journal articles, citation count of the articles from Web of Science, current-ness of the article and relevance ranking algorithms from different index fields.

5.5. WorldCat Local

WorldCat Local is most easily thought of as a localized version of WorldCat.org. The Library Technology reports defines as the WorldCat Local as the first product in the field of Web-scale discovery products. In 2009, it entered into partnerships with various providers to include substantially greater amounts of article-level content into its centralized index. The service is provided in two versions, Worldcat Local and WorldCat Local "quick start". For the libraries with subscription to WorldCat Catalogue and FirstSearch, the service is provided free of costs. The WorldCat Local does not require authentication for searching through the database and the local libraries have to configure the authentication level of the users, whether to authenticate at the point of search or at the time of retrieval of full-text. The WorldCat Local interface is presently provided in six languages and gives options to the users to refinement of search results based on facets, export of records into various citation formats, RSS feeds for searches, spelling suggestions etc. It gives social networking features like sharing search results on facebook, Delicious and many other social networking websites. It also provides option to for visibility of books in Google Books search.

6. ADVANTAGES OF FEDERATED SEARCHES

There are certain advantages of using Federated Searches. Federated search is affordable, proven discovery technology. In a number of situations, federated search has been linked with the discovery layer to provide a more unified user experience. Federated search tools present the user with a single, simple interface, often very similar to what a user would find in Web search engines eliminating the visit to various databases with varied interfaces. The federated search tools give an option for the libraries to group various resources to provide a customized subject specific search to the users. It redirects the users directly to the native source searched for accessing the resource. Following are some of the other advantages using Federated Searches :

i. Federated searches qualify the authenticity of the information. For example, anyone can write a report on a topic and post it on the Internet. That does not mean that information was checked or accuracy. By using this new add-on feature to the school's library's automation system, students can better ensure the information they use for their research is accurate. With a federated search engine, the information has been checked and verified by educators and professionals.

ii. It is difficult for most students to choose appropriate, relevant sites from hundreds of thousands of hits. Using a federated search engine can be a huge time saver for researchers. Instead of needing to search many sources, one at a time, the federated search engine performs the many searches on the user's behalf.

iii. Targeted searches are usually filtered for quality. Federated search engines show their value best in environments in which the quality of results matters, such as libraries, corporate research environments, and the federal government. In the case of the federal government, the constituents of the government benefit greatly from such applications. A major difference between a federated search engine and a standard search engine like Google is that the client who contracts for the federated search service selects the sources to search. In almost every case, the sources will be authoritative. Google, on the other hand, has very minimal criteria for source selection.

iv. The federated search includes books and other materials that already may exist in the school library. Thus, the federated search engine acts as a helpful librarian does, directing users to excellent quality.

v. With federated searches, not as many results come up with a specific search related to their topic compared to the abundance of unrelated results with Google. In addition to filling out forms and combining documents from multiple sources, another important benefit of federated search engines is that they search content in real time. Real time data is crucial for researchers who are searching for up-to-the-minute content or for content that changes frequently. As soon as the content owner updates their source, the information is available to the searcher on the very next query.

7. ISSUES WITH THE FEDERATED SEARCHES

Following are some of the issues with the Federated Searches :

i. Federated Searches cannot cover all online library resources. The goal of one-stop shopping cannot be achieved completely by any federated search.

ii. It may not make sense to add to a federated search menu the very specialized databases that most general users would not be interested in, or the databases that require special software.

iii. Many libraries have databases on a pay-per-search basis, and libraries normally do not want them to be searched by a federated search for budgetary reasons.

iv. Some databases have a limited number of concurrent users, and if these databases are included in a federated search, the limited seat(s) is/are taken immediately whenever someone logs into the federated search, and no other users can use these databases. Libraries normally do not want to include databases with a very limited number of concurrent users in the federated search.

v. Some databases work with one federated search product but do not work with the other. If databases require a login, they will not work with the federated search.

vi. The biggest constraint of conventional real-time federated search engines is the time it takes to fetch search results from multiple resources it searches in comparison to search engines like Google and Yahoo. Since federated search engines send the search query to different databases and fetch results in a real-time environment, the speed with which search results are delivered depends upon the response time taken by multiple databases being searched. At times, a few databases from amongst the databases being searched are too slow to respond, as such the user get timeout message or zero hits for those databases causing frustration in users. As the federated search solutions are mostly provided on-campus networks, for off-campus users the searching becomes much slower as the users have to pass through authentication procedures of the library. Besides, with increase in number of subscribed databases in bigger institutions, time taken in executing a search through federated search interfaces increases dramatically.

vii. The coverage of the resources is another limitation of the federated search it searches, inability of inclusion of some of the databases, such as SciFinder Scholar, that require specialized interface. Besides, there are issues with the ability of these interfaces to merge, de-duplicate and rank retrieved search results appropriately.

viii. Verification, authentication, and certification can be difficult for the federated search vendor. Since federated search engines don't hold the data locally, meaning the engines perform the search and send the results back, the federated search engine must be able to access multiple, password-protected databases behind the scenes, all at one time, and show users their results in one easy-toread interface. The challenge for federated search vendors is to ensure that only licensed users can access databases in an appropriate manner, as specified by their license. This may require a library or a corporation to set up multiple areas where only certain licensed users can access a federated search.

ix. The number of different cookies a subscription database uses makes the authentication process either a simple or complex procedure. All the user needs to provide is the ID, password, and files to be searched for each subscription database. The federated search engine will handle the rest of the authentication procedure. However, the initial setup process can take a number of hours to a number of days, depending on the complexity and number of subscriptions.

x. Most of the federated search vendors allow clients to create their own "look and feel" for the search interface and results pages. However, if you do not have the staff resources, they will often allow a more static look where little decision making on your part needs to be done.

8. CONCLUSION

Federated search technology is an integral component of an Information Portal, which provides the interface to diverse information resources. With growing number and variety of electronic resources available in the market, libraries are required to look for search and discovery tools that provide seamless and coherent access to all resources that a library subscribes to as well as those that can be accessed through open access channels. Individual end users will benefit from federated search technology. This blends e-journals, subscription databases, electronic print collections, other digital repositories, and the Internet. Federated searching reduces the time it takes to search and usually displays results in a common format. Most complete federated search solutions support multiple search protocols. Typically they offer integrated OpenURL resolution, spell checking, saved searches, alerts, de-duping, and single click access to the native interface.

The very problem of the libraries, the discovery of resources by the users has changed with changing library resources and the library user perspective. When the generation Y, who are more web-savvy and referred the web search engines as a replacement to the libraries, the federated search solutions have once provided the library to give a single search box to the users to come back to the library for access to the scholarly and authentic information sources. But it lack with the coverage of the content of the resources. But the success of discovery product always lies in the coverage of the content which the library subscribes. With the web-scale discovery tools which provides an integrated discovery for all the resources available in library, whether directly held by the library subscribed e-content, or print material in form of catalogue, or other information sources like repository, ETDs held in the library or other openly available contents. The users who always assume the search box on library webpage for searching everything might be right now with this new technology.

REFERENCES

1. Burke, J. (2010). Discovery versus disintermediation: the new reality driven by today's end-user. VALA 2010. Available: *http://www.vala.org.au/vala2010-proceedings/vala2010session-1-burke* . (Last accessed 30th Jan. 2014).
2. Chen, Xiaotian. (2006). MetaLib, WebFeat, and Google: The strengths and weaknesses of federated search engines compared with Google. 30 (4) p.422-423
3. Clarke, Eddie. (2010). Resource Discovery Tools Guide and Evaluation. Available: http:// *www.staffs.ac.uk/COSE/DICE/ResDisToolsandEval.pdf* . (Last accessed 30th Jan. 2014).
4. EBSCO Discovery Service™ (EDS). Available: *http://www.ebscohost.com/discovery/edsabout.* (Last accessed 30th Jan. 2014).
5. EDS Content - EBSCO Discovery Service™ (EDS). Available: *http://www.ebscohost.com/discovery/eds-content.* (Last accessed 30th Jan. 2014).

6. Ex Libris the bridge to knowledge. Available at *http://www.exlibrisgroup.com/category/PrimoOverview.* (Last accessed 30th Jan. 2014).
7. Gibson, Ian., Goddard, Lisa and Gordon, Shannon. (2009). One box to search them all Implementing federated search at an academic library. Library Hi Tech. 27 (1), pp. 118-133.
8. *http://en.wikipedia.org/wiki/Federated_search* (Last accessed 30th Jan. 2014).
9. Mercun, Tanja, and Maja, Dumer. (2008). New Generation of Catalogues for the New Generation of Users: A Comparison of Six Library Catalogues. Program: Electronic Library and Information Systems 42.3. pp. 243-61.
10. Morgan, E. L. (2009). Web-scale discovery indexes and "next generation" library catalogs. Available: *http://infomotions.com/musings/web-scale/* . (Last accessed 30th Jan. 2014).
11. Nagy, Andrew. (2009). A Conversation With Karen Schneider: VuFind and Summon.Available:*http://www.wils.wisc.edu/events/wworld09/sessions/anagy.pdf.* (Last accessed 30th Jan. 2014).
12. Open Archives Initiative Protocol for Metadata Harvesting. Available: *http://www.openarchives.org/pmh/c* . (Last accessed 30th Jan. 2014).
13. Pomerantz, J. (2006). Google Scholar and 100% Availability of Information. Information Technology and Libraries, 25(1), 52-56.
14. Sadeh, Tamar. (May 31-June 4, 2005). Google Scholar Versace Metasearch Systems.Available: *http://elag2005.web.cern.ch/elag2005/media/workshop8.pdf.* (Last accessed 30th Jan. 2014).
15. Summon™ Content & Coverage. Available:*http://www.serialssolutions.com/ summoncontent-and-coverage/* (Last accessed 30th Jan. 2014).
16. Vaughan, Jason. (2011). Ebsco Discovery Services. Library Technology Reports. 47(1). pp. 30-38.
17. Vaughan, Jason. (2011). Ex Libris Primo Central. Library Technology Reports. 47(1). pp. 39-47.
18. Vaughan, Jason. (2011). OCLC WorldCat Local. Library Technology Reports. 47(1). pp. 1221.

19. Vaughan, Jason. (2011). Serials Solutions Summon. Library Technology Reports. 47(1). pp. 22-29.

20. Wisniewski, J. (2010). Web Scale Discovery: The Future's So Bright, I Gotta WearShades.Available:*http://findarticles.com/p/articles/mi_hb3328/is_201007/ai_n54716433/*. (Last accessed 30th Jan. 2014).

21. WorldCat® Local. Available: *http://www.oclc.org/worldcatlocal/* . (Last accessed 30th Jan. 2014).

22. Yang, Sharon Q. and Wagner, Kurt. (2010). Evaluating and comparing discovery tools: how close are we towards next generation catalog?. Library Hi Tech. 28 (4), pp.690-709.

13

Use of Information Technology in Public Libraries

1. INTRODUCTION

Information Technology (IT) is a dynamic and unending resource. It plays a significant role in education, research and development. Use of modern technology has assumed greater relevance in the context of fourth law of library science 'Save the time of the user' wherein Dr. S.R. Ranganathan had underlined the need for internal efficiency of the library. The new technology which today is available is just a new tool to produce, store and distribute information. It also makes the communication more effective and rapid. That is why we should call it now days ICT (Information and Communication Technology) and not only IT, Information Technology. As means of communication this new technology is comparable with the book. Thus, recent computer and telecommunication technologies have highly revolutionized the field of library and information services, facilitating collection, storage, organization, processing analysis, presentation, communication and dissemination of data more quickly and in greater volume than ever before.

2. INFORMATION TECHNOLOGY AND ITS NEED

Information technology simplifies the coming together of the disciplines of electronic, computer hardware and software, communication (in particular telecommunications), artificial intelligence and human machine interface. UNESCO has defined information technology as

"The Scientific, technological and engineering disciplines and the management techniques used in information handling and current interaction with men and machines and associated social, economic and cultural matters."

It acts as one of the major tools to shape our society and our institutions- particularly our libraries as one of the most important influences in education, culture and society. Information technology, through the melding of computer technology with communications, digital imaging and full-motion video and sound, can be a powerful ally to improve education and thus improving skills for gainful employment. Cut, in order to do this, libraries and librarians will have to change. If the right changes are made by libraries of every persuasion, there would be a good information technologies. These systems would become major information delivery systems to a wide variety of societal segments.

The term 'Information Technology' is widely used in U.K, U.S.A and India. 'Telematics' is used for the same in France and 'Informatics' is widely used in Russia and other socialist countries.

Libraries are using Information Technology to automatic the technical services, to provide efficient reference and information services. IT helps the growth and development of libraries in different directions. According to *P.A. Cochrance* some of the use of IT to the libraries are follows: -

- To increase efficiency.
- Ultimately may save/ generate money
- Eliminates some uninteresting and repetitive work.
- Helps to increase the range of services offered.
- Helps to avoid duplication of efforts with in a library and between libraries in a network.
- To facilitates co-operation and the formation of library network.

According to - *ALA Glossary*, - 'Information Technology is the application of Computers and other technologies to the acquisition, organization, storage, retrieval and dissemination of information'. Information Technology is electronic technologies used for collecting, storing, processing and communicating information. IT brought in many services to libraries to speed up their activities. These includes: telecommunication technology, telex, videotex, teletex, e-mail, CD-Rom technology, Internet, Library Network networks, online retrieval services. The advance in technology will continue to improve the effectiveness of the libraries.

The rapid and exponential growth of information has made it necessary for librarians and information scientists to employ new techniques to cope with the massive proliferation of literature in all subject fields. Research in the science and social sciences has led to high productivity in document publication. To bring this case amount of information under bibliographic control and to render it useful and accessible to potential users is a great task. The information is valuable only if its is retrieved timely and cost effective. The scientific application of knowledge has necessitated to keep abreast of the latest information and makes necessary to keep interaction with working in advanced and frontier areas. So, in this age of information explosion/overload, keeping track of information resource and managing the same are the key to achievement and success.

Acquisition, organization, delivery and storage of information have always been the main tasks of any real library. Emerging new technologies offer new ways of handling these tasks.

3. INFORMATION TECHNOLOGY AND PUBLIC LIBRARIES

The UNESCO Public Library Manifesto 1994 considered - 'The public libraries as a living force for education, culture and information, and as an essential agent for the fostering of peace and spiritual welfare through the minds of man and women'.

Public libraries have to play a triple role in this modern age. They have to identify the information needs of the society and this has to be done at all levels. The publications which the public needs have to be procured and provided to those who need them. The public libraries have to modernise their facilities using Information Technology so that they can render better services to their users. The information is increasing in volume every day at various levels and on various subjects. Hence computerization is very much needed in public libraries especially to offer new services to the users, to provide efficient and accurate services, control the rapid growth of information, facilitate cooperation and manage increased work load.

According to *M. Vijaykumar* following are some of the important impact of Information Technology on libraries:

- IT application improves the quality of library services.
- IT improves the efficiency of the library.
- IT uses to enhance the knowledge and experience
- IT makes integration within the organizations.
- IT applications use essential to improve the Communication facilities.

- IT application are helpful to obtain the right information at the right time in the right place at the right cost.
- IT applications improve the studies of library.
- IT application takes over the traditional way of information handling in the library.
- IT helps in effective resource sharing and networking.
- IT application allows more control over the library.
- Utilization of IT applications makes the library more stable.
- IT helps to attract the library users.

4. ADVANTAGES OF INFORMATION TECHNOLOGY TO LIBRARY USERS

The use of IT in libraries has tremendously increased, because it provides enhanced user satisfaction, cost effectiveness, faster and simpler programmes, rapid response and easier operational procedures. IT provides numerous benefits and advantages to library users. According to *F. Henderson* some of the advantage are as follows: -

- Provides increased flexibly.
- Provides speedy and easy access to information.
- Provides remote access to the users.
- Provides information flexible to be used by any individual according to requirement.
- Provides more up to date information.
- Provides access to unlimited information from different sources.
- Facilitates the reforming and combining of data from different sources.

5. BARRIERS OF INFORMATION TECHNOLOGY IN PUBLIC LIBRARIES

It is estimated that a large number of library professionals are still not even aware of the use of information technology in public libraries. To implement Information Technology in the public libraries for providing the effective and efficient services to the users, following may be some of the barriers :

- Lack of long-term approach to computerization,
- Lack of professional recognition by the library authorities,
- Lack of sufficient trained specialized manpower to use the computers and library softwares,
- Sometimes library staff members are not interested in IT adoption in the libraries,
- Lack of technical skills to develop local library in house database,
- The high cost involved, especially, for accessing the remote database,
- Installation of computers in libraries is still considered as a costly affair,
- Some time library staff members are not interested in learning information technology application in the public library due to poor salary,
- Lack of information technology knowledge and interest on the part of users.

6. CONCLUSION

Most of the public library in India do not have computers and the librarian working in the libraries in general, are not conversant with the application of computers in libraries. Public libraries are facing the challenging task of satisfying the increasingly complex and diverse information need of the users. Public library can use today a wide variety of technology options that exist now. Fruitful result can, however, be obtained only when we make the best use of the technologies.

REFERENCES

1. Banerjee, K. Utpal (1992). Information Technology for a Common Man. New Delhi : Computer Society of India.
2. Cochrance, P.A. (1992). Information Technology in libraries and Ranganathan's five laws of Library Science, *LIBRI, V.42*, pp. 235-241.
3. Haravu, L. J.L.(1993). Library automation and networking in India : An overview of recent developments. *Annals of Library Science and Documentation, V.40(1) , pp.* 32-40.
4. Henderson, F (1992). Relationship with users of IT in special libraries, edited by Margarate Britting. London : Rontledge, p. 98-106
5. Kannappanvar, B.U. and Vijaykumar, M. (2001). Use of Information Technology in Agricultural university libraries of Karnataka : A comparative study. *DESIDOC Bulletin of Information Technology, V.21(1).* pp.21-26.
6. Kumar, P.S.G.(1991). Computers and University Libraries in India. *In,* Outstanding Studies in University Librarianship, Ed. by Sood S.P. and Sharma, C.L. Jaipur : RBSA Publishers, p.176-186
7. Kumbar, M. (1996). Use of Information Technology in library sciences. *Herald of Library Science V.35(1-2),* January-April pp.17-23.

14

Networking and Resource Sharing in Library and Information Centres

1. INTRODUCTION

Library Resource Sharing is an essential appendage to effective library services. No library can have all the books which may be in demand by its clientele, neither it is possible for a library to meet such smaller libraries. Resource Sharing has a long and noble tradition, but in recent times, resource sharing has become a central focus of interest to the libraries. On the other hand it leads to the information scientists and a direction for future development.

Library resource sharing is a partnership where several libraries share one or more of their functions, for example, acquisitions, processing, storage and delivery of services. Each member has something useful to share, is willing to share and a plan exists to accomplish this Major goal of resource sharing is to augment the local holdings by providing access to collections of other libraries. Libraries have always been under tremendous pressure to share their resources. Inflation, almost static or dwindling library budgets, information explosion and escalating prices of publications have all contributed towards this situation. No library, however richly endowed in resources, is in a position to meet all the requirements of its users from its collections alone. What can libraries hope to share? These can be categorized into mainly two types materials and services and procedures. Resource sharing of materials includes cooperative acquisitions, which requires access to the catalogue, on-order and in-process information of participating libraries, inter-library loan, which mainly involves finding the location of the required document, verifying its availability and physical transfer; and sharing of common storage for less used material. Resource sharing of services and procedures includes; bibliographic access to holdings catalogues for cataloguing and classification.

How do we measure in library resource sharing is successful? Two main criteria are speed and cost of resource sharing. Resource sharing procedures must occur with sufficient speed so that the client has the desired material in hand well before the need has evaporated. Cost should be less or at least equal to the cost of purchasing the same material for the local collection. Several key requirements need to be met for successful resource sharing. These include availability of appropriate communication, technology and delivery systems, formal agreement among the participating libraries for implementing cooperation (in terms of acquisition policy, sharing of materials, bibliographic control, loan period, renewals etc.) and strong management and governing mechanism. More importantly, as it has been repeatedly demonstrated, successful resource sharing has to do more with behavior modification than technology. In the pre-Internet years, resource sharing mainly dealt with technical processing (e.g. shared cataloguing) and inter-library loan. Less dominant were resources sharing for acquisitions and storage. Printed and card-based union catalogues were not uncommon Library automation and computerization of union catalogues was carried out on main frames using proprietary software, communication protocols and user interfaces. Towards the later part of 1980's and early 1990's many resource-sharing networks distributed their union catalogues on CD-ROMs to the participating libraries. With the availability of the Internet, librarians quickly realised that they need not spend their efforts and resource to develop proprietary networking solutions. Internet and Web technologies have been effectively used in resource sharing efforts with several additional benefits. Key advantage is that the Internet can be used as the carrier network by all member libraries of a resource-sharing network. They just need to have good Internet connectivity. The common users interface provided by the Web browsers enable integration of access to shared resources (e.g. union catalogues) and also to local library collections and services. Integration of messaging and file transfer protocols in the Web enable easy support for inter- library loan and cataloguing efforts. Since Internet offers platform independent protocols and public domain tools, development of new applications and services and value addition to existing services becomes quite easy.

A library collects information pertaining to different subjects and events. Information is available in the form of books, journals as well as modern packages like films, tapes, disks and other computer files in the library.Earlier, a library was considered to be a place where books and written documents were kept. But now it selects, collects, stores and distributes the documents or information to meet the demands of users. Library provides on loan the latest and rare documents required by the students, scholars, professionals and others.

Resource sharing is now a common term in the information parlor, which denotes apportioning of library materials, manpower and money. The term, resource sharing was developed out of the age old concept of library co-operation. This was made possible by the advent of tele-communication technology.

The formation of new subjects by splitting or cohesion and the high rate of growth of published materials lead to a situation where, no library in this land is self sufficient to serve all its users. It has to depend on external sources for the information requirements of its users, particularly in the field of science and technology. In its most positive aspects, resource sharing entails reciprocity, implying a partnership in which each member has something useful to contribute to others and which is ease to willing and able to make available when needed. Resource Sharing maximizes the use of materials and minimizes the cost.

Resources can be shared by libraries and information centers in many ways like acquisition, cataloguing, classification, storage and preservation. Preparation of Union Catalogues, Current Awareness Service (CAS), Abstracting, Indexing, Selective Dissemination of Information (SDI), Bibliographic Services, Current Contents Services, Inter-library Loan Service, etc.

At present time when the Computer and Communication Technology has gained the central role in all walks of life and drastically changed the way people think, communicate and do business, it became indispensable to computerize and network the libraries just to survive. The entrance of these new technologies in library premises rescheduled the functioning of libraries and provided a new dynamic shape to the age-old concept of resource sharing. Lack of effective and efficient technology has been a major hurdle for resource sharing in India, besides the lack of co-operation among the participating libraries. Now by the use of Information Technology, it became possible to create co-operative functional resource sharing library-network which is the—most important requirement at this juncture where the economic consideration, information explosion and specialized users needs are forcing the libraries to co-operate.

2. CHARACTERISTICS OF A NETWORKED LIBRARY RESOURCE SHARING SYSTEM

Following are some of the characteristics of a Networked Library Resource Sharing System :

2.1. Speed

The resource sharing system should be speedy. It should be based on the latest means of data communication systems and programs. It should be able to judge tile timeliness and urgency of user's information need, because the use of information depends on whether it is provided at right time or not.

2.2. Accuracy

The resource sharing system should be able to locate and provide the accurate information. It should be reliable and error free.

2.3. Cost/fee

The information provided should be cost effective. It must be less than the original cost of document.

2.4. Staff courtesy / knowledge / assistance

The professionals engaged in the resource sharing activities should be knowledgeable and prompt to handle the queries. The speed and accuracy of manual resource sharing system depends on these professionals.

2.5. Consistency of service and reliability

It must be consistent and reliable. The resource sharing activity should be adopted as an important component of present library system.

2.6. Communication (provision for status reports

The union catalogues should be able to provide the status report regarding availability of the document.

2.7. Delivery and request options

The resource center should be able to deliver the needed document! Information through required mode of delivery i.e. via e-mail, fax, courier or by post.

2.8. Self-service options

It will be easy to use, so that user can handle it without any problem.

3. NEED OF RESOURCE SHARING

No single library can incorporate all the information required. As information is a social wealth which knows no boundaries hence it is obvious and makes sense to share what others generate in their own countries. The need for sharing the resources has been necessitated by other resources too, such as information; inadequate space in the libraries; proliferation of subjects; influence of technological advances on the communication; collection, storage and dissemination of information; UBC (Universal Bibliographical Control) and growth of library network.

In the opinion of *Bhattacharya* "There are certain activities traditionally associated with libraries-such as acquisition, serial control, cataloguing and circulation. Today the 'Library Automation' is used extensively to refer primarily to the use of computers to perform some of the traditional library activities such as those mentioned above. Conventionally, some related fields-such as information retrieval, automatic indexing and abstracting automatic textual analysis, etc. do not fall within the preview of library automation or computerization in libraries".

- The explosive growth of all forms of literature.
- Increasing demands on information.
- Inflation in the cost of materials.
- Increasing cost of information.
- To help less equipped libraries.
- To share the valuable resources
- To boost the distance learning and more.

Today, yet the roles played by telecommunication technology and the reprography technology are of great significance because of the extent of support they offer to computerization in libraries and it is the effective source by which the resource sharing can be carried out.

- Impossible to be self sufficient to meet increasing demands of its users from own collection and it is not desirable to develop huge collections anticipating future demands.
- To reduce the cataloguing cost.

4. REQUIREMENTS FOR RESOURCE SHARING

Following are the requirements for resource sharing:

- There is need for electronic catalogue and indexes for print resources available in the library.
- The technology or equipment to link libraries and to make users aware of collection of owns library and other libraries.
- Standardized software hardware and databases.
- Operating policies on the type of information and archives which users can access (books, journals, reports, catalogue, indexes, publications etc.)
- Training of own staff members and end users for effective use of electronic media.

5. PROBLEMS AND PROSPECTS OF RESOURCE SHARING

If we look at the usefulness and strength of resource sharing among libraries, we find a very enthusiastic picture, but on the other hand when we analyze the ground realities of the present situation of our academic institutions and libraries, it seems worthless to talk about these services and activities. We have to accept the realities to reform them as soon as possible, because the growth of IT will not leave space to do anything after some years. The major problems to be eliminated before may be identified as:

- The required technology and needed organizational structures are not presently available to provide the required level of service, comparable to that available today without the concept of resource sharing.
- Resource sharing will affect the economics of publishing by increasing unit pricing as library orders decline. A substantial part of the prospective saving from resource sharing will thus evaporate.
- A large library may become more and more of a lender (rather than borrower) of materials, causing resource sharing to be a drain rather than a source of additional material.
- If all libraries turn to resource sharing, none will acquire sufficiently and have books to lend;

In spite of these lacunae we have started to move in the direction. At this stage it is essential to develop some sort arrangements to stream line the movement.

Followings might be recognized the prerequisites of a functional resource sharing system.

5.1. Common code of conduct

Apart from similar software and networking protocols the participating libraries have to evolve a common code of conduct regarding the collection development (Acquisition Policy) and resource sharing. There are several basic agreements among libraries that must be developed to operate a co-operative resource-sharing network. It includes.

a) Agreement to share currently owned materials will protocols, limitations and priorities.

b) Financial agreement, to safeguard tl1e individual recognition of the libraries.

c) Agreement on acquisition policies to ensure consistent development of holdings and to avoid redundancy.

d) Agreement of record keeping to streamline and to ensure the smooth operations from acquisition to borrowing and lending.

5.2. Infrastructure

It includes the installation of required hardware and software to create bibliographical, contents pages, abstracts and full text electronic databases and their networking. It is also needed to create various union catalogues and to develop efficient software to handle on-line users query. In addition to these a sound document delivery system could also be needed to send the required information to its end user. In nut shelter library wants to be part of resource sharing network should have to have computers, printers, modem, scanners, database creation and networking software of specified standards, telephone connectivity, network access, photocopying machines, fax and a reliable postal system. The cost effectiveness of resource sharing is diminished at the present, because it has to run in parallel with other running system.

5.3. Legal copyright and photo copying laws

It is noticeable that the resource sharing activities should violate the copyright and photocopying laws.

5.4. Trained manpower

The establishment and organization of resource sharing activities are not possible without the competent, trained and dedicated manpower. At present it is needed to organize massive education and training programs via different modes to fulfill the required need.

5.5. Aware users

The user is the most important component of any system. Keeping in view this fact, participating libraries and nodal agency simultaneously have to develop and organize user education / orientation programs in changing context, to ensure the maximum utilizations of the resource sharing activities.

In addition to above said prerequisites it is essential to adopt some professional ethics to run the system smoothly. There is no procedure to impose this idea on participating libraries, but it is worth noticeable that in future only those libraries will survive whose professionals will be guided by this idea.

7. STEPS FOR SUCCESSFUL RESOURCE SHARING

The following steps are necessary for successful resource sharing:

- There should be legislation or agreement for sharing of resources.
- Communication facilities and postal facilities should be at reduced rate.
- All library facilities should be made available to the readers of participating institutions.
- A data bank may be established at one center selected by mutual consultation.
- Draft the data collection format on mutual basis.
- Subject specialization will facilitate resource sharing.

- Update the Union catalogues with computer.
- Compile and maintain union catalogue at local, regional, state and national level.
- Interlibrary loan form should be uniform.
- Provide reprographic facilities including microfilming and microfiche facilities.

8. FUTURE OF RESOURCE SHARING

The library profession has never been exposed so much in the past to the changing information scenario as it has been exposed now. In this age of information explosion the technology has progressively replaced the old methods of information collection, storage and retrieval. Today the walls of a library are giving way to electronic environment to establish link with information and virtual libraries that are getting shopped on the Internet. Each individual library is acting as a place for storage and service to the users. This advance scenario is not firmly entrenched in India yet, although a number of libraries have The Internet connections and access to other electronic resources. This scene is going to grow rapidly in the 21st century.

9. CONCLUSION

Though India was relegated to backwaters as Third world countries, but much before entering the new millennium, India proved itself as one of the front ranking countries from this world which possess advanced information technology undertake library activities of high repute. But, unfortunately while comparing with other highly developed countries of the world and in particular, in the domain of resource sharing and the employment of computers in library services, what one finds is that India haven't made a big leap in this directions.

In case of libraries the automation and networking should be considered as the first and second dimensions and the resource sharing as third dimension, which opens the doors of services where imagination is the only limit. We have started to move in this direction due to this various library networks have emerged. Now it depends on librarians and libraries whether they want to survive or not, if yes they must adopt IT and actively participate in the resource sharing movements, because the concept of libraries in physical boundaries is going to be part of history.

REFERENCES

1. Abraham, Alexander(1982). Resource Sharing in university libraries : a myth or reality. *In,* G. Devaranja and others, *eds.* Resource department in academic libraries. New Delhi:Ess Ess Pub. p. 77-84.
2. Chandel, A.S. and Saraf, Veena (1986). Planning in Library Resource Sharing. Lucknow : Print House, 237p.
3. Kaul, H K.(1999). Library Resource Sharing and Networks. New Delhi : Virgo Publications, 336 p.
4. Kaul, H.K.(1999). Library Resource Sharing and Networks, New Delhi:Virgo Pub. p.284.
5. Kent, Allen and Galwin, Thomas J. *eds.*(1977) Library Resource Sharing. New York:Marcel Dakker, p.18.
6. Khurshid, Anis(1982). Resource Sharing of University Libraries in Pakistan. *Herald of Library Science, 21(3-4),* 169-182pp.
7. Rajan, A.C.(1992) Resource Sharing among College libraries in Kerala. *In,* G. Devarajan and others, *eds.* Resource department in academic libraries. New Delhi :Ess Ess Pub. p. 77-84.
8. Shukla, H.K.(1996). Studies in Librarianship. Jaipur: RBSA. p.152-3.
9. Vishwanathan, T.(1991). Information Management in Library and Information Centres in India. *IASLIC Bulletin, 36 (4),* 139 -144pp.
10. Chopra, H.R.(1991) Resource Sharing in university libraries in India. *In,* S.P. Sood and C.L. Sharma, *eds.* Outstanding Studies in University Librarianship. Jaipur:RBSA. p.146-51.
11. Kent, Allen *ed.*(1974).Resource Sharing in Libraries : why, how, when, next action steps. New York:Marcel Dekkar, 224 p.

15

Industry-Institution Relationship

1. INTRODUCTION

Exploration of resources for the benefit of mankind was the most important contribution of man to the society. With the rapid changes in global and nation scenario especially due to manifold increase in population and fast developments in information technology, industrialization, urbanization the needs of people have gone beyond expectations-unable to be created by the limited resources. That created the need for exploitation of more and more resources and also sharing the resources among different sets of people like of people from institutions, industries, government etc. There are many such type of symbiotic resource sharing process going on around the world. Once such process in industry-institution relationship. Industry-institution relationship is the means by which institutions and colleges achieve the dual purpose of making technical education relevant to the needs of the country and solving the problems of the industry by utilizing the resources of the institution. The need for such Relationship is recognized worldwide and is very strong in the developed countries. It is generally regarded as a major contributor to the rapid advancement of technology. Recent surveys of the alumni of engineering Institutions and industries indicate that there is both recognition of the weakness of that Relationship as well as a realization that such relationship is very desirable.

In this document the author tried to examine the various issues related to this relationship in the context of technical institutions and industries in India. The word 'Institution' has been used throughout for universities, colleges or institutions offering technical education in India. While the word 'Industry' has been used throughout, the scope of the relationship should not be limited to industries in the R & D laboratories of the government. Technical manpower is trained at three levels in India-certificate, the diploma and degree levels. The certificate courses are offered by it is and at the school level organization. Diploma courses are offered by polytechnic colleges. At the degree level there are universities, institutions of national importance like IITs and engineering colleges which are either affiliated to some universities or are authorized to give their own degrees. Generally these institution employ teachers of a high caliber. The involvement in R & D work of the teachers will keep the technical education at the forefronts of technology and enable the graduates to cope with the fast changing technology. Simultaneously and involvement of industrial workers in the institution will keep them abreast with the theoretical knowledge. Thus among the relationship there can be mutual sharing of resources.

2. NEED OF THE POLICY STATEMENT

Due to Liberalization and globalization of economy the need for the industry and institution relationship has been provided in various policy statements of the Government in India. During the preparation of National Policy of Education (NPE), 1986 a document entitled "Challenge of Education–A Policy Perspective" was prepared by the Ministry of Education which had noted that "The Relationship between industry and technical institution which is so essential for ensuring relevant quality and cost effectiveness remains weak despite exhortations for closer cooperation."

Subsequently NPE adopted by the parliament in 1986 emphasized the relationship by stating that "The curricula of technical and management programmes will be targeted on current as well as the projected need of the industry or the user system. Active relationship between technical or management institution and industry will be promoted in programme planning and implementation and exchange of personnel, training facilities and resources, research and consultancy and other areas of mutual interest...Networking will have to be established between technical education and industry, R & D organizations, programmes of rural and community development and with others of education with complementary characteristics.

The draft policy statement suggests various steps for encouraging Relationship which include:

- Funding national laboratories and academic institution through online projects;
- Promoting university-industry relationship by diverse means, including adjunct positions for necessary personnel;
- Encouraging the use of national laboratory facilities and their enterprises by industrial units by way of contract research project appropriately paid by the industry;
- Developing the consortium approach involving academic institutions, national laboratories, including those of the mission agencies namely the Department of Atomic Energy, Space and Defence Research and Development wherever feasible, and the user industry for global oriented programmes and product development;

- Facilitating easy mobility of personnel among universities, industry (including R & D institutions connected with industry) and the ministries; and
- Assigning multi-dimensional responsibility to the existing technical institutions.

In the industrial and postindustrial societies, technology and total expert knowledge of business, is one of the most crucial factors determining the wealth of a nation. To compete in the world market, Indian industry/ business has to be up-to-up with the latest technology/ information to provide a cutting edge. The quantum jump in technological development information technology and break-through can be best achieved through a synergetic relationship with mutual benefits between academic and research community on the one hand and the industry/ business on the other. The small and medium enterprises (SMEs) in particular would be most benefited by Relationship with the academia for upgradation of existing technology, evaluation and adaptation of new technology, information problems solving R & D in the areas of products, process and quality.

Mechanism of university–industry relationship

There are various ways in which Industry and Institutions can help each other.

The Institutions can

i. Set up Liaison cells that have adequate databases on facilities, equipment and expertise, available in the universities as also on the type and important teachings of industries in the region;
ii. Provide material characterization, testing and certification facilities;
iii. Keep the industry informed about new discoveries developments and innovative scientific work being undertaken;
iv. Undertake research related to technology transfer

in collaboration with R and D units in industry;

v. Help small and medium–scale industries to induct and maintain modern technology;

vi. Provide training programs for technicians, scientists and engineers; and

vii. Develop specialized continuing education programs for updating skill and knowledge.

The Industries can

i. Assist teaching programs by giving endowments.

ii. Support research programs , especially those on applied research;

iii. Make available sophisticated and costly equipment to the institutions for research.

iv. Provide financial assistance for the development of the university;

v. Assist in the development of curricula and syllabi.

vi. Participating in teaching programs.

3. RESOURCE SHARING

Institutes need to be enterprising winners rather than a hope loser. The proverbs "Unity is strength" and "Small is beautiful" clearly indicate that there is no substitute for team work. Team work means sharing resources among the team members. These members share goals culture, learning, effort and information. Including this type of mindset among staff can turn the institute into a global winner. The AICTE approaches encouraging multi-use of facilities represent this resource sharing culture.

Networking of institute and industry based on the principles of small group working has also been proposed. The capital investment done in building, equipment, library, etc., can most effectively be utilized by avoiding duplication of resources. University structure can be suitably divided into certain zones or units say three districts make one unit. The colleges in this unit can allocate their available resources in terms of, say, funds and library, and develop a few areas of excellence in their institutions. In short the concept of resources sharing can advantageously be used in all the five areas mentioned earlier namely, goals, culture learning, efforts and information.

Information Support Services

The activities under this heading would be to provide access to the national and international information and database relevant to the requirement of specific organization and their personnel.

Providing information support to the industries/ business houses establishing networks and links with international/national database like DIALOG and INSDOC can be undertaken through various forms such as : periodic status reports, occasional monographs and bibliographic/abstracting services and newsletter.

Computer networking facility and vast library resources at university would provide the necessary inputs for these services.

4. INDUSTRY-INSTITUTION RELATIONSHIP-METHODOLOGY

Industry-institution relationship can take place at different levels, each having its own mechanism, objectives and difficulties. It has become very clean that the institutions and industries need each other and cannot survive without each other, through the liaisoning agency was missing. A liaisoning agency was created in the form of the industry-institute Relationship cells. I.I.I. cells have been created under World Bank aid project and have started functioning but they are facing initial teething troubles. The objectives have been identified but the methodology to be adopted for achieving these objectives has to be more clearly pronounced and defined.

The objectives and the proposed methodology are being summarized as under :

4.1. Implant training of teachers

Technology is changing at a fast pace and every teacher should compulsorily be sent every five years to an industrial unit for three months of implant training. Industrial units, where the desired training facilities are available should be identified. For this purpose industries associations may also be involved as a liaisoning agent.

4.2. Implant training of students

This training can be arranged during vacations. In case of sand alone which courses, one or two full semesters can be devoted for this purpose. Industry alongwith the number of seats available in each should be identified. For this purpose the assistance of industries association should invariably be sought. Students should also be encouraged to put in their own efforts in achieving the aforesaid objectives.

4.3. Curriculum development with the assistance of industry

The industrial units should help by projecting their requirement and then by extending their co-operation in designing of the curricula, which should be reviewed every five years. Technically qualified personnel from the industry should be drawn for revision of curricula.

4.4. Delivering the expert lectures by institutional faculty

Teachers from institution can go to the industrial units and share their knowledge and similarly professionals from the industry can come to the institution and work as visiting faculty to impact their experiences. It is a known fact that the industry personnel have good practical knowledge but they may lack the expertise on delivering lectures.

4.5. Project assignment to the institutional faculty

This is the most difficult and tedious of all the objectives but most fruitful in terms of establishing and maintaining the relationship between industry and institution.

Industries Association should be asked to identify a list of industrial projects, which they would desire the institution to undertake. The project should be very clear in terms of its objectives and time schedule that industry is prepared to offer.

4.6. Imparting continuing education to the industry personnel

Industries have a large number of people who would like to enhance their knowledge, so that they can equip themselves for advancement in their career. In many cases, industries may also be interested in imparting continuing education to their employees, so that they can perform better.

4.7. Advancement of campus interviews

Industries should be requested through their Association, to come to the institution for conducting Campus interviews of students' candidates for the purpose of filling vacancies in their organization. Campus interviews can be arranged in which experts from the concerned industrial unit and the relevant faculty of the institution can jointly interview the student candidates.

5. THE BENEFITS OF RELATIONSHIP

It goes without saying that the training of technical manpower in the Country must be consistent with the needs of the country, both in terms of numbers and the nature of work that the graduating students are expected to undertake. The vast majority of the graduates of the engineering colleges and diploma holders of polytechnics are employed by industry, both in the private sector and the public sector. Relatively smaller numbers go into enterpreneurship: Some fiend employment in government organizations; only a few go in for higher education. The academic institutions can render various problems of the industry. These may relate to research and development or manpower training through continuing education. The excellent faculty and other facilities available at the educational institution can be a source of great benefit to industry. The institutions can provide testing facilities as well as advice and guidance in matters relating to state-of-the art technologies and technology forcasting.

Relationship also benefits the institutions greatly in that the faculty develop firsthand knowledge of the state of our industry and their problems and this information gets passed on to the students. Another aspect of importance to industry is that the faculties have free access to information on the state of the development of technology in another countries. This helps them to get information, which will otherwise be considered confidential for being commercially emploitable.

Another very important aspect of information, which has become much more urgent in view of the resource crunch is the financial inputs which can be provided by industry to educational institutions. This can be in several forms such as–

i. Sponsored research funds with the built-in provision for overhead costs added to the cost of the proposal;

ii. Continuing education programmes which can be tailor-made for the needs of industry and which are funded generously by industry to provide substantial financial inputs;

iii. Creation of faculty positions in the forms of chairs, and

iv. Contributions to buildings for specific research laboratories, campus recruitment facilities, etc.

10. PROMOTION OF INDUSTRY-INSTITUTION RELATION

During the last decade the institutes of technology and some leading universities in India have formulated programs to promote relationship between institution and industry. A few illustrative examples are given below:

- The Indian Institute of technology, A center for Industrial Consultancy and Sponsored Research (IC&SR) was established at IIT, Madras 1973. Industries from all sectors utilize the expertise and facilities of the Institute through institutional consultancy, retainer consultancy and research based industrial consultancy.
- The IIT, Delhi established a foundation for Innovation and Technology Transfer (FIIT). It acts as an interface between the institute and industry. It offers programs of product development; technology initiatives, technology advancement and human resource development.
- The BITS, Pilani has created a number of institutionalized linkages in the industry. Under its practice school programme students of the first-degree engineering attend two courses in the industry. PS-I is for two months after the second year and PS- II for 5-1/2 months for the final year. In addition it has developed Distance Learning Programmes, for persons working in industry leading to B.E/ M.E., M. Phil. and Ph.D. Degree. It has also developed a technology innovation center where persons from industry can spend time to update their knowledge.
- The Tiruchi R.E.C, Triuchi set up in 1989 by the Department of Sciences and Technology the Triuchi R.E.C. Science and Technology Enterpreneurship Park (TREC-STEP) conducts one month long entrepreneurial development programmes. It has

64 industries units set up by those who have undergone training at TREC-STEP. It also imparts training to youth under the Mass Employment Generation Programme.

- The University of Poona, Pune has established in 1986, a University of Poona Sciences, Technology and Enterpreneurship Park (UPSTEP) to provide test and certification facilities and consultancy services. It has made significant achievements in high power silicon devices, surface modification and microprocessor-based instrumentation.

11. CONCLUSION

Summing up, we may say, that the industry and institution can be brought face to face so that there is prefect understanding of the complementary roles and functions of each so that can work in perfect harmony and can serve country and the people with better manpower, particularly in the new environment of open market, globalization and privatization.

The recommendation made by ISTE Section of the Karnataka State on 1-3-94 which have been made on the basis of a brain-storming workshop, wherein 20 industrial representatives and 30 institution participated. At the end of these recommendations, the committee has made a 12 point action plan for Industry-Institute partnership to be acted upon by various agencies – the DTEs, the Institutions, the CII, the AICTE etc. etc., But the question remains who will bring together all these on to a platform, make them talk, act and work in coordination on a continuous basis? The answer to this is technical university established by the leading organization of the industry – the CII to which all Engineering Colleges are affiliated and the University will be a mechanism to ensure continuous dialogue, deliberations, discussions and conclusions so as to ensure perfect meeting between the supply of engineering personnel and the fast changing needs of industry.

REFERENCES

1. Mathur, Naresh C.(1995). Institution–Industry Relationship. *Journal of Higher Education, 17 (3)* .pp. 341-350.
2. IIT Preview committee Report, *MHRD,* 1986.
3. Singh, Nirmal (1995). Types of Consultancies and Consultancy Rules *In,* Liaison Cells for University–Industry Relationship in Liaison Cells for University–Industry Relationship. New Delhi : Association of Indian Universities, pp.21-31.
4. Mathur, Naresh C.(1995). *Op. Cit.* pp. 341-350.
5. Khalsa, R.S. (1995). Industry-Institute Relationship methodology. *Indian Journal of Technical Education. Vol.18 (3).* pp. 55-58.
6. Power, K.B. (1995). Need for Establishing Liaison Cells. *In,* Universities for University–Industry Relationship in Liaison Cells for University–Industry Relationship. New Delhi : Association of Indian Universities, pp.13-15.
7. Waghodkhar, P.H.(1999). Industry–Institute partnership : Impact on globalization, *India Journal of Technical Education, Vol.22 (3).* pp-63-67.
8. Singh, Nirmal (1995). *Op. Cit.* pp. 21-31.
9. Natrajan, R (1993). Factors promoting Industry–Institute symbiosis. *India Journal of Technical Education, Vol.16.* pp. 1-5.
10. Venketeswaran, S.(1994). A working partnership in between University Research Labs and Industries, *CURIE.* pp. 6-12.
11. Ganpathi, V.(1994). University-Industry Research Relationship, *Research Management, Vol.21.* pp. 35-41.

16

Marketing of Library Products and Services

1. INTRODUCTION

Developments in information technology especially Internet and communication media have challenged the concept of traditional library. In the era of networking technology, one can access information on any segment of knowledge across the world within no time from his desktop. This easy access and instantaneous availability of information has crossed the geographical as well as time barrier and influenced the reading habits of peoples. This has brought library services into the field of competitive market. Libraries have been using various aspects of marketing such as publicity and public relations for many years. But, the use of marketing as a technique is of recent origin and is gaining interest among the library professionals. It has been observed that the application of marketing techniques to library services has considered library as a service organization and not as a business house.

For many years marketing techniques that were considered to be belonging to profit motivated business and industrial products have been extended to the non-profit organisations.*Kotlar* and *Levitt* are the pioneers to extend the application of marketing techniques to non-profit organisations. *Walters* states that the marketing approach to services means that we talk to our customers and that we develop specific products and services as a direct result of listening to their needs.

Marketing is an exchange process whereby two or more individuals or groups exchange goods or services for items of value. In library or information centre one of these individuals is almost always a Librarian. The other individuals include students, faculty or in case of special libraries, fellow employees.

2. USE OF MARKETING CONCEPT IN LIBRARY AND INFORMATION CENTRES

Library is a social and service institution providing information to its users/members. Its traditional functions include selection, acquisition, storage, processing, circulation and reference. Over a period of time, due to change in the nature of demands by the clients, libraries have expanded their functions to include documentation, document delivery system and some other services also. *Seetharama* indicates, the activities and services/products of library &information centres –

a. Selection and collection of documents - includes bibliographies and current awareness services,

b. Indexing and abstracting-deals with Indexed bibliographies, abstracting bulletins, custom searches,

c. Extraction–digest extracts, descriptive reviews/ state-of-the-art report/trend report, compilation,

d. Evaluation -Critical Review of area

   Critical compilation of data

   Criteria for experimentation

   Recommendations

Solution of problems

Correction of data

Prediction of properties,

e. Other activities - Translation, editing, publishing and reprographic services.

Dr. S.R. Ranganathan's concept of *Five Laws of Library Science* had the Marketing concept at their core.

A focus on customer needs (2nd Law) and wants through saving of time (4th Law) is clearly emphasized in these laws as far back as 1931. Also, third law relates to finding a reader, probably implying that the library should reach out to the customers. A closer examination indicates that modifications are needed in interpretation of the laws. *Firstly,* the definition of a customer, only as a reader, needs to be widened to include the purpose of reading and ways of using the information. *Secondly,* in today's the process of use of information (like use of computers/ information technology) to process the information obtained from the library & information centers) may give rise to totally new needs and wants (like getting information through INTERNET, E-Mail, which can be used directly on the personal computer. *Thirdly,* given the usefulness of information in one library and information centres to customers in different and far off locations, reaching out to customers is becoming far more important.

Thus, though customer focus has long been advocated in the Library profession, it may be refined to suit the current context of the market. The size of the unit and activities undertaken govern the design of the organization of a library and information centres into various sanctions like acquisition, circulation, etc. It may be noted that many functions in a library and information centres are back office functions. Only limited members of staff interact with customer and that too, mostly at the interactive of the customers themselves. There would be hardly any library and information centre where there is a function /section called *Marketing.*

3. WHY MARKETING IN LIBRARY AND INFORMATION CENTRES ?

Today, marketing is extremely important for any business sector. It is not only essential for manufacturing industries but also service industries, government enterprises and non-profit organizations like libraries. It has also become an essential component of library services to enable them to survive and succeed. Due to the rapid change in the scenario of constraints, resources, cost inflation and competition, marketing has become necessary for libraries. Increasing competition of commercial information suppliers has compelled libraries to consider implementing marketing techniques and their services. Library marketing consists of users and library activities and exchange relationship created through the creation, distribution, promotion and pricing. The concept of tools of marketing have often been successfully applied by the premier institutions like DESIDOC, INSDOC, IITs and other special libraries in India but, still many libraries are failure in satisfying their users requirement and many resources are underutilized.

The marketing known as the four P's is a combination of interrelated elements that help organisation meet their objectives. These elements are basic and controllable as the marketer is able to make change. The four P's are- Product (or Service), Pricing, Place and Promotion. So, marketing is not just advertising but its about identifying, anticipating, supplying and meeting customer needs and demands.

3.1. Product- The first 'P'

Product/service is the first 'P' in the marketing. Generally, a product/service is defined as "a task or activity performed for a buyer, an intangible that can not be handled or examined before purchase". Basically, the term 'Product' refers to core product, tangible or physical product and augmented. The product includes all services, ideas, and goods made available through the library. These products might include materials and services provided by the staff of library and information centres. So, information is the core product of library and information centers. The product also includes physical objects places, organisations and persons. The ways in which Libraries organize access points between the client and information are also the products of the library. So, cataloguing, classification, circulation, indexing, OPACs, indexing, abstracting, translation services, SDI, CAS, CD-ROM searching, Internet searching etc. all are the library products. We can again categories the products into three categories –

i. Physical information products/services – it includes books, periodicals, etc.

ii. Electronic information products/services – it includes CD-ROMs, DVD, etc.

iii. Online information products/services – it includes OPACs, LAN, Internet, etc.

Components of Library Product

The product consists of the following three component:

a. Marketing support services : No product is complete without support services, although its level may vary depending on the nature of the product /service. For example - supplying the full text of an article which is requested on the perusal of an index of articles (Product) could be a major support service to the product.

b. Benefits that the product/service offers : Each of the elements mentioned, as a product attribute, by itself, does not have meaning unless it either individually or collectively, offers some benefits to the customer.

c. Attributes that the product/service contains: Following are some examples of attributes of products/ services in the library-

f. number of journals covered,

g. contents of the journal,

h. extensiveness and exhaustiveness of the information provided,

i. number of books that a client can borrow, etc.

Need of Planning of Library Product

The need for product planning arises due to the following reasons :

- Changes in technology
- Change in customer needs and expectations
- Change in customer profile
- Change in competition of products.

3.2. Pricing of the product – The second 'P'

Pricing is one of the important decision areas of marketing. It is a dynamic and multi-stage process. Pricing decisions are based on the demand and supply of goods on one hand and cost of production and benefits gained by the consumers on the other. So, pricing policy of library and information products and services mainly depends on the goals and objectives of organization. Pricing decisions mainly depends on the cost of production, the demand for the product and the price of other competitors.

Price helps in appropriately positioning the product/ service/information center in the mind of the target segments vis–a–vis the competition. Price goes by many names like function, fee, rent, fare, toll, interest, dues, salary, wages or commission depending on what is being exchanged. The price services includes direct and indirect costs needed to produce the product.

Pricing policy depends on the policy of library. In public library, all numbers, all the offered services are available free of cost, but some of those services in academic libraries and special libraries are priced. In, special library environment, price relates to what the client must given to use the product/services offered. Here price refers to the overall cost of the library in relation to the value of the service. In library & information centers, the following are fee based services – Online database search, translation service, document delivery, training and consultation, downloaded information, presentation of abstracting and indexing services, etc.

These may be some methods of fixing the price of service/product-

- Unit price method
- Per item method
- Fixed price method

3.3. Publicity and Distribution of Product-The third 'P'

Publicity and distribution is one of the important aspects. After identifying the products' cost and price the next step is to connect each product with the target clients. Getting products to the consumer at the right place and at the right time. With commercial products, this will be a thing like using different channels of distribution to get the goods from the manufacturer to the consumer.

One has to make the clientele aware of the services provided. Traditional means of making people aware of services such as newsletters or the distribution of bookmarks. These method are by no means obsolete, but libraries of the future may take advantage of mailing lists programs, demonstrations in people's offices through the use of portable computers like circuit-rider libraries, demonstrations for passer-bys in well populated place throughout institutions. So library and information centre should provide different channels of distribution which will meet the clients need in term of both time and convenience. Placing the library products in the market. Place is a complex endeavor. The library should take care of the quality, time priority, convenience, and format of presentation.

3.4. Promotion and Communication – The fourth 'P'

Promotion is the fourth 'P' in marketing, after Product, Price and Place i.e. the communication activity. Promotion of an information product is the essential communication process to let the prospective client become not only aware of the new products and services available, but also to motivated them to actually subscribe to the products/ services. So, 'Promotion is an essential fourth piller among the four 'Ps' of marketing. So, it is essential to communicate the community and the potential clients that the library has identified their needs and has developed cost effective products. This can be done by effective public relations, publicity and advertising. In other words, we can say that the things that everyone instantly links with marketing are - advertising, promotions, offers and public relations.

The basic purposes of promotion are to –

- To motivate the users/clients to actually buy the product or services,
- To attract and heed the attention of clients,
- To make the clients aware of the product or services.

Dr. T. Viswanathan, formerly Director of INSDOC, New Delhi, gave an example of what would happen if promotion is not done. Speaking at a workshop on 'Marketing of Information products and services' held at IIM, Ahmedabad, and the International Development Research Centre, Canada in Feb. 1994, he pointed out that INSDOC'S CAPS (Contents, Abstracts and Photocopies Services) could only achieve 50 per cent of the target in the first two years.

Following are the promotional tools for library & information product- Internet, CAS, LAN/WAN SDI, Newsletter, Telephonic service, Oral presentation, Seminars, Exhibitions, Reprography, Posters and presentation, Acquisition list, Celebration of library week, Library display, News release, etc.

The promotion of all services are carried out mainly through personal contacts and publication of brochures etc. The success of these services is measured by the benefit accrued to the recipients. Library & information centers have to motivate the promotion not only to their clients, but also to their own staff and to the managers of their sponsoring organizations by providing special incentives gifts, bonus etc. Without the internal bridges, the external promotion activity will not be effective.

4. BARRIERS OF MARKETING

It's not an easy work to implement the four 'Ps' for the success of the marketing of library and information products as it has been observed that there are four barriers for adoption of the marketing approach which are :

4.1. Attitude

Information professionals like many other professionals, have been inward looking-happy with satisfying a limited clientele, that too when asked for, and happy with jealously guarding their importance.

4.2. Structure

The staff which comes into contact with the public or clients are the counter clerks and less frequently, the reference librarians and the librarian. As a result, there is no staff to reach out and capture the point of view of the client. To introduce any such layer would be resisted from the existing staff and the turf holders. Moreover, the library and information centres are a part of a large organisation which does not follow the, marketing approach as well. Also traditionally security of the job, common to public institution and lack of involvement of professionals in the management of the library or information centre, in developing countries is conductive to a no charge syndrome.

4.3. System

Library and information centres, so far, have been more storage security, and audit conscious. They do not allow the client or clientele point of view inside the system. Guarding or protecting the information is more important than utilizing it for the satisfaction of its clientele.

4.4. Environment

The culture, especially in the developing countries, still believes that information should be free and sought by client's themselves. Marketing and payment for variety of service, like education or information, is considered infra-dig both for the giver and taker.

5. CONCLUSION

Library and information centres, as the resource centres play an important role in providing the information products to its clientele. Library and information managers need to give adequate attention to market the services in order to survive in the highly competitive world. It helps us to focus the efforts, ensures the use of resources and make a professional impact. Every organisation needs marketing, whether they intend on making a profit or not. Library and information services need it too, either to increase the use of their service and materials or for social benefit. The main function of marketing is generation of product, pricing of product, distribution of product and promotion of product. Library and information managers of today can make their library more responsive and service oriented towards users needs and wants to improve their users satisfaction with library. The final and the most important thing in marketing of library and information products and services is that it should be supplies at the right time and place, otherwise it would be of no value to the user. It will loose its utility.

REFERENCES

1. Linda M.G.(1995). "Trends in marketing Services". *Library Trends, Vol.* 43(3). p. 498.
2. Helton, Rae and Esrock, Stuart(1998). "Positioning and marketing Academic Libraries to Students". *Marketing Library Services,* Vol.12(3)
3. De Saez, E. E. (1993). Marketing concept for libraries and information services. London :Library Association, pp.3.
4. Kinnear, Thomas C. and Bernhardt, Kenneth L. (1986). Principles of marketing. Glenview III : Scott, foreman, pp.40-50.
5. Zikmund, William G.(1996). Marketing. 5th ed. Minneapolis : West Publishing. p.170.
6. Jain, Abhinandan K. and others(1996). Marketing of information product and services, IIM, Ahmedabad. New Delhi : McGraw-Hill, 462p.
7. Ranganathan, S.R.(1931). Five Laws of Library Science. Madras : Madras Library Association.
8. Smith, D. (1995). Practice as a marketing tools : four case studies. *Library Trends,* Vol. 43(3).

10 Broady-Preston, Judith (2000). Strategic marketing for library and information services. London : Library Association Publication.

11 Kolter, Philip (1994). Marketing management: analysis, planning, implementation, and control. New Delhi : Prentice-Hall.

17

Physical Stock Verification of Library Collection

1. INTRODUCTION

In the previous time libraries were considered as being simply a warehouse of books. The books in the libraries were kept locked in almirahs and they were preserved and not issued; consequently the chances of their loss were very rare. As the libraries now provide open access service to make the holdings available to the users, the loss, damage, and misplacement of books is inevitable. To know and replace the lost books, and to maintain balance between various subjects, and to take adequate precautionary measures, it is necessary to do periodical inventory and accounting of the library collection. The term stock verification thus came into existence with regard to libraries. The modern technology has enabled automation and integration of the various processes of libraries and information centres to reduce or avoid human intervention and to increase the efficiency and speed *(Dhiman,* 2000).

2. STOCK VERIFICATION (SV) - THE TERM

The term stock verification is also known as 'stock taking', 'physical verification or checking', 'stock inspection', and inventory taking, etc. Stock verification is largely applicable for ascertaining the position of stores in government and commercial organizations. The term SV refers as being the process of checking as to what is in stock in relation to what it was. The emphasis is being put more on finding which items are missing than on how much is the loss calculated in rupees. It may be an insignificant aspect of librarianship as far as teachers, research scholars and the library experts are concerned.

Shorter Oxford Dictionary defines Stock verification as "Periodical examination, inventorying and valuation of all the stock goods in a shop, warehouse, etc." *(Dhiman, 2000)*.

In the context of libraries, verification of stock is different from the verification of stores in private or government business organizations, so far as the purpose of the job and the difference in the meaning of 'Store' and 'Stock' are concerned. The collection in the libraries contains the various types of information sources.

The library is a public institution and these are subjected to accounting and checking, verification and reporting. The rule 99 in the chapter 8 of General Financial Rules (GFR) read with rule 116 make the difference between 'Store' and 'Library collection' much clearer "The position of library books, etc. is different from the other stores.

3. ADVANTAGES OF STOCK VERIFICATION

The stock verification has some major advantages as mentioned below:

i. Stock verification discloses the position of the loss of documents so that the replacement may be made in case of important document loss.

ii. Stock verification provides adequate account of the percentage of inevitable loss.

iii. Stock verification provides opportunities to weed-out long un-used, very old editions of books from the library.

iv. Stock verification helps in reviewing the precautionary measures already taken in preventing loss or mutilation occurred. It helps in planning the method to provide adequate safeguards to check future losses.

v. Library users can browse entire collection because misplaced books are restored in their proper place and this result in the rectification of stock.

vi. Periodic stock verification leads to the cleaning and dusting of books and thus prevents their deterioration.

vii. Stock verification provides an opportunity to the staff members to acquaint themselves with the holdings of the library which results is the better reference service to the users.

4. FREQUENCY NORMS OF STOCK VERIFICATION

The holdings of the library may be checked at regular intervals. Library should conduct periodic stock verification in order to:

i. have an up-to-date record of library holdings;

ii. have concrete data on rate of loss;

iii. assess strengths and weaknesses in the collection.

Stock verification may be done at the end of the academic year or on a continuous basis throughout the year. Stock verification task should be planned to ensure its completion with the least interruption to the library services. For example, using a continuous inventory system entails closing off only one section of the library to circulation for a limited time while the rest of the library remains open for the users as usual. It may be observed that the size of collection is considered as the only basis for deciding frequency of stock verification in libraries is not sufficient consideration. Size of the library collection can only serve as an indicator of the total work load involved in the operation.

It is desirable but not necessary to conduct stock verification of the entire collection every year; however, stock verification schedule should be established and implemented as per the norms mentioned in the General Financial Rules (GFR).

Libraries of Govt. of India and its other organisations have to do a mandatory physical verification of all their holdings as per the following guidelines *(GFR, 2005):*

"Complete physical verification of books should be done every year in case of libraries having not more than twenty thousand volumes. For libraries having more than twenty thousand volumes and upto fifty thousand volumes, such verification should be done at least once in three years. Sample physical verification at intervals of not more than three years should be done in case of libraries having more than fifty thousand volumes. In case such verification reveals unusual or unreasonable shortages, complete verification shall be done.

(ii) Loss of five volumes per one thousand volumes of books issued/consulted in a year may be taken as reasonable provided such losses are not attributable to dishonesty or negligence. However, loss of a book of a value exceeding Rs. 1,000/- (Rupees One thousand only) and rare books irrespective of value shall invariably be investigated and appropriate action taken."

So it can be observed that the frequency of stock verification depends upon the size of the stock, the human and material resources available for the exercise.

5. METHODS OF STOCK VERIFICATION

Libraries traditionally perform the periodic stock verification by adopting any one of the methods enumerated as follows:

i. By accession register;

ii. By separate register with accession numbers in consecutive order;

iii. By slips containing accession numbers;

iv. By numerical counting of documents on the shelves;

v. By shelf-register cards or shelf-list cards;

vi. By sample stock verification;

vii. By making stock verification as a continuous process; and

viii. By using computers and library management softwares, and other automated methods.

In general, there may be three type of environments for stock verification of documents in the Library:

a. Manual library environments : Without the help of computers, only staff involved.

b. Semi-automated library environments : Partial use of computers.

c. Complete automated library environments : Fully use of computers, Library Management Software, Barcode Technology, etc.

The manual methods are cumbersome, time-consuming, and more staff members are to be involved. Besides chances of errors is very high and sometime's libraries are closed partially, if not fully. As a compelling need, computers replaced the manual methods. But even with computerized stock verification, the accession numbers are to be keyed into the computers. When barcodes are used for this purpose, the data entry is automatic, errorless, and saving in time is ensured.

6. NORMS FOR INEVITABLE LOSSES

Detection of losses may be called as one of the prime objective of stock verification. Norms for deciding inevitable loss may be laid on the size of library collection, and quantum of use of library material. In the case of library, the material can be either used in the form of circulation (check-in and check-out of library documents) or consultation (Reading of documents in the library). Since the library collection is different from the 'Store' and the libraries are service institutions, it is more logical to make the quantum of use the basis. Following are some of the recommendations made by the conferences/ workshops/committees for the inevitable losses of the documents in the libraries:

6.1. Dr. S.R. Rangnathan (1942)

Dr. S.R. Ranganathan in his book entitled "School and college Libraries" published in 1942, stated that, "In an open access, some loss must be expected in spite of the greatest vigilance on the part of the staff." Hence unless there are reasons to suspect foul play or wanton negligence on the part of the staff ,the management must be prepared to write –off some books every year, say about one volume for every 2000 volumes issued for consultation or loan"*(Ranganathan,* 1942).

6.2. Library committee of U.G.C. (1965)

In 1965, University Grants Commission has framed a library committee about "University and College Libraries". Report submitted by this committee states about the inevitable loss of documents as follows(*U.G.C.,* 1965):

"Even the best of safeguard, the most human treatment possible and vigilance of the highest order, there will be some loss. The authorities of a library should be prepared for it. In British libraries, Loss of one volume for and issue of 1000 volume is now, considered tolerable. The fact is that loss due to miscreants will take place even at higher percentage of loss".

The committee also added that, "Loss of 3 books per 500 issued books should be treated as negligible loss."

The Ranganathan committee of UGC forcefully

recommended to write-off an inevitable loss @ 2 for every 1000 books issued in an open access library.

6.3. U.G.C's Workshop from 5th to 7th March of 1979

UGC's Workshop on formulating standards for college libraries was held at Khandala from 5th to 7th March 1979. In this workshop, recommendations about loss of books are as follows :

- In consultation with the heads of department, weeding out of obsolete and unusable library material should be done on a regular basis;
- If missing books are not traced within a period of three years, they should be written off in consultation with library committee;
- Four books per thousand issued should be treated as negligible loss;
- The librarian and the library staff should not be held responsible for the loss of books unless gross negligence is proved.

6.4. Government of India (1981)

The meeting in respect of losses of books in libraries due to open access system and weeding out of books was held in the chamber of special secretary of Govt. Education Dept. on 10th Feb 1981. In this meeting, it was accepted that due to open access system in libraries, there will be some inevitable loss, it is difficult to say that what is the limit of acceptable loss in open access system in a particular library. The Joint Director of College Education Department did however bind in a survey conducted by the department that in college libraries, the quantum of the losses of books varies from 6 to 18 books per 1000 books issued. Keeping in view this, it was resolved to recommend that as a unified policy, 4 books per 1000 issued be treated as inevitable loss in the open access system and this loss should be written-off by the any authority concerned *(Grover,* 1998).

6.5. Resolutions of the Seminar (18th Nov. 2000)

The Seminar on Collection management and loss of books in academic libraries was held on 18th Nov 2000 at Thiruvanathpuram. The resolutions of the seminar includes the following points :

- The practice of holding librarians responsible for the unavoidable loss of books in libraries is a factor that seriously hinders the realization of the basic objectives of the libraries i.e. putting books to the maximum use for the benefit of its members therefore this practice should be discouraged.
- The provision in the General financial Rules of the Govt. of India for treating three books for 1000 books circulated as a reasonable loss as a guideline to be observed by the colleges. However, the fixing of the upper limit of price at Rs. 200/- per book for writing off stipulated in the provision which was made 17 years ago in 1983 has to be altered in view of the steep rise in the cost of books. Considering the present level of book price, it is reasonable to raise the upper limit to Rs. 2000/- and Rs. 1000/- in the case of foreign books and Indian books respectively.
- The responsibility for the loss of books exceeding the norms fixed in the General Financial Rules of the Govt. of India should be made operational only in situations where negligence on the part of the library staff has been established. The such cases, unlike the practice at present in which the chief librarian is made accountable, the entire concerned library staff should be held responsible.

6.6. Norms as per Govt. of India, General Financial Rules (GFR)- 2005

Weeding is as important activity in the selection and acquisition because it helps to keep the collection fresh, alive, current and relevant and therefore academic libraries should realize the importance of weeding policy to keep the library collection alive. Following norms should be adopted for Writing-off lost books as per GFR :

- Rule no. 116(2) (ii): "Loss of three volumes per one thousand volumes issued/consulted in a year may be taken as reasonable provided such loss can not be attributed to dishonesty or negligence on the part of Librarian. Loss of a book of the value exceeding Rs.200 (Rupees Two hundred) and the books of special nature and rarity shall invariably be investigated and consequential action taken. All such losses will however be written-off only by a competent authority. *(GFR, GOI, OM -23, 1984).*"
- "Loss of books up to 5 books per thousand books issued/ consulted can be considered reasonable."

However in an open access library, annual loss of 3 volumes for every 1000 issued should be considered as a normal loss in normal circumstances as recommended by Dr. S.R. Ranganathan. In case of the losses go beyond it, all steps may be taken to find-out reasons thereof and necessary precautions or measures be taken to minimize the loss.

7. PROCESS OF STOCK VERIFICATION

Keeping in view, the above automated stock verification procedure was adopted by the libraries by employing barcode and Library Management Software(LMS) facilities so that stock verification could be performed easily with less manpower. Earlier, manual stocktaking was an exhausting exercise as each and every book's detail had to be manually entered into the system or registers. Now with the introduction of new technology, it is very easy for the library staff to just place a scanner on the barcode; the scanner automatically passes the scanned information to the common database or server. Following process was involved for stock verification of documents in the libraries:

i. Barcode scanners are being used for data capturing - Scanning of barcode label (accession number) of documents.

ii. Putting month and year stamp at the inside back cover to ensure that the document is physically verified.

iii. Returned documents during the stock verification period are also verified before shelving.

iv. Besides, identification of damaged and wornout documents for repair, binding of obsolete volumes, and rearrangement and cleaning can also be done simultaneously.

v. Once the data capturing is over, the verification and generation of report with Library Management Software(LMS) could also be done in a short period of time.

The barcode technology using Library Management Software(LMS) played a significant role in the automated systems in spite of having some limitations of the technology. This technology is an appropriate technology for the management of learning resources and library services.

Stock verification has become easier by using the hand held barcode scanners. The accession numbers in the form of the barcode can be scanned and matched with the document or information resources database. The information about missing resources can be easily accessed. Weeding-out rescurces and updating of records also becomes simpler through this process. This is how barcode technology helps to verify the stock of the library systematically, quickly and accurately.

After generation of stock verification report through Library Management Software(LMS) following steps could be followed :

i. Approval of stock verification report by Competent Authority

ii. Withdrawal of written-off items
iii. Remarks in the accession register
iv. Remarks in the library catalogue/online catalogue
v. Remarks in the shelf-list record
vi. Disposal of damaged documents
vii. Information to the Accounts Section
viii. Information to the Teaching departments/centers
ix. Information to the Book Selection Committee
x. Improving safety arrangements

The Stock verification has been neatly justified and summarized by Smith in following words:

"The desire to give the be best possible library service and the public relation angle so inextricably tried to good service were the most important reasons for taking an inventory... keeping the catalogue an accurate index of the entire book collection was considered of utmost importance in giving good library service. This includes catching books that were improperly catalogued as well as withdrawing catalogue cards for missing books...fruitless searching for books can become more costly in the long run than an inventory would be."

REFERENCES

1. Chandel, A.S. and Walia, R.K.(1993). Computer-Assisted Stock Verification System. *Libri,* 43(2), pp.108-122.
2. Dhiman, A.K.(2000). Stock Verification: Some problems of electronic publications. *DESIDOC Bulletin of Information Technology,* 20(6), pp.3-5.
3. General Financial Rules (GFR), Government of India(2005).
4. Grover, V. K.(1998). Weeding Collection in a University Library: their methods, problems types and solutions. *Indian journal of information Library and Society,* 11 (12), pp.1-7.
5. Hyde James H. (2003). Library collection Management. New Delhi: Dominant Publishers, pp.253-254.
6. Kumber, M.(2000). Stock Verification and loss of books in

college libraries: A survey. *Annals of Library Science Documentation*, 47(2), pp.67-73.

7. Mittal, R. L.(1987). Library Administration: Theory and Practice. 5th ed. P.357-359.
8. Ramakrishna, Reddy K. (1995). Weeding out of documents in libraries: General procedure and guidelines, *CLIS Observer*, XII (3-4), July - Dec. 1995, pp.32-36.
9. Ranganathan, S.R. (1942). School and college libraries. Madras : The Madras Library Association, 432 p.
10. Sridhar, M.S.(1991). Library Stock Verification: A ritual and occupational hazard. *IASLIC Bulletin*, 36(3), pp.103-10.
11. UGC (1965). University and College Libraries containing the report of the library committee of the U.G.C and the proceeding of the seminar on from Publisher to Reader held on March (4-7), 1959, New Delhi : University Grants Commission, pp.46-47.

18

Weeding-out Library Collections

1. INTRODUCTION

Weeding the library's collection is an essential part of a library's collection development and maintenance; it helps to ensure a current, useful collection. It can be a difficult, even painful, process for some but the weeding process is respectful to the library's mission and its service to the users.

Weeding is the process to evaluate each item in the library collection against criteria stated in a collection development policy and discard those items that do not meet the criteria.

Weeding is defined as the practice of discarding excess copies, rarely used books, and materials with incorrect information or no longer relevant to the curriculum or needs of students. Weeding should not be used as a means for withdrawing materials which are of a controversial nature or needing re-evaluation.

Weeding is a problem with many libraries due to rule not permitted the same. American Centre and British Libraries demonstrated in the country how a carefully maintained active collection by weeding-out unwanted as well as less used ones periodically improves the overall functioning and serviceability of the library. Library professionals know the difficulties of maintaining active collection with less/never used titles in the same stack area creating many practical problems in the stack maintenance. The less used books in the stacks encourage users who want to misplace and hide useful books in such areas.*(Jeevan, 2010)*

2. NECESSITY OF WEEDING?

Weeding is necessary to prevent a library collection from becoming obsolete. At the same time, weeding is necessary because a library has limited physical spacc. It is simply not possible for a library with limited space to collect and to house all print materials.

Weeding-out of materials is absolutely necessary in a library. There are some very good reasons for weeding library collection collections in an academic environment. Keeping the collection current and/or appropriate to the primary needs of the teaching and research in the institution; preservation or conservation purposes; or, to make space on the shelves for more titles. Most academic libraries are not blest with unending space, so space on the shelves becomes a mandate of sizeable proportions.

If we use a public library as a model we find that librarians need to weed out materials that have become obsolete. New scientific findings, medical data etc must be kept current to properly inform the concerned community because there are frequently changing so weeding-out the outdated and replacing with current materials is a duty of the library. In regards to fiction, a library must manage the space of such collections and there are many schools of thought on criteria. The popular way to handle weeding of old fiction this question in a public library is to use circulation data in the weeding process; it is also popular to exclude classics in this endeavor. The following are major established reasons for weeding:

(i) To Improve the Quality of Collection : Careful and regular weeding will enhance the quality and up-to-datedness of the collection, thereby building library users' trust. It has been said that many patrons feel that the experts select library books and the mere fact that the book is in the library lends authority to it. To foster and ensure this reputation, weeding is a necessity. The collection needs to evolve in order to adequately support the curriculum of academic institute.

(ii) To Save Space and Money : Weeded materials no longer cost money for cleaning, binding, mending, extra stacks, extra files, and all the other hidden costs of maintenance and space, none of which are cut by lack of use. Crowded shelves can be avoided. There can be more space for tables and chairs for in-house research, and study.

(iii) To Save Time : Collection weeding will save time for patrons and staff. Crowded shelves, full of ragged books with torn markings, cost time if one is trying to use the collection for research or looking for a particular book or trying to shelve books. An overload of useless books increases all library housekeeping.

(iv) To Make the Library More Appealing : Attractive new books will replace old and unattractive ones as a result of weeding. Weeding-out library materials improve the appearance, appeal and browsability of the collection;

(v) To Provide Feedback on the Collection's Strengths and Weaknesses : Systematic weeding increases staff knowledge of the collection. This can be extremely helpful in collection building practices and to get feedback on the collection's strengths and weaknesses.

3. WEEDING-OUT LIBRARY MATERIALS : GENERAL GUIDELINES

The collection development policy should state the overall purpose for the collection. Weeding is a part of that development and maintenance—removing inaccurate and non-useful books to make space for the newer books. Library policy should address practical issues related to collection development and weeding. Weeding of collection in the libraries should be regular activity every year in order to maintain materials that are still useful and timely. Some of the general guidelines for weeding are as follows:

(i) Last date of circulation : If the material has not been in general use during the past five years (depending on the type of material).

(ii) Physical condition : If the condition is badly worn or excessively dirty, the item may be weeded, and a decision concerning replacement should be made.

(iii) Timeliness : This is one of the most frequent criteria:

(a) out-of-date materials, particularly in the sciences and technology. A rule of thumb is to reconsider almost anything more than three to five years of age,

(b) materials no longer in demand, or that no longer support the curriculum or current community needs

(c) older editions no longer used, and out-dated textbooks, where they are part of the collection.

(iv) Ephemera : Certain subject areas, this type of fad literature should be weeded, particularly when it is found that a title no longer circulates, is no longer timely, or the information seems unreliable.

(v) Duplicates : Where there are duplicates and none seem to be circulating or used, a single copy may be all that is needed. At a later date (one to two years) the single copy should be reconsidered for weeding.

(vi) Reference works should be given special attention in order that all the above criteria be applicable in all of the special areas. Current information in this area is critical.

4. WEEDING-OUT CRITERIA FOR GENERAL/ TEXTBOOKS/REFERENCE COLLECTION

There are several criteria that might be used for weeding-out materials from the Library. CREW (Continuous Revision, Evaluation, and Weeding) method is often used by the libraries, bases the decision on the value of the book, length of time since it was last checked out, and the condition of the book. Length of time since the last checkout is a pretty good predictor for whether or not the book will be checked out again anytime soon; if it hasn't been checked out in five years, there probably is not going to be a stampeded to check it out today or tomorrow!. Based on the available resources / documents following material need weed out from the library:

- Older and superseded editions that contain outdated or inaccurate content.
- Materials, which no longer support the academic curriculum.
- Materials used very rarely and have no potential use.
- If the latest edition of a book is available in the library collection and the book is not heavily used to the issue record slip.
- All old and superseded editions of the book should be withdrawn.
- Textbooks may be weeded out if all of the following conditions are applicable:
    i. They are no longer part of the present curriculum at the Institute;
    ii. Their contents have become obsolete (e.g. computer science books);

   iii. They are old and latest edition is available;
   iv. Consent of the concerned academic departments is obtained;

- All worn-out, mutilated volumes should be withdrawn from the library collection. If necessary, replacement copies may be ordered based on the demand and usefulness of the book.
- All monographs should be considered for withdrawal provided; if they have not been circulated for the last 10 years, but with the consent of the concerned academic departments
- Books/conference proceedings available in both formats (print and CD-ROM) will be retained for 3 years. However, print copies may be withdrawn from the collection after three years and distributed to concerned academic departments through Gift & Exchange.
- Outdated materials e.g. Computer Science older than 5 years (except UNIX, Open VMS, Cobol, Fortran), Science after 10 years except History of Science, Botany and Science, Technology and Applied Science older than 5 years, Library Science after 10 years except for theory and history, Travel books older than 10 years, Health, Medicine, Nutrition and Drugs older than 5 years, Psychology older than 10 years (not including Biography, History of Psychology, and Psychological Theory), Physical Education older than 10 years.
- Books not checked out in more than 10 years.
- Social Sciences need to be weeded heavily.
- Duplicate and multiple copies of directories, guidebooks, yearbooks, etc.
- If indexes/abstracts, catalogs, bibliographies, etc. are available in both formats (print and CDROM) the print copy can be discarded. Those indexes/

abstracts available on the Internet, free of charge, will be considered for withdrawal.

- Materials which are badly worn out, defaced, or otherwise in poor condition should be replaced new copies, if used, or discarded, if not used.
- Atlases older than 10 years
- Incomplete Series (either order the missing volume or delete the set)
- Older volumes of reference publications, particularly serials, such as directories and yearbooks. If online editions of encyclopedias, directories, yearbooks, etc. are available, hardcopies ofprevious editions of these materials shall be weeded out from the library collection.
- All monthly, quarterly, and semiannual statistical handbooks should also be withdrawn, if their yearly cumulative publications are available in the library collection.
- Bibliographies with narrow subject scope.

5. FOLLOWING MATERIAL NEED NOT WEED OUT FROM THE LIBRARY

- Primary sources of Information
- Methodist history and theology unless duplicated or in a new edition
- Regional materials (history, literature, geography, economics, art, music, etc.)
- Classics in each field
- Core materials in each discipline
- Literary classics
- Works deemed to be of historical value by the library professional staff

6. HOW MUCH LIBRARY SHOULD WEED-OUT?

Most of the existing standards mentioned weeding without explaining how to do it or when to do it. They limit their statements to a sort of general agreement that weeding is beneficial and ought to be done.

How much should be weeded ? - It will depend on the library, its collection, and how long it has been since the collection was weeded. However, according to "In Service to Iowa: Public Library Measures of Quality (3rd ed) general guidelines:

"Every item in the library's collection is evaluated for retention, replacement or withdrawal at least every three years to determine its usefulness according to the library's collection development policy. Three percent or more of the collection is withdrawn each year."(Morgan, 2001).

Several standards recommend the creation of written weeding policies without offering further details about how to proceed.

The "Tennessee Minimum standard for Non-Metropolitan Public Libraries" divides their libraries into Six levels, depending upon the population being served. In each level the same statement appears recommending that at least 5 percent of the collection to be weeded out yearly. *(Morgan, 2001).*

7. WEEDING-OUT LIBRARY MATERIAL - INDIAN SCENARIO

In Indian scenario, there is lack regular weeding of unused, destroyed, old version of new copies, copies of books no longer relevant to the curriculum. For this the libraries facing space problem and easy sorting and replacement of documents are hindered. Though some libraries have some selected copies of useless books the librarians have not got any order form the competent authorities for their destruction or removal and these authorities are not giving any such order as there is no definite rules for weeding of library materials. But this miserable condition should not continue if the library is to keep up to date and for this there should be provision for weeding of library materials in a regular basis and there should be some power vested to the principal to write off certain percentage of books every year to cope with the missing books caused by the users.

In India, Public funded libraries have stricter rules for weeding and hence librarians fear to tread on that path often leaving the library with many older and less used books. Some librarian tried to get over this problem by identifying less used title from the active collection and keeping them in a remote stack. Though libraries did it by considering circulation statistics and assessing books normally taken out for reading in the stack rooms by users, senior users have academic ways of explaining why some books used less are of more academic worth. Sometimes these remote stacks are not accessible all times like normal stacks. This end users interest to have all their books of interest in one place make it practically difficult for libraries to proceed with remote stacking of less used collection. Some libraries involved users to identify the titles of less interest without much success. Though difficult to arrive at a consensus by library professional, it is advisable to have a very active stack area for more current and frequently used titles leaving the less used as well as old books to a separate area, which should be done only after convincing the users and library committee of the benefits of such a step. Provision may also be made at the same time for not denying any user access to the less used books in the remote stacks upholding the spirit of five laws of library science. *(Jeevan, 2010).*

8. CONCLUSION

Weeding-out of books should be a regular feature and should be carried out with the approval of the competent authority, at least once in a year. During annual stock taking, weeding-out of collection should also be carried out. Weeding a library is like weeding a garden; one looks over everything and carefully selects those things which need to be removed. In a library, weeding is a shelf-by-shelf and book-by-book review and withdrawal of certain books in a library's collection. Weeding can be either scheduled regularly or irregularly, as the need arises, or can be constantly ongoing.

Today it is more important than ever for libraries to maintain their relevance in the age of instant access, electronic databases. But while our print collections continue to grow, many library collections are drowning in obsolete, unused, and unwanted materials. Most libraries keep up with deselection by weeding systematically all year round, but many of us run into obstacles ranging from dwindling materials budgets to long-term administrators and governing officials reluctant to let go of materials. Others understand the importance of weeding but are reluctant to cull as many items as they should because their budgets won't allow them to replace the weeded materials. But consider this: if your library contains shelves of useless books that are of no interest or use to your patrons, why not just put up wallpaper with a book pattern on it? Chances are it would look better and it would be no less useful than what you already have. The best way to avoid this problem is to weed continually.

The wedding-out and stock verification has been neatly justified and summarized by Smith in following words :

> "The desire to give the be best possible library service and the public relation angle so inextricably tried to good service were the most important reasons for taking an inventory.. . keeping the catalogue an accurate index of the entire book collection was considered of

utmost importance in giving good library service. This includes catching books that were improperly catalogued as well as withdrawing catalogue cards for missing books...fruitless searching for books can become more costly in the long run than an inventory would be."

REFERENCES

1. Brooks, Colette (2002). So many books, so little space. *New York Times,* Oct. 26, 2002, p.9.
2. Grover, V.K.(1998). Weeding Collection in a University Library: their methods, problems types and solutions. *Indian journal of information Library and Society,* 11 (12), pp.1-7.
3. Hyde James H. (2003). Library Collection Management. New delhi ; Dominanat Publishers, pp.253-254.
4. Jeevan, V.K.J.(2010). A Critique on Stock Verification in Libraries. *IASLIC Bulletin,* 55(4), 2010. p. 229-237.
5. Minutes of the Advisory Committee for Library (ACL), 2006.
6. Morgan, Steve (2001). Weeding library collections: library weeding methods. *Journal of Documentation,* v.57, no.4 (July 2001), p.561-564.
7. Ramakrishna, Reddy K. (1995). Weeding-out of documents in libraries: General procedure and guidelines, *CLIS Observer,* XII (3-4), July - Dec. 1995, pp.32-36.
8. Slote, Stanley J.(1989). Weeding library collections: library weeding methods. 3rd ed. Englewood, Colorado : Libraries Unlimited, Inc., p.23.

19

Improving Quality of LIS Education

1. INTRODUCTION

With the rapid changing requirement for information by the users and radical changes in information technology together with its impact on the society have led to the recognizing and rethinking for LIS Education. This paper is an attempt to highlight, how library schools can gear up to take up the challenge of new millennium to prepare right type of professionals. The purpose of professional education is self-defined to prepare individuals for practice a profession. Education is a complex profession. It may refer to formal schooling or to the life long process of learning from experience. Education of the testing level aims at the all round development of the individual mental, moral, social or cultural for adjusting oneself to different working situation. It is expected at this level that the individual learner gains knowledge acquire skills to develop himself to find his place as a worthy member in the profession. For such type of education a planned programme is of vital importance and it is reflected in the curriculum that is designed for this purpose.

2. LIS EDUCATION IN INDIA

LIS Education in India has its tracings to 1911 when the first training course was started in Baroda by W.A. Borden and the birth of full time P.G. Courses dates back 1931 in Madras University, mainly through the efforts of Dr. S. R. Ranganathan. Since then this profession is progressing steadily. Now after Eighty years Library Science Profession is at a crossroad of diversified factors involving management of several different tasks hitherto not handled.Library science education as such came through universities at a slightly later stage. Now it is taught at different universities and training centers, such as :

- Post matriculate Certificate Course.
- Post higher secondary polytechnic course.
- Postgraduate Library and Information Science.
- Post B.L.I.Sc. - Master of Library and Library Science
- M. Phil Programme
- Ph. D Programme
- Associateship offered by INSDOC, New Delhi and DRTC Bangalore.

According to a compilation by *Rawtani* [1] there are 105 Library science schools in India offering BLISC, 85 M.L.I.Sc. or its equivalent, 14 M. Phil. and 51 Ph. D. programmes. While detailed content analysis of LIS syllabi not the objective of this paper , it has been observed that LIS Education in India universities including the open universities gives an impression of diversity in the course curricula of LIS Education.

3. CURRICULA

The syllabus of any course has to be structured within a fixed framework. Every professional training has a life cycle and a transitory period. The quality of future professionals' habits depends much on having up-to-date curriculum. It needs to be so oriented that it is able to cope up with the rapidly changing needs. The syllabus of LIS studies taught at University level is varying. In the recent past advanced topics like computer application and networking technologies have been included in the courses. The increasing use in the number of electronic information materials such as CD-ROMs, especially in the area of science and technology and R & D information systems necessitated for their inclusion at the postgraduate. Since it is a process than purely a product, it is expected to take into consideration the trends in the socio-economic front and link it with the needs of the profession. The important changes taking place in higher and tertiary level education are the changes in learning process. There is an increasing trend of adopting to combination of teaching methods and a skill from 'Chalk and talk' method. The traditional teaching methods are supplemented by project work, seminar, group discussions, fieldwork, tutorials, in-service training, internal assessment etc. The Library Science profession is demanding specialized skills from the professional in addition to simply disseminating information. These skills have to be acquired through learning process. For example, when students are expected to give seminars based on their project work, they are dissemination the information what they have understood. It needs skill of presenting what they have grasped, justifying what they have to say and understanding human interactions learning and grasping abilities of students are generally checked three means.

Writing Skill : Generally revolves around memory and retention power.

Doing skill : One learns best by 'doing' something.

Thinking skill : Involves interpreting the facts 'doing' by trial and error and seeking solutions.

One of the most important activities in higher

education institutions, more precisely in universities (where Library and Information Science is taught), is learning through research, may be in the form of project work, dissertation, investigation work and so on. Today, library is a part of worldwide network and the requirements of the users cannot be predicted with absolute certainty. Therefore, LIS Education needs to be structured in such a way that the professionals develop necessary abilities and skills to withstand the pressures, while they are in learning process.

4. QUANTITY Vs QUALITY EDUCATION

The gradual improvement in LIS education in the country has manifested more in quantity rather than in quality. Although the number of departments and professional association and other institutes alongwith the students enrollment as steadily increased, but the quality of outgoing students leaves much to be desired. The current course content of LIS programs show no relevance of the subject to our present day informational demands of the society. Keeping in view the veracity of the curricula, few years' back UGC has constituted a committee, curricular development committee in LIS education, which has partially focus on the steps to be taken to bring out necessary improvements in curriculum standards so that the quality could be maintained in LIS education.

5. SKILLS REQUIRED FOR THE LIS EDUCATION PROFESSIONALS

Libraries are undergoing transformation and so also users' expectations due to rapid technology changes. Skills and competitions acquired during early career stages are not likely to suffice beyond 10-15 years. The Market Place of libraries is partly determined by their ability to disseminate the knowledge. Libraries deal with the information in contents. In addition to access the information, they are expected to add value to it and create repackaged information. They will be having a dialogue with specialists in computing, networking, finance, marketing and so on. The services will be more customer based and they will have to acquire skills such as :

- Excellent communication skill–both oral and written with polite aggressiveness.
- Professional attitude to critical thinking for problem solving.
- Broad knowledge of networked information and deep knowledge of specific subject field.
- Knowledge of setting up web sites for libraries.
- Developing attitude towards 'Marketing of information'.
- Knowledge of writing on-line publications using SGML code.
- Skill for developing multimedia packages.

6. TRAINING FOR QUALITY SERVICES

Quality in Education is an evaluation of the process of educating, which enhances the need to achieve and develop the talents of the customers of the process, and at the same time meets the accountability standards set by the clients who pay for the process or the outputs from the process of learning. The six sigma approach developed by Motorola is a statistical unit for measuring quality. Although it is aimed at up gradation of business recesses with nearly zero defect, there should not be any difficulty in applying the quality concept involved in it for giving quality services from the libraries. It may achieved partially by adopting the following means:

- Making conscious efforts for improving communication skill-verbal, written or even through body language.
- Teaching critical thinking and problem solving.

- Making a plan for computer assisted instructions.
- Developing "Intelligence Learning Technology" by having self teaching guides.
- Organizing library's collection with new zero effect, which is absolutely essential for speedy information retrieval.
- Managing library budget with no duplication with every conscious effort to avoid overhead expenditure.

7. CONCLUSION

The information organization has an important role to play new ideas, new concepts, and develop an attitude to have a desire to continue to learn throughout the working career. Technology is just not the answer for everything. Computers can store and process vast amount of information but they are not creators, neither intuitive. Quality Management is not merely sophistication of equipments but it is managing the change, which needs a change in philosophy and developing right attitude. The curricula in Library Science should provide sufficient scope for continuous learning, as well as it may be designed in such a way that every professional feels confident and comfortable over handling technology. Special efforts may be done to identify such professionals who have strong leadership qualities and have the potential of being visionaries to take the profession ahead successfully. Information Management in the view millennium will then be rewarding experience.

REFERENCES

1. Hoy, Charles and others (2000). Improving quality in Education. London: Falmer: p. 10-26.
2. Gokhale, Pratibha (1999). Quality Management Through Library & Information Science Education. *Workshop on Information Management*, held on6 – 8 Jan 1999 atDRTC Bangalore.

3. *http://www.ukoln.ac.uk/services/lic/new* library quality Management through LIS Education.

4. Kohli, Manoj (1998) – 'The six sigma solution'. *Business India*, June 29 – July 12, p. 87

5. Satyanarayana, N.R. (1997). LIS Education: change or status quo ? : Information and Society (Essays in the Memory of Prof. P.G. Rao). New Delhi: Ess Publication p. 112-120.

6. University Grant Commission, Review committee Library Science in Indian Universities. New Delhi, 1965.

7. Dutta, Bydyarathi and Das, Anup Kumar (2001). Higher Education in Library and Information Science in India. *ILA Bulletin, 37(1)* : 25-30.

8. Rawtani, M. R. and Others (2002). A Regional study of Library and Information Science education in India : some observations. *ILA Bulletin, 38(4)* : 108-117.

20

Emerging and Innovative Technologies for University Libraries

1. INTRODUCTION

The importance of a user or a customer has been increasing as the world is becoming more competitive. University Libraries too have to constantly search for users who keep their holdings on the move. We have been constantly shifting and advancing ourselves from a superior technology to a more superior one. Users could be considered as the power base for the libraries. Genealogy of library shows that services that the libraries provide keep on changing in accordance with the needs and expectations of the users. Libraries have always innovated their services along with the advancements in information technology and the changes that take place in communication behavior due to such advancements. Technological advancement has brought about a huge transformation in the nature of media and the patterns of communication. Such transformations keep the nature of resources that the libraries acquire, services they provide and the nature of users they serve in a constant flux.

The ultimate role of the library is to provide service to the users. With the advancement in information technology, there have been a lot of changes in the concept of traditional library work as well as service. The recent trend and change in the information related field especially in collection, storing, processing and dissemination of information have resulted in to the evolution of digital libraries. The recent developments in the Internet and in Web Technologies have brought significant changes in the concept of traditional reference services and a number of web based "expert services". Information services are provided to the users on demand as well as anticipating the user needs including various forms of current awareness and selective dissemination of information services. Such services are provided to the users to keep them abreast of the latest developments in their field of interest through online search services in digital information environment.

With the invention of E-resources quantity and quality of research both have been affected. Different search techniques are used by library users to search and locate relevant information. To understand how users of libraries search and locate relevant documents, we librarians, need to understand the search techniques and what resources and sources of information they generally use and require. Information professionals and users both suffer from the problem of exhaustive information, from a wide range of sources and shortage of time to find, manage and evaluate. Sometimes users search internet indiscriminately without knowing the facts. Here librarian plays an important role by making the users aware of the importance of the evaluation of the retrieved information by guiding them, how to retrieve, what to retrieve and how to further use that retrieved information, which is called evaluation of information. The challenge posed by the information explosion is being successfully met by electronic information sources. Further this information explosion, diversity of user need, financial crunch and impossibility of self-sufficiency has led to the formation of consortia at local, regional, national and international level.

Communication is the basic activity on which most of the library operations are based. After all, libraries exist for communication of information. The change in the nature of communication due to technological advancements and the society's response towards it forms the very basis for the libraries for designing its services. Web 2.0 introduced the concept of two way communication. With the help of web 2.0 technologies, a person is able to produce contents on the web, edit the already exiting contents on the web page, interact in real time, work in collaboration at one point in time, and share multimedia files and many other things.

Library service reflects a transition within the library world in the way that services are delivered to users. The focus is on user-centered change and participation in the creation of content and community. Library service has to be constantly updated and re-evaluated to best serve library users. It also attempts to harness the library user in the design and implementation of library services by encouraging feedback and participation.

Changing needs of users have changed the role of a librarian, which has transformed a librarian into information professional. Librarians have always acted as an electronic middleman between knowledge source and its users. They are now helping the readers in the best possible way by using the latest technology and searching techniques. There has been a considerable growth in the technology and trends in library in the past. The forthcoming emerging technologies will have a deep impact on library administrations, resources, services and instructions.

2. INNOVATIVE TECHNOLOGIES FOR UNIVERSITY LIBRARIES

New tools and techniques are useful for university libraries in providing services and making existing services available in new and interesting ways. Implementation of some of these tools and techniques are likely to improve reputation and standing of libraries in the community. Some of them may successfully attract new patrons to the library, others may help to retain existing members or make libraries even more important as centres of the culture and history of their cities and academic institutions. Some of the new services may remain unused, however, since feedback and public opinion may be a vital component, such services may be abandoned in favour of other services that are better accepted by the users. Some of those changes may be viewed as disruptive, while others may not be feasible or applicable to all libraries. These new services and ongoing changes are likely to make libraries more interesting, more relevant, and better acceptable place.*(Arora, 2009).*

Library 2.0 technologies may facilitate useful tools for university libraries to stay relevant and remain useful libraries have to adapt to changing user needs and expectations. Through library 2.0, libraries can be able to attract constant reputation and standing in the society. Library 2.0 also will bring a meaningful and substantive change in libraries, in its collection, in its services and in information delivery method. Using Library 2.0 tools library could provide better, relevant and valuable information to its users. Library 2.0 also attempts to harness the library user in the design and implementation of library services by encouraging feedback and participation. Library 2.0 applications are to provide more and more interaction and user-centric library and information services to users. Libraries are using social networking, SMS, blogs as tools for promotion, publishing and outreach services.

2.1. Library 2.0 Tools and Technology : with possible implementation in a University Library

Library 2.0 encompasses several technologies and its possible implementation in academic libraries. Web 2.0 technologies can help university libraries to create collaborative and participative environment that is necessary to deliver user-centric library services and to create new resources and build-upon existing ones using collective intelligence of users. Availability of technologies gives libraries the ability to offer improved, customer-driven services to their users. Library 2.0 applications (IMs, RSS feeds, Streaming media, Podcast, SMS, Blogs, WIKI, Social networks Social networking sites, API and Ajax, etc.) are able to provide more and more interaction and user-centric library and information services. Both library users and library staff can add or edit the contents through web browser. The main objective of library 2.0 applications is to move towards technology based services environment so that large number of users can be benefited and to change the library and information services by making them more personalize, Interactive, collaborative, web-based and needs driven by users desired.

Following are some of the tools and technologies that are used in library 2.0 may provide opportunities for the university libraries to reaching out its users:

2.1.1. Instant Messaging (IM)

IM is a form of real time communication between two or more people based on typed text, images etc. IM has become increasingly popular due to its quick response time, its ease of use, and possibility of multitasking. Libraries are already deploying IM for providing 'real-time reference' services, where patrons can synchronously communicate with librarians much as they would in a face-to-face reference context. Libraries can benefit greatly by adopting this technology as it evolves since it facilitates reference services in an online mode quite similar to traditional reference services of the physical library.

Possible implementation in University Libraries

IM (e.g., Google Talk) could be adopted by the users of university libraries. The reason behind its popularity may be because it can easily be implemented in reference services to replace traditional methods like email or telephone. With IM, librarians and users would not only communicate with each other but could also keep a script of their exchanges if they so wish. In addition, IM offers synchronous communication whereas email does not. University library can offer live reference services like Instant Messaging (IM) around the clock in a collaborative manner for example: INFLIBNET Centre is using Google talk support for users of SOUL software.

2.1.2. RSS Feeds

RSS stands for Real Simple Syndication or Rich Site Summary. RSS is a family of web feed format used for syndicating content from blogs or web pages, RSS uses an XML that to blogs or websites, which are interested by the users. Many web browsers have built-in-feed readers or aggregators, and can easily add feeds to web page. It summarizes information items and links to the information sources. The technology, on one hand allows a web site (or e-publisher) to list the newest published updates (like table of contents of journals, new articles) through a technology called XML, on the other hand, it facilitates a web user to keep track new updates on chosen website (s). Like a personal search assistant, RSS feed readers visit pre-defined web sites, look for updated information and fetch it automatically on to the user's desktop.

Possible implementation in University Libraries

We can use RSS in following ways in a university library :

- University library can generate RSS feeds for users to subscribe to knowing updates on new arrivals, new services and newly subscribed databases.
- Announcement of the availability of new books and other resources in a given subject area.
- Librarians can subscribe to RSS from the sources for compiling their customized alerts.

2.1.3. Streaming Media

Streaming multimedia is sequential delivery of multimedia content over a computer. The streaming of video and audio media is an important application of Library 2.0. As media is created, libraries will be responsible for archiving and providing access to them. Libraries are already beginning to explore providing digital repository applications and digital asset management technologies using such application.

Possible implementation in University Libraries

"YouTube" could be used in the University Libraries to upload multimedia video files and recorded events for the benefit of users.

2.1.4. Podcasting

Podcasting is a multimedia service that a library can provide to the users using web 2.0 technologies. A storytime, book discussion, author's speak organized by the library can be recorded and uploaded on the website or on any online space where the library is present. Users can subscribe to the podcasting service and they will be notified whenever a new audio or video file is uploaded. By subscribing to the podcast, the users will be assured of always getting updates when new recordings are released. Library users don't have to continually check back to the programming page of Web site to see if any new stories have been released. Recording can be done on a simple digital recording recorders or open source software like 'audacity' can also be used. Audacity allows you to record live audio and then cut, copy, splice, and mix it before converting it to MP3 format. Such recordings can also be added to library collection and serve as a resource for physical library users.

2.1.5. Vodcasting

The "VOD" in Vodcasting stands for "video-on-demand". It is identical to podcasting. While podcasting is used for delivering audio files, vodcasting is used for delivering video content. Like podcast content, vodcasts content can be played either on a laptop or on Personal Media Assistant (PMA).

2.1.6. SMS Enquiry Service

Short Message Service (SMS) is a mechanism of delivery of short messages over the mobile networks. The SMS enquiry services in a library allow patrons to use their mobile phones to SMS their inquiries to the library. The reference staff deployed to attend to such queries can respond immediately with answers or with links to more in-depth answers.

Possible implementation in University Libraries

The user can get help on finding even when the learning resources centre/library is closed. Short message service (SMS) is very popular; learning resource centers /libraries allow patrons to use their mobile to SMS their demands or queries to them.

2.1.7. Blogs

A blog (an abridged form of term web log) is a website, usually maintained by an individual, with regular entries of commentary, descriptions of events, or other material such as graphics or video.

Blogs can be considered to be the best example for web 2.0 technology. Its global proliferation has great implication for libraries. They enable the rapid production and consumption of web based publication. Today, blogs have become a significant form of publication. It has become inevitable for libraries to include them in their collection. Not only as a resource can the blogs be used by the libraries but also as a significant channel for communicating with the library users. It can serve as a first point of contact between library users and the librarian. Interactions with the readers help in understanding them in a better way. Such an interaction can serve as a resource for the users and the librarians to solve their day to day problems. Libraries can make an archive of such interactions and analyze the questions for understanding the user needs. The answers given by the librarians will be available for the whole community of users to view and respond. Libraries can make use of the blog for listing the upcoming events. Current events can also be discussed on the blogs. A blog can also be integrated to a library website main page. Whenever somebody visits the library website he/she will be shown the library blog. Users can also subscribe to RSS feed facility which almost every blog provides. By subscribing to this facility, users can be notified as and when new content is uploaded on the blog.

Possible implementation in University Libraries

- University Libraries can use blogs as a tool for promotion, publicity and outreach services.
- Discussions on various books can be initiated and readers can be encouraged to read them using blog.
- Blogs serve as a platform where the users can file their concerns, queries and suggestions regarding the services and activities of the library.
- Libraries can disseminate information to their users, make announcements for its new resources and events through its blogs.

- Blogs can be used to initiate debates and interaction amongst users and staff. Moreover, library staff and user can be encouraged to use Library blogs to get to know each other and interact at personal level.
- Blogs can also be used for the collection development where the users request the resources.
- Blogs can be used as tools for marketing of the information as well as the library.
- It can also be used as tool for posting Minutes of the Meetings for necessary actions.

2.1.8. Wikis

A wiki is a collection of web pages designed to enable anyone who accesses it to contribute or modify content, using a simplified markup language. Wikis are often used to create collaborative websites and to power community websites (Wikipedia, 2013).

Like blog, wikis also help the library capture its community's knowledge and collect it in a manageable way, making it accessible to everyone. Wikis can work as a repository for documents and multimedia files. Libraries can design wikis for making a space for readers with specific subject interest. Just as blogs, wikis are also web based application that can be formed using the services of the company that provides the facilities. Also open source proprietary softwares are available in the market that can be used to design a wiki and uploaded on the libraries server or the host server that provides the facilities. The best example of a wiki is Wikipedia which is managed with the help of contributions from the users and is used by the community themselves. In other words the individual's knowledge is harnessed and used by the community. The permission to edit the content of a wiki can be restricted to members of the library.

Possible implementation in University Libraries

- Using wikis, library can provide detailed information on activities, functions and services of the Library. Moreover, the users of the Library are also encouraged to contribute to the Wiki with their contents and suggestions on services and activities.
- Wiki provide a quick, low-tech method to generate and maintain web based library subject guides and act as communication tools to enable social interaction among library and information professionals and patrons.
- Wikis can be used for social interaction and discussions among the librarians & users as well.
- Wikis can also be used by the users to share information and enhance the contents, and a record of these transactions is archived for future reference.
- Wikis can be used for creating subject guides, subject gateways.

2.1.9. Social Networking

A social network service is web-based software that facilitates creation of a virtual social network for communities of people who share interests and activities or who are interested in exploring the interests and activities of others *(Wikipedia, 2013)*.

Social networking is another web 2.0 space where many of the library users are found. Libraries have started exploring the potential of this space too. Social networking sites like facebook, my space, twitter, Flikr, etc are used extensively. The gaining popularity of social networking sites gives a reason for libraries to get themselves visible on that space. Libraries, outside of the virtual space have always been a social space that provides an opportunity for the people to socialize and share. Social networking could enable librarians and patrons not only to interact, but to share and exchange resources dynamically in an electronic medium. According to Maness, "the face of the library's web-presence in the future may look very much like a social network interface." Maness, (2006) Libraries can use the social network for interacting with the users, for getting more readers by promoting library services, for listing library events, for initiating a discussion on books and current events, for uploading library images and videos, etc. Such a space has a tremendous power of increasing the popularity of library among the users.

Possible implementation in University Libraries

- The Library can have a Facebook Page, which includes links of relevant parts of Library website, link to RSS aggregation services and search applications.
- Libraries can create a page to reach to new users.
- Social networking could enable librarians and patrons not only to interact, but to share and change resources dynamically in an electronic medium.
- For building network among the interested group in discussing the common things user content can be added to the library catalogue, including book reviews or other comments.

2.1.10. Tagging

A tag is a keyword that is added to a digital object (e.g. a website, picture or video clip) to describe it, but not as part of a formal classification system. The concept of tagging has been widened far beyond website bookmarking, and services like Flickr (Photos), YouTube (video) and Audio (podcasts) allow a variety of digital artifacts to be socially tagged. The University of Huddersfield, West Yorkshire, UK, for example, has introduced Web 2.0 features into their library catalogue and options for rating the books as well as dynamic floor plans showing locations of subject areas with an aim to make the catalogue more interactive tool.

Possible implementation in University Libraries

- Tagging can be applied to the Library Management System editing the subject headings from the user point of view and thereby enhancing the indexing and relevancy of the searches, making the collection more dynamic.
- Tagging would greatly facilitate the lateral searching.

2.1.11. Social Bookmarking Services

Social bookmarking is a method of storing, organizing, searching and managing bookmarks of web sites using descriptive metadata. In a social bookmarking system, users can save links to web pages that they want to remember and /or share with other users. These bookmarks can be made public, or saved privately or shared only with specified people or groups of people. The authorized people can usually view these bookmarks chronologically, by category or tags, or via a search engine *(Wikipedia, 2013).*

itList, Blinklist, Clip2, ClickMarks, HotLinks, del.icio.us, Furl, Simpy, Citeulike and Connotea, Stumbleupon, Ma.gnolia, Blue Dot, Diigo, etc. are some of the popular bookmarking services.

Possible Implementation in University Libraries

Libraries can make use of social bookmarking sites using RSS feeds for subject disciplines or in areas of specialization relevant to them.

2.1.12. Mashups

A mashup is a web application that combines data from more than one source into a single integrated tool. Content used in mashups is typically sourced from a third party via a public interface or API (web services). Other methods of sourcing content for mashups include Web feeds (e.g. RSS or Atom), and screen scraping. Many people are experimenting with mashups using Amazon, eBay, Flickr, Google, Microsoft, Yahoo, YouTube and APIs, which has led to the creation of the mashup editor *(Wikipedia, 2013)*.

Possible implementation in University Libraries

It allows the user to edit OPAC data and metadata, saves the user's tags, IM conversations with librarians, wiki entries with other users (and catalogues all of these for others to use), and the user is able to make all or part of their profile public; users can see what other users have similar items checked-out, borrow and lend tags, and a giant user-driven catalogue is created and mashed with the traditional catalogue.

There are a number of mashup platforms that can be used to create mashups, e.g. Intel Mash Maker, Google Mashup Editor, LiquidApps, Microsoft Popfly, Serena Mashup Editor, Yahoo pipes, etc.

2.1.13. *Ajax (Asynchronous JavaScript and XML)*

Ajax (Asynchronous JavaScript and XML), or AJAX, is a group of inter-related web development techniques used for creating interactive web applications. The technology facilitates web pages to interact with users by exchanging small amounts of data with the server "behind the scene" so that entire web pages do not have to be reloaded each time there is a need to fetch data from the server. This is intended to increase the web page's interactivity, speed, functionality and usability *(Wikipedia, 2013)*.

Possible implementation in University Libraries

Ajax is a cross-platform technique usable on many different operating systems, computer architectures, and web browsers as it is based on open standards such as JavaScript and the Document Object Model (DOM).

2.1.14. Application Programming Interface (API)

An application programming interface (API) is a source code interface provided by an operating system, library or service to support requests made by computer programs. Language-dependent APIs are available only in a particular programming language. They utilize the syntax and elements of the programming language to make the API convenient to use in this particular context. Examples of API are Windows API, Scopus API that enables a user to select Scopus data elements to your own mashups.

2.1.15. Library Tool Bars

A toolbar is a graphical user interface consisting of a panel of buttons, icons, menus or commands that are used more often in an application. Toolbars are used in common applications such as Microsoft Word, and as add-ons for web browsers such as Internet Explorer and Mozilla Firefox.

Possible implementation in University Libraries

The Libraries can develop its tool bar to show-off its e-resources, databases, products and services.

2.2. Other Innovative Technologies and Services for a University Library

Following are some of the other new and innovative services those could be implemented in a university library to reaching out its users and improve the quality of services:

2.2.1. Federated Search and Discovery Tools

Federated Search and Discovery tools could be made available to enhance searching of e-resources by the users. With growing number and variety of electronic resources available in the market, libraries are required to look for search and discovery tools that provide seamless and coherent access to all resources that a library subscribes to as well as those that can be accessed through open access channels. Individual end users will benefit from federated search technology.

Federated search helps users to find resources across library collections. Federated search applications excel at finding scientific, technical, and legal documents whether they live in free public sites or in subscription sites. This makes federated search a vital technology for students and professional researchers. For this reason, many libraries and corporate research departments provide federated search applications to their students and staff. The user does not need to know of the existence of particular databases, nor does he/she need to know how each individual search interface works. In the basic search mode, federated search provides a single search box offering a Google-like experience.

Discovery tools should not be confused with federated search products. The former 'promise to provide a single interface to multiple resources based on using a centralized consolidated index to provide faster and better search results', while the latter search remotely, rely on connectors, and provide 'only partial and limited solutions'. In addition, a federated search tool usually requires user logon and works in a protected environment, while a discovery layer is open to the public. A discovery tool is often referred to as a stand-alone OPAC, a discovery layer interface, an OPAC replacement, or the next generation catalog (NGC).

2.2.2. Implementation of 'Six Sigma' to Enhancing Service Qualities

Modern library management lays great emphasis on objectives to be accomplished by the system. In library and information centres, the first and foremost objective is to satisfy the need of its users.

Six-Sigma stands for Six Standard Deviations (Sigma'(ó)' is the Greek letter used to represent standard deviation in statistics) from mean. It is statistically based methodology for improving product quality to meet the users' needs. Six-Sigma is a method for improving quality for reducing errors that result in quality service with reducing costs. Using Six-Sigma, university library can improve their services to the users by reducing defects and minimizing cost involved in library services. This will satisfy users as well as the funding organization.

In the IT influenced environment, libraries are extremely under-pressure to justify their existence as well as their importance for the organization. For this library must satisfy user's need as well as meet their expectations. Moreover, libraries should constantly strive to provide quality services to the users by cutting the cost. As a disciplined process, six sigma provides two standard process models, i..e DMAIC(Define, Measure, Analyse, Improve, and Control) and DMADV(Define, Measure, Analyse, Design and Verify).*(Ahmad Ali and Imtiaz, 2010).*

2.2.3. Institutional Repository

Institutional repository could be created for hosting full-text of research publications of university faculty and researchers of the university using Dspace or any other such software. It provides a platform for faculty and researcher to deposit, reuse and share their research publications. The repository also has the ability to capture, index, store, disseminate and preserve digital material created in any part of the University. Using repository faculty and researchers can register themselves with the digital repository and submit their pre-prints (pre-refereed version of an article), post-prints (post-refereed final version) and publisher PDFs (if allowed by the publisher). Web of Science/SCOPUS databases could be used for updation of records regularly. It may also include other resources like ETDs, Institutional publications, Minutes of meetings, etc.

2.2.4. Library Website

A library website can be designed to accommodate all the features of web 2.0 technology. Over and above, these facilities of subject chat rooms can be provided where users having common subject interest can chat with each other. A facility of instant messaging could be implemented where librarians can instantly reply the questions asked by the users.

2.2.5. Personalized Library OPAC

Library catalogue is the space through which the user generally initiates venturing to the library website. This can be the place where the library website can take and provide the opportunity for the user to participate and interact with the librarian as well as other library members. The data regarding the user's interest area can be collected while accepting the application form. Such data can be used for providing personalized service to the user through library website. Such a data can assist in displaying the literature recently acquired by the library on the particular user's interest on his personal page whenever he/she 'signs in' in his/her account. Such a service can assure a personalized approach towards library users and will also make them aware about the recent books on his/her interest. Library catalogue can also provide the room for user participation by providing the opportunity to rank the library resources. Users can also make a comment or write a review on the particular resource used by them. That comment can be reflected on the catalogue entry and other reader can respond to it. Such a facility can encourage the users to participate in user discussion and the librarian comes to know about the views of the readers on a particular resource. Users can also provide the keywords that they feel should be included in the keywords for a particular book over and above the key words provided by the librarian so as to make the searching better.

2.2.6. RFID Technology

Radio Frequency IDentification (RFID) based is the best automated library automation system used world wide and is an effective way of managing collections of the library and providing enhanced services to the users having benefits like: self check-out, self-check-in (book drop), to control theft, to find misplaced reading material, sorting, inventory accuracy, stock verification procedures, security control, video surveillance, people counter, Smart Card issuance, etc. It *is an automatic data capture technology that uses tiny microchips and miniature antennas affixed to documents.* RFID plays a vital role in redefining the library processes to make everyone's job easier right from the users to library staff.

The implementation of RFID technology certainly improves service efficiency for university libraries and enables more diversified applications and service modes. The benefits of RFID technology cannot be ignored in today's tight staffing and funding climate in recession.

2.2.7. Shibboleth/EZproxy- Remote Login facility to the users

EZproxy is widely used to provide access to off-campus users. It helps provide users with remote access to Web-based licensed contents offered by libraries. EZproxy is a web proxy server that could be used by university library to give access from outside the library's computer network to restricted-access websites that authenticate users by IP address. This allows library patrons at home or elsewhere to log in through their library's EZproxy server and gain access to the databases subscribed by the library. It is a middleware that authenticates library users against local authentication systems and provides remote access to licensed content based on the user's authorization. More than 2,500 institutions in over 60 countries have purchased EZproxy software.

Shibboleth leverages the main campus identity management system, protects user privacy and data security, and provides fine-grained access control. It is standards based, open source software package for web single sign-on across or within organizational boundaries. It allows sites to make informed authorization decisions for individual access of protected online resources in a privacy-preserving manner.

2.2.8. Subscription to E-resources

The use of e-resources is very common among the faculty and research scholars in university system and majority of the faculty and research scholars are dependent on e-resources to get the desired and relevant information. But practical use of e-resources is not up-to the worth in comparison to investments made in acquiring the resources. Infrastructure and training programs should be revised as per requirements.

University Library could make available books in electronic form to its users. Library users' expectations are changing as they become more wired and more dependent upon technology as wireless technologies have become more advanced and readily available. The libraries must think beyond the paper book and utilise the capabilities of the E-Books.

2.2.9. Users' Meet

Library can provide a space in the library premises to its community of users' to organize discussions, meeting, book talks and other events that the users' would wish. This can prove to be a good service to meet the expectations of users who believes in physical library environment. Such events can be publicized on library websites, blogs, social networking sites and other venues. Such gathering can also be a meeting place for discussing on the services that the library provides. The audio/video recording of these meetings can be uploaded on the library website and blogs for the community to use. This way the online as well as the physical library users can also interact with each other. This service will provide the opportunity for the physical library users' that are significant in number to take part in the library operations.

2.2.10. Users' Speak

Library can also provide a space for the users' to share their views in the library newsletter or journal. This can provide the opportunity to the physical library users to interact with each other. It can be a short article or a personal view on library service and the person willing to respond to the article can come up with it in the next issue.

3. CONCLUSION

User behaviour, driven by change in technological environment, gives a meaningful direction to the services that the libraries provide. The best way a library can approach user with its services at this point in time would be through a social network interface designed according to the user's need that provides them the facilities of web 2.0. It can be a personalized OPAC that includes facilities provided by instant messengers, RSS feeds, blogs, wikis, and social networking sites within the library's network or can be an independent visibility on such spaces. It can be a virtual space where one can not only search for books and journals, but interact with a community, a librarian, and share knowledge and understanding among them. Movement towards serving user will require libraries to open not just access to their catalogs and resources, but access to their control. Libraries will move from centralization to decentralization. Such an approach demands libraries focus less on secured inventory systems and more on collaborative discovery systems.

Library 2.0 proposes to bring revolutionary changes in libraries that are bound to bring about conceptual, cultural and physical changes in libraries to keep pace with the changes in communities and their information seeking behaviour. Library 2.0 technologies may provide useful tools for university libraries to stay relevant and remain useful libraries have to adapt to changing user needs and expectations. We conclude that library 2.0 will provides better, relevant and valuable information to its users.

The primary objective of libraries is to organize and provide access to information, and it remains the same although the format and methods have changed drastically. Under the present scenario of declining budgets and higher subscription costs of journals in India, it is becoming very difficult to meet the demands of library users. The only solution to the problem is the pooling and sharing of resources print as well as electronic by way of consortia. New technologies have provided great opportunities for delivery of services. More and more libraries must unite, which of course requires a change in the attitudes, practices, and policies to get the maximum benefit. Researches have to be carried out with aid of technological advancement to compete the fast growing environment. The library movement in India is rapidly increasing and the traditional libraries are now on their way to digitization in a phased manner. In a developing country like India where resources are limited, funds are inadequate; the library professionals have to take careful and judicious decisions in selecting library materials. Also the library and information professionals have to keep on watch for newer technological developments and noticeable changes in the use of many information platforms such as Internet, multimedia and digital library. Thus the library personnel should develop their professional proficiency and communication skill in order to meet the challenges emerging out of library services. Use of ICT has changed the conventional way of thinking about library and information profession where only libraries involve in generating the content and services for user shifted to the side of the user where library and information professionals will enable to users to generate then for themselves.

Mossop rightly said, *"there's never a 'best time' to adopt any new technology – today's facilities are always better, cheaper and faster than yesterday's, but whatever you buy today is almost guaranteed to have been superseded by something even more ideal by the time tomorrow comes"(Bradley, 2007).*

REFERENCES

1. Ahmad Ali Al-Zubi and Imtiaz Basha(2010). Six Sigma In Libraries: A Management Perspective, Canadian Journal on Computing in Mathematics Natural Sciences, Engineering & Medicine Vol. 1, No. 3, April 2010 .
2. Arora, Jagdish(2009). Library 2.0: Innovative technologies for building libraries of tomorrow. Proceedings of national seminar open acccss to textual and multimedia content bridging the digital divide. Jointly organized by INFLIBNET Center and CEC, New Delhi, Jan.29-30, 2009. p.49-69.
3. Bradley, Phil(2007). How to use web 2.0 in your library? London, Fact publishing, 2007.
4. Casey, M. E. and Laura C. S. (2006). Library 2.0: Service for the next-generation library. Library Journal, January 1. Retrieved on March 30, 2013 from *http://www.libraryjournal.com/article/CA6365200.html*
5. Casey, M. E. and Laura C. S. (2007). Library 2.0: A Guide to a Participatory Library Service. New Jersey: Information Today, Inc.
6. Dora, Malkarjun and Maharana, Bulu(2008). A-Lib 2.0: New avatar academic Libraries with web 2.0 applications. Proceedings of international conference CALIBER, 2008.

Jointly organized by INFLIBNET Center and Allahabad University, Allahabad, 28th Feb to 1st March, 2008, p.469-75.

7. Maness, J. M. (2006). Library 2.0 Theory: Web 2.0 and Its Implications for Libraries. Webology, Volume 3, Number 2. on March 30, 2013 from *http://www.webology.ir/2006/v3n2/a25.html*

8. O'Reilly, T. (2005). What Is Web 2.0? Design Patterns and Business Models for the Next Generation of Software. on March 30, 2013 from *http://oreilly.com/web2/archive/what-is-web-20.html.*

9. Wikipedia(2013). Web 2.0. Retrieved on March 30, 2013 from *http://en.wikipedia.org/wiki/Web_2.0.*